The Philosophy
of
Welfare

The Philosophy
of Welfare

Selected Writings of
Richard M. Titmuss

Edited by
BRIAN ABEL-SMITH and KAY TITMUSS

with an Introduction by
S. M. MILLER

ALLEN & UNWIN
London   Sydney

Allen & Unwin (Publishers) Ltd,
40 Museum Street, London WC1A 1LU, UK

Allen & Unwin (Publishers) Ltd,
Park Lane, Hemel Hempstead, Herts HP2 4TE, UK

Allen & Unwin (Australia) Ltd,
8 Napier Street, North Sydney, NSW 2060, Australia

First published in 1987

British Library Cataloguing in Publication Data

Titmuss, Richard M.
   The philosophy of welfare : selected
   writings of Richard M. Titmuss.
1. Welfare state
I. Title II. Abel-Smith, Brian
III. Titmuss, Kay
361.6'5   HN17.5
ISBN 0–04–361063–3
ISBN 0–04–361064–1 Pbk

Set in 10 on 12 point Sabon by
Columns, Caversham, Reading
and printed in Great Britain by
Billing and Sons Ltd, London and Worcester

Contents

Preface

The idea of producing this volume came from Professor Mike Miller, who has kindly contributed the introduction. He pointed out that much of what Richard Titmuss had written in the 1950s and 1960s has a special relevance for the 1980s, when governments on both sides of the Atlantic have been cutting back spending on social services. Yet Titmuss's writings were no longer readily available to readers in the United States. We saw a similar need to republish Titmuss's core messages in the United Kingdom, because his widely read volumes *Essays on the Welfare State* and *Commitment to Welfare* would soon be out of print.

The problem which presented itself was how to choose what to include in one volume of manageable size. We consulted colleagues and friends on both sides of the Atlantic and found a wide degree of consensus on which articles appeared most frequently on booklists and thus were still being recommended to students. This helped us to select particular chapters from the two volumes of essays mentioned above. But we wanted to go further and include other essays which crystallized Titmuss's contribution to thinking about social policy, and particularly some of his later writing, which is scattered around in a variety of different journals, and was completed after the second volume of essays had been compiled.

In making the selection we have been guided by the title we have given to the book. Of course we are not trying to assert that there is or could be only one Philosophy of Welfare. What we aim to set out is Titmuss's own personal philosophy of welfare and show how he defended and justified it. This does not of course cover the totality of his academic contribution. He also made important contributions to demography, social medicine and history and this work was far from being ephemeral. Indeed his daughter, Ann Oakley, has referred to some of his early statistical work in her recent history of ante-natal care.[1] We debated whether we should include one or more of his contributions to the history of British social policy, in view of the fact that his largest single work had been historical – *Problems of Social Policy*, the social history of the Second World War inside Britain.[2] We finally decided to restrict the volume to philosophical or contemporary writings, partly to give it a unity and partly because the history might only have been intelligible to those with some detailed knowledge of Britain's institutions. Finally, we could not resist including the introduction to one of the last lectures he ever gave, though it is still in print in *Introduction to Social Policy*. It says so much about the man who wrote it. We call it the Postscript.

Richard Titmuss was appointed Professor of Social Administration at the London School of Economics in 1950 and remained in this post until his death from cancer in 1973.[3] His appointment was unusual as he had never studied at a university and had no degree. In fact he had left school at the age of 14. His father had been a small farmer in Bedfordshire until the agricultural depression drove him out to try his luck in London. A haulage business in Hendon, first with horses and then with lorries, proved a failure, and he died in 1926, heavily in debt. It was the precarious financial position of his parents which made it impossible for Richard Titmuss to continue his education. After his father's death, he secured a clerical position in the County Fire Insurance Office. He remained with the company for sixteen years, and achieved the rank of inspector at the unusually early age of 32. This gave him practical knowledge of how insurance operates in practice, and it also gave him the freedom to organize his own working hours. But it made him highly critical for the rest of his life of the social impact and power of insurance companies. This is reflected in the third and twelfth essays republished in this book.

It was after Titmuss's marriage in 1937 that he developed the drive and confidence to start writing on social conditions and social needs. For five years he led a double life – earning his income from the insurance company and during the rest of his time ferreting out statistics and pondering on social problems. Out of this period came three books on the related themes of poverty, ill health, demography and family planning – interests which are particularly reflected in the fourth essay of this book. These books attracted the attention of, among others, Sidney and Beatrice

Webb, Eva Hubback and R. H. Tawney. The latter became a family friend until his death, and Titmuss was later to build on and widen Tawney's philosophy when he himself moved into the London School of Economics. Titmuss makes his tribute and acknowledges his debt to Tawney in the first essay in this book.

It was Eva Hubback who recommended Titmuss to Professor Keith (later Sir Keith) Hancock, who had become supervisor (later editor) of the official civil histories of the Second World War. By this time Titmuss was settling war damage claims, and was in an occupation which was considered essential for the war. Hancock took what some would have thought a considerable risk, by supporting Titmuss's appointment to author the volume on the development of the social services during wartime Britain, despite his complete lack of formal tutelage, in either history or social policy. The result was the masterpiece *Problems of Social Policy*, which led to his appointment to the new chair of Social Administration at the LSE in the same year. Titmuss reflects on the relationship between 'War and Social Policy' in the fifth essay of this volume.

At the LSE, Titmuss did not spend all his time in that concrete tower reflecting on the subtleties of social policy, though he was surprised to find that all his contract of service required him to do was 'to advance knowledge of his subject'. He busied himself in teaching and administration and built up a large academic department. His students varied from early school leavers, whom he smuggled into the University on the basis of commitment and practical experience, to Princess Margaretha (later Queen) of Denmark who had concerns of a different kind. ('If I am going to spend my life opening and shutting social institutions, I had better learn what it is all about'.) He was greatly in demand as a member of official committees and commissions (e.g. health visitors 1953–4, Medical Education 1965–8, One-parent families 1970–3). From 1965 until 1971 he was a member of the Community Relations Commission. From its establishment in 1966 until his death he was a member and later deputy chairman of the Supplementary Benefits Commission, which was responsible throughout Britain for the scheme of social assistance, or what would be called in the United States 'Welfare'.

He was also in demand for public lectures first in the UK and, as his reputation grew abroad, as the keynote speaker at vast international conferences. Often conference organizers chose the subjects on which he was to address them. 'The solutions to the problems of the whole world packed into fifty minutes' he would say with a grin at the pretentiousness of others. Thus many of the essays reproduced in this volume were written for distinct occasions and separate audiences; he did not set out to write books of essays. Hence the criticism that the present volume does not all add up to one totally coherent theory misses the mark. Perhaps, if he had lived longer, he would have brought it together in a different way. But sadly he did not. He survived a severe attack of tuberculosis in 1958, thanks to therapies not available thirty years earlier, but succumbed to cancer before the age of retirement from the LSE.

Thus the essays need to be understood in their context of time and place. The second essay in the book was originally a public lecture in honour of Eleanor Rathbone, who had fought so long and hard to have family allowances introduced in the period between the two world wars. This essay, 'The Social Division of Welfare', is perhaps the most influential piece he ever wrote. While, up to 1955, the Labour Party had seen its social policy objectives as the establishment of a floor of benefits and services as of right with the aim of reducing and perhaps eventually abolishing means testing, from 1955 onwards there emerged the aim of extending to all many of the fiscal and occupational benefits currently enjoyed by the middle classes (what in the United States would be called tax expenditures and fringe benefits). The Labour Party's policy for pensions adopted from 1956 onwards derived in part from this essay of Titmuss's. So did the integration of allowances for children in the income tax system with family allowances in the Child Benefit Act of 1975.

The third essay, 'The Irresponsible Society', applies the principles of 'The Social Division of Welfare' to the pensions field in more detail. It was written largely as a searching critique of the *Report of the Committee on the Economic and Financial Problems of the Provision for Old Age* published towards the end of 1954. Titmuss shows that the then current concern about 'the burden' of an ageing population was largely misplaced; he criticizes the inequity of financing state pensions to an increasing extent from flat rate contributions, 'which, unlike direct taxation with its elaborate search for equity between two taxpayers with

different dependencies, pays no regard to individual circumstances', and argues that private pension schemes are 'a second
"social service" with a similar purpose but quite dissimilar
principles and methods'. The gradual transition from flat rate
contributions to wholly earnings-related contributions to national
insurance took place between 1961 and 1974. Titmuss concludes
that 'Already it is possible to see two nations in old age: greater
inequalities in living standards after work than in work: two
contrasting social services for distinct groups based on differing
principles, and operating in isolation of each other as separate,
autonomous, social instruments of change'. The partial assimila-
tion of occupational pensions with state pensions was provided
for in the National Superannuation Bill 1970, which failed to
reach the statute book when a general election was held in June
1970, but was achieved by the Social Security Pensions Act 1975.

In the fourth essay, Titmuss describes the effects of demographic
changes on the social position of women. He documents the sharp
decline in the period spent in childrearing over only two
generations, the extent of women's increasing expectation of life,
the growing extent of marriage, particularly earlier marriage, and
discusses the changing expectations of the marital relationship.
This essay was one of the first to comment on these changes, and
to speculate on their meaning for future relationships between the
sexes.[4]

The fifth essay on 'War and Social Policy' contains Titmuss's
wider reflections on the influence, not just of the Second World
War on social policy, which he had so masterfully documented,
but of earlier wars and of wars in other societies at other times.
He traces the growing interest of governments as the scope of war
expands in questions of manpower. First, the concern is over the
quantity of manpower, later the concern extends to the quality of
manpower – to national fitness – and finally to the health and
well-being of the whole population, to those injured in bombing,
those injured in factories and the dependent needs of certain social
groups. Titmuss shows how each of the three wars in which
Britain had engaged in this century at the time he wrote
contributed to an expansion in the scope of public social services.

In the essays which make up the central part of this book
Titmuss makes his contribution to a debate which has underlaid
the development of social policy for well over a century and is by

no means concluded, if it will ever be concluded. How much redistribution should there be in society? What role should private insurance and tax concessions play in the redistribution? How far should redistribution by government be selective (if so, by what criteria) and how far should universal benefits be provided? How far should redistribution be in kind or cash? And, if we were to achieve an acceptable redistribution of cash, should people be left to make their own choices on what services they purchased? During the 1960s the tone of the debate was influenced by an important underlying assumption – that Western societies were achieving and would continue to achieve relatively rapid economic growth. As people got richer could they be expected to buy their own social services? Would affluence lead to an end to ideological conflict in society? It was also influenced by a technological development – the growing use of the computer. Did this development make it possible to operate selective services in both a more efficient and more acceptable way? Could the income tax system be transformed into the sole agent of redistribution, doing all the giving as well as the taking so that social insurance, public assistance and all other means-tested schemes could be abolished?

Chapter 6 represents Titmuss's reply to those who were arguing that ideological differences between left and right had come to an end with the acceptance of the Welfare State. One reason for including it is to represent some of the thinking in the book he published in 1962, *Income Distribution and Social Change*, which has long been out of print.

Titmuss expanded on his reply in the next five chapters. He took issue with what was then the new Chicago 'school' of liberal economists of which Professor Friedman is the best-known exponent – a school of thought which was later to have a substantial influence on the thinking of both President Ronald Reagan and Prime Minister Margaret Thatcher. Chapter 7 on 'Universal and Selective Social Services' is still regarded by many people as the most penetrating article which has yet been written on this much discussed subject. In it Titmuss shows that income tax coding cannot simply be adapted as a means-testing mechanism to replace all others. Nor is this conclusion refuted by the demonstration in 1971 that a system of tax credits was operationally feasible in Britain. Even this tax credit scheme would have only replaced one means test on those at work – the family income supplement scheme which had not yet been introduced when Titmuss wrote this essay.

On the international level he shows in Chapter 8 some of the consequences of the international migration of doctors, which has constituted a major hidden subsidy from the poorer countries to the richer. He goes on to question the morality of preaching family planning to developing nations while attracting away the skilled manpower needed for services to provide birth control and death control. He then analyses the functions which social service benefits fulfil.

Chapter 9 'Choice and "The Welfare State" ' was originally a lecture delivered to the Fabian Society in 1966 and concentrates on four questions. Can economic growth by itself solve the problem of poverty? Can private welfare markets solve the problems of discrimination and stigma? Do they offer consumers more choice? Are social services in kind different from goods on the private market? The original text of the lecture ends with the example of human blood. We have omitted this here as the subject is covered in greater detail in what we have included as the next chapter which summarizes part of the argument in *The Gift Relationship* 1970. This book had a substantial impact on policy in the USA. Within months of publication the United States Secretary of State for Health, Education and Welfare (Eliot Richardson) had asked to see Titmuss when visiting London. The issue of the quality of blood used for transfusion has since come into prominence again because of the AIDS epidemic.

Chapter 11 was a lecture delivered to the American National Conference on Social Welfare in 1966 (significantly in Chicago itself) devoted to the question of whether economic growth can be expected to lead automatically to social growth and make it possible to dismantle the Welfare State. In Chapter 12 Titmuss returns once more to the theme of the relationship between private and public insurance.

Chapter 13 turns to the wider role of social security systems. How do these systems respond to demands for equity and adequacy in societies with more unemployment and more 'resting' between jobs, more divorce, separation and cohabitation and changing roles for women? Titmuss provides us with an analysis of the societal conflict between maintaining incentives to work, on the one hand, and the obligation to maintain dependents and prevent poverty, on the other. His perspective was clearly informed by his experience as deputy chairman of the Supplementary Benefits Commission.

Chapter 14 began as a lecture which Titmuss gave in the summer of 1970 in his Supplementary Benefits Commission role at the annual training scheme for civil servants administering the British Social Security Scheme. In it he argued, unfashionably at the time, that the attempt to codify all regulations for social assistance ('welfare' in the USA), so that they would all become 'rights' interpreted by lawyers, would be a retrograde step. Despite his warning, this is what was done from 1980 onwards. In 1985 the British government proposed to return to discretion, though within the financial limits of a fund established for this purpose.

Chapter 15 reprints the keynote address he gave in 1972 to a vast international audience gathered in The Hague for the International Conference on Social Welfare. This represents a magnificent summary of the essence of Titmuss's approach to social welfare.

The final chapter is the last piece of any length he wrote. It was delivered at the start of the series of lectures he gave at the LSE a few months before his death. It shows that in these months he felt his work and the work of others (as he would insist on adding) had not been entirely in vain. In particular, the British National Health Service was practising the moral principles in which he believed so passionately.

B. Abel-Smith
K. Titmuss
January 1986

Notes

1 Oakley, A., *The Captured Womb* (Blackwell, 1984).
2 Titmuss, R. M., *Problems of Social Policy* (London: HMSO, 1950, reprinted by Kraus, Liechenstein, 1977, with full references).
3 For a biography see Gowing, M., 'Richard Morris Titmuss 1907–1973', *Proceedings of the British Academy*, London, vol 61, (1975).
4 In 1986 the Titmuss Memorial Lecture held at the Hebrew University of Jerusalem was given by Titmuss's daughter, Ann Oakley, on the subject of 'Social Welfare and the Position of Women'; the lecture takes as its starting point this 1958 essay. (A. Oakley 'Social Welfare and the Position of Women' Thomas Coram Research Unit Occasional Paper, 1986.)

Introduction:
The Legacy
of Richard Titmuss

S. M. MILLER

I read Richard Titmuss's essay on 'The Social Division of Welfare' with great excitement when it appeared in 1956. At that time attention in the United States was centred on 'the affluent society', which had made great strides in raising income standards, avoiding the continuation in the postwar period of the Great Depression of the 1930s and expanding the social security system. American capitalism was described as producing an 'Income Revolution' of rising and more evenly distributed incomes.

In that seminal essay and many other writings Titmuss provided a way of analysing the surprising development within capitalism of the welfare state and the presumed great improvement in living standards and reduction of inequalities. He widened the understanding of how government affected the distribution of resources over time. His analysis was eye-opening; it provided a way of analysing social programmes and the Welfare State rather than of praising or demeaning them in ideological terms.

In starting to re-read Titmuss's works almost thirty years after that initial and welcome Titmussian shock, I wondered if they would appear either so dated or so incorporated into policy and political thinking that it would be hard to understand why Titmuss was once fresh, challenging, innovative, and inspiring. I could hear his voice as I read. And it was vivid because his messages were still pertinent to these days of Welfare State austerity in contrast to the flush of expanding social programmes of the 1950s and 1960s when Titmuss wrote much of his work.

1

Early on he was engaged in argument with the believers in the free market, centred on the Institute for Economic Affairs in London but importantly shaped by the thinking of the American economist Milton Friedman. Those who promoted private markets in health, education and welfare have since gained political and intellectual influence on both sides of the Atlantic. Titmuss took them on and his arguments still have power and significance.

Titmuss delved into the inner workings of social policy and provided us with modes of analysis and a set of relevant questions. We use many of them today but not as fully and as deeply as he advocated.

Titmuss wrote about *purpose*, a question that never dies, though it may be answered in different ways at different times. Frequently, the fact that an answer has changed may be only dimly understood. The fact that new circumstances require new goals may be only belatedly recognized. Titmuss concentrated on the fundamental issues of what social policies should do and on the effects of any choices that are made. In a period when social policies are harried by Thatchers and Reagans, they can be defended and transformed into more effective instruments only by clarifying what their purposes should be.

Why a Welfare State?

One view of the Welfare State which still underlies much contemporary thinking is that it should be residual, declining over time, succumbing gracefully to economic growth. General economic improvement will reduce poverty and the need for social programmes. Titmuss vigorously argued against this position, for it misconceives what the Welfare State is about and the processes of economic and social change.

In Titmuss's view, the dynamics, issues and results of the Welfare State can be understood only in the context of changes occurring in the society in which it operates. Although distributive questions are at the heart of the Titmuss analysis, it is not restricted to the social stratificational questions of who has been helped or harmed. His perspective is much broader. He placed the need for social policies in the context of the whole social structure of society and showed how changes in that structure produced

2

pain and dislocation. He stated social policies are now 'an integral part of industrialisation' and its processes.

The strains of industrial society, the nature of the economy, the changes in community functioning, demographic shifts and pressures on the family resulted in daily life burdens which individual families cannot cope with alone. State help was needed for all, at one time or another, if families and individuals were to be able to function effectively.

From his earliest writings before the Second World War (including a book with his wife Kay), he stressed the importance of demographic changes – the changing age structure of the population, particularly the growth in the number of the aged; the lengthening of longevity; the reduction in the number of children in families, especially working-class families. Numbers count. Such changes affect the character as well as the scale of need.

Changes in family structure are independently important. The number and spacing of children and longevity of parents influence needs. Who produces and receives income for the family are variables which influence familial behaviour. Working mothers require a wide variety of supports, particularly if they are single parents.

Titmuss saw that issues of work create needs for social programmes. Workmen's compensation arose from the dangers of the work situation. Alienation on the job produced strains on the family. Unemployment created the need for public aid.

In contrast to the feeling that growth solves most problems, Titmuss emphasized the costs of growth. He discerned disservices, disamenities, disutilities, and uncompensated pain within the presumed affluence of a rising gross national product. Affluence and economic change generally produce 'diswelfares', 'disutilities', and 'illth' as well as wealth. Economic growth produces costs. If the burdens and prices of change are 'left to lie where they fall', then the vulnerable populations will bear the costs of the advances of others. This axiom obviously applies where the dwellings of the low income groups are destroyed in order to make possible high value commercial buildings. The poor are then left alone to compete for the limited and low quality stock of low rent housing, resulting in homelessness and spurts in the percentage of income going for housing. The investors in the commercial enterprises benefit; those with low income suffer. Obviously, there is a case

3

here for compensation to cover the pain and costs of dislocation.

A wider example is the use of unemployment as an anti-inflation device. In order to curb inflation and thus benefit exporters in particular, many suffer a severe drop in income. This decline is not due to anything that the unemployed have done. They are bearing the burden for the rest of society of an anti-inflation programme. To placate the anti-inflationary gods they are sacrificed on the altar of the Phillips Curve so that 'all' of the economy could presumably benefit. A disservice has been done to the sacrificed which should be atoned by unemployment benefits without stigma.

The costs of economic growth and stability are not evenly distributed. Most policies benefit some and penalize others. 'Macro benefits' accrue to those who are advantaged by governmental policies to buy military goods or to increase the interest rate; free trade aids export industries and harms firms and their employees oriented to domestic markets. The capitalist 'gales of creative destruction' which Schumpeter admired devastate human lives. If a society leaves 'the costs where they lie', if it does not attempt to shift burdens from the immediately vulnerable to all of society, especially those who directly benefit from the prices paid by the vulnerables, then the least well off bear the burden for the beneficiaries of growth.

True, individual polluters could be charged with the costs that they produce for society, as David Reisman argues. But for many diswelfares, the culprit is harder to identify, or a governmental policy is more difficult to construct and enforce. Here, public policies are indispensable.

The Welfare State, then, is an adaptation to the economic and social processes and changes of an advanced industrial society. It is compensation for the vulnerables who pay the prices of 'progress'. (Prevention of distress and need and reduction of inequalities are other roles of the Welfare State and we shall discuss later Titmuss's views on these two issues.) The Welfare State is not a 'handout' to the improvident as many of its critics choose to view it; most of us need its aid at some point because of the character of contemporary society; many suffer for the benefit of others.

The Welfare State is not a stopgap measure that developed in a society wildly bullish about its economic prospects; it is intrinsic

4

to the very functioning of modern society. Large scale business structures limit the options of people and make them vulnerable; governmental and business choices harm many families. Modern society has enlarged choices and enhanced standards of living for many; it has made most of us more vulnerable at the same time.

The Objectives of the Welfare State

Currently, discussions of the Welfare State revolve around what should be the level of expenditures and where to make cuts; only occasionally is the question raised of what additional aids or protection are needed. The question of what size and kind of Welfare State should be placed in the context of what should be the objectives of the Welfare State. A major part of Titmuss's attraction and usefulness is that this question of goals animated his analyses.

The post-Second World War Welfare State was initially propelled by broad, if also politically useful, concerns. The promulgation of the idea of the Welfare State during the Second World War in the official Beveridge Report was an effort in the UK to declare that there would no longer be 'Two Nations' of well-to-do and poor after the war, that the solidarity of the war effort would continue in the recognition of the responsibility of the state and citizens for the well-being of all. In France as well, the Welfare State programmes developed after 1945 were seen as a means to create one society after the rifts of defeat, collaboration and resistance.

Today, this binding mission of the Welfare State has been largely ignored. Titmuss never lost this vision. He regarded the Welfare State as the main engine of greater equality in both a quantitative and qualitative sense. The cash transfer systems of the Welfare State could not only even out the command over resources during the life-cycle of individuals but it could also reduce the income differences among households. The Welfare State's medical care and social services ('in-kind', non-cash activities) could reduce disparities among households in the accessibility and utilisation of these important resources. The lower income groups would benefit more than the higher income groups. A truly progressive tax system to provide funds for social expenditures would reduce income differences while the social expenditures themselves would be deeply redistributive. Titmuss may have understressed the importance of reducing inequalities in the original distribution of income and wealth in his belief that government, through social and tax decisions, could have a profound effect on the reduction of inequalities if it had the political will to do so.

Qualitatively, the public services of the Welfare State would treat everyone as a citizen worthy of equal respect. The differential treatment in institutions and daily life that the lack of money causes could be eliminated. A true Welfare State would avoid discrimination and stigma.

For Titmuss equality was a crucial goal but it was also a means. For he sought different relations among people. His objective was to restore and deepen the sense of community and mutual care in society. Without equality this spirit of common concern for other people, even for 'the stranger', could not be achieved. Money equality by itself did not assure the sense and practice of community. Institutions were needed which daily expressed the common bonds among people, which built interactions as moral transactions not only as market exchanges. The Welfare State provided the possibility of such institutions.

Titmuss's analysis did not centre on power or on the commanding heights of the economy as much as on the pursuit of community. He envisioned the Welfare State as a way of building links between persons, providing a common endeavour, a feeling of responsibility for one another. Rather than seeing the Welfare State as an opponent of voluntarism, that spontaneous feeling of responsibility for fellow beings, he regarded the Welfare State as empowering people to manifest concern for one another. In *The Gift Relationship* he portrayed the American system of market relationships in blood as reducing the quality and quantity of blood when compared with the British system of voluntarism based on the mutuality of the National Health Service.

Solidarity and friendship are the leitmotifs of a better society; they are exhibited in the daily life of people and their interactions, not in economic statistics. That is not to say that economic relationships are unimportant. The reduction of inequalities is central to the task of building solidaristic social relations and developing a web of relationships which fosters our concern for other people.

Why are solidaristic relations important? Because their absence divides people from one another, deprives each of the other's qualities, creates domination and subordination where they need not exist, makes each of us less of what he or she can be. Inequalities limit each of us, even those who are in the dominating positions, because we cannot have full relationships with others. The privileges of inequality as well as its disadvantages diminish all of us. And they make society grimmer. Economic gain becomes so centrally important either to protect what we have or to gain what we think we lack. Inequalities make economic goods too important in daily life and sustain the commercialization and banalization which occur in a growing number of societies today. (Titmuss was drawn in part to Third World societies because he hoped that their traditional values of solidarity would not be lost.)

Clearly, Titmuss did not think that equality assured better social relations; but he also clearly did not believe that in the absence of equality a satisfactory base for improved social relations could develop. Equality was not only worthy of itself but, for Titmuss, it was also a means to a qualitative advance in human relations, the emergence of a community based on mutual concern. While he was concerned with economic relations, he saw them in the broader context of social relations and civic virtue, the idea of a community rather than of an aggregate of isolated individuals tied together only by a momentary and strained cash nexus. Like Marx and Durkheim he saw the cash nexus and the business contract as alienated forms of community. This vision led him to criticize sharply the dangers of stigma and market imperatives in social policy.

Those who believe that he was heavily influenced in his aspirations for the Welfare State by the contributions of social policy to the integration and cohesion of society during the Second World War may be right. So may be those who see a religious element in his work and a hope that his England could be a beacon for the world. More important than the origins of his objectives is the profundity of his vision, the effort to provide a philosophical and moral direction for the Welfare State. In a period when the Welfare State is thought about in terms of cutting programmes, in protecting almost mystical 'incentives', or as a financial burden, when only 'money talks' and 'efficiency' is the basis for choice, the broader view of the possibilities and meanings of the Welfare State need to come to the fore. Few today speak and write about the Welfare State in terms of the broad potential that Titmuss envisioned. He would test what the Welfare State is and is being made against what its role might be in softening and challenging the economizing and commercializing of society. This orientation is, in my opinion, the greatest legacy of Titmuss.

The Economist Mode

Titmuss was critical of the growing domination of the mode of thought of the economist as *the* 'sound' way of approaching social policy and of the ideology of the market as the best or preferred way of dealing with social need and the constructing of social policies. In both respects, his warnings are pertinent to the current period in which economists and their ideological acolytes rule the discussion of social policy.

The economistic mode is exemplified in cost-benefit or cost-effectiveness analyses in which the benefits accruing from a prospective policy are compared with the costs of that policy. A cost-effective policy is one in which benefits outrun costs and the policy with the highest benefit surplus is to be preferred over policies with lesser net returns. The problems of cost-benefit analysis have been sounded many times[1] but the Titmuss critique is still worthy of attention, especially since the simple cost-effectiveness mentality still prevails.

The foundation of his scepticism is his suspicion of statistics, official and otherwise. Like most investigators who are close to the data that they use, he was aware of their grave limitations and distortions. In a period when economists with their econometric techniques are willing to measure confidently every tendency currently appearing, forecast with great aplomb trends and the outcomes of every possible change, a heavy dose of agnosticism is needed. Not only was Titmuss critical of the instruments of estimation and predication, but he also forced attention to the basic quality of data: he recognized early on the computer world's once widely accepted wisdom of 'garbage in, garbage out'. Titmuss emphasized that data are a product, not an uncovering.

The shakiness of the structure of data on which analysis and policy are based is well known but largely ignored. We know less about the world than we think and much of what we 'know' is wrong. Harsh agnosticism, no doubt, but needed scepticism. The Titmuss suspicions of data and measurement are needed ingredients of policy analysis and an antidote to the assuredness and assertiveness with which the economistic mode is employed.

What particularly bothered Titmuss was the homogenization of dispersion that is endemic in econometric exercises. There are no average families, he argued, and social change, such as in work patterns, can be profound and swift, eluding their modelling. The complexity of personal situations makes what he termed 'computerama' difficult (here he was referring to what he considered naive notions of a negative income tax offered by economists that obviate the need for a variety of policies to deal with income deficiency). Models are muddles for they largely ignore the issues involved in the administration and implementation of programmes. Economic models of human situations and distress are misleading and do not provide a reliable methodology for making choices. We should avoid the hardening of categories and the simplification of reality.

The cost-efficiency approach relies on the quantification of everything. Not only is Oscar Wilde's comment on those who know the price of everything and the value of nothing appropriate but the quantitative goal approach biases the choice of policies towards the quantifiable. What cannot be measured tends to be ignored or downplayed, especially negative effects upon the society in general, e.g. commercialization of life, and upon the poor in particular, e.g. increasing stigma. The methodology ordains the ingredients of choice.

The Market

Market criteria and private enterprises in the social sector result in the loss of equality as a goal. Profits and narrow efficiency-cost criteria displace the objective of developing a society which moves toward greater equality. The private sector is not just an alternative to the public sector in providing services – a contention of many marketeers – but it also subordinates the equality objective; it changes the goals of the Welfare State.

The call for markets and privatization is misleading because, as Titmuss stressed, the state offers many incentives (especially in the form of reduced taxation) and supports to private markets in the social sector. An outstanding current example in the United States is the exemption from taxation of up to $4,000 a year for couples who invest in Individual Retirement Accounts, a budding alternative to the public Social Security system. The public–private split in thinking is misleading.

Titmuss's criticisms of reliance on the market and privatization (transforming public services into profit-making, privately owned enterprises) as the way of handling social needs are certainly relevant to the religious devotion to the private market exhibited by many today in Britain and the United States. He strongly questioned the appropriateness and effectiveness of the market for dealing with the conditions that social policies confronted. Market and profit criteria should not determine the quality and nature of care that individuals experience. At one level, he argued that the market has characteristic failures: it does a poor job with excluded low income people; it leads to a two tier system as lower-income people are shunted out of the private market into specially constructed and second-rate social programmes, strengthening stigma, social and political exclusion and inequalities; the market does not do well on the important issue of prevention, tending to neglect it completely as the external benefits are too widely dispersed to provide the limited resource and demand and supply conditions necessary for market operations.

The market is not a reliable allocator of resources. The dollars that consumers are willing to spend on a particular service may not coincide with social need. Information on what is useful is not widely or evenly disseminated; the adding up of individual decisions about the purchase of social services does not guarantee that what is desirable over the long run, or even the short run, will be accomplished.

Titmuss's most profound criticism of the market is in the tradition of Polanyi's *The Great Transformation*. The market has become independent of society and treats individuals as isolated, unsocial and chopped-up beings. The consumer of social services or other commodities is seen as operating in different markets and performing a variety of roles from worker to consumer, from family member to voter. Titmuss hit hard at the underlying sociological assumption of this way of conceptualizing economic and social life, declaring that 'People . . . do not "play" roles like actors. A role is something that a person is'.[2] The market mentality does not treat people as members of a community, experiencing intermingled activities and choices.

His perspective here is part of his broad approach to exchange which is basic to the market and to other transactions. He regarded, as anthropologists emphasize, that exchange is a social transaction. As Durkheim emphasized in *The Division of Labour*, the exchange that takes place through a contract, a market device, depends upon assumptions about the reliable behaviour of the participants in the contract, the social and legal norms and practices about contracts, its ultimate enforceability through a legal system. Exchange and market relations do not concern only the movement of a commodity or service against monetary bids. Exchange was historically a moral transaction[3] and retains much of this quality. When this moral quality is shorn from the exchange, not only do vulnerable people suffer and inequalities grow; society is then less cohesive, more selfish, and more commercial, losing the sense of what is important in human interactions. Exchanges have always a social dimension[4] and social policy is always a moral transaction[5] affecting social and community relations. The private sector seeks to ignore and escape this moral quality.

To be critical of markets and the private sector is not to argue that they have no function in the social policy sphere. Rather, it is to separate the private sector as an ideology from the private sector as a functioning mechanism. As ideology, the private sector is seen as always preferable to the public sector in dealing with a human problem and as offering the optimal use of resources, even from a long term or social perspective. As a functioning mechanism the question is under what circumstances and for what ends is a private market desirable? There is no predetermined assurance that the market always produces the most desirable results. The predisposition to a market and private sector mentality and solution was, for Titmuss, an imposition of ideology rather than a reasoned response to a specific situation. This is certainly an appropriate caution when the private market is apothesized.

One implication is that social policy should not be treated as an economic instrument, an adjunct to the market. Directing social policies mainly so that they facilitate market relations, e.g.

training and 'rehabilitating' young people so that they could work more effectively even when employment is lacking for them, is a distortion, in Titmuss's view, of what social policies are about: aiding the individual to realize human potentialities and binding individuals together in a more caring society. Currently, the efforts to convert social programmes to selective and temporary economic programmes for young people having difficulties in gaining employment may lose the essential social objective of social policies as well as failing to achieve their more specific goal of gaining a secure foothold in the labour market for the disadvantaged young.

Titmuss's writings can be seen as an effort to provide an alternative approach to that of the economists. He not only offered a different value base than efficiency in looking at social phenomena. He sought different modes of analyses, breaking down the distinction between economic and social policies (as in 'The social division of welfare' where he argued convincingly that governmental and market policies which had similar effects in terms of the distribution of income should be considered together as alternatives rather than treated separately as social benefits, tax benefits and fringe benefits), insisting on the role of large scale societal changes in individual behaviour which made microeconomic analyses and remedies misleading.

Titmuss did not complete the task of working out a comprehensive analytical alternative to the economic mode of thought. To some extent, every generation has to develop its own social mode of analysis as conditions and competing modes of analysis change. But Titmuss pushed along the road of developing a theory of social policy. He refused to accept the domination of social policy by economic theory as the one 'rational' mode for public discourse and offered alternative modes of analytical thought and political discourse.

Stigma and Selectivity

In Britain and the United States in the 1980s political pressure is strong to increase means-testing and reduce or eliminate universal programmes available to all. Means-testing would restrict public programmes to those below a low income level and thereby reduce costs. The Titmuss argument against this selective orientation centred largely on the dangers of stigma.

Stigma threatens the person stigmatized, the programme, and the society which condones stigmatization. The stigmatized person experiences the fact of being separated from the rest of society, of being treated as someone different, marginalized, as less than others, as not worthy of the everyday exchanges and transactions that make up the community. This experience often produces a 'spoiled identity', a self-image which is damaged and diminished, impeding the autonomous actions of the individual. 'If people are treated as burdens', Titmuss declared, 'they will behave as burdens'.[6] He could have added that if they are treated as untrustworthy, subject to harsh checks of their eligibility, they will often fulfil that prediction.

As is now well known, programmes aimed at stigmatized people tend to be of low quality; programmes only for the poor tend to be poor programmes. Emergency rather than preventive care is the focus. Funds tend to be inadequate; staff demoralized by the overwhelming demands on them and the low status and economic rewards accorded their work. Programmes exclusively for the poor tend to be politically vulnerable, subject to erosion, frequent and disturbing changes, and serve as a popular target for attack. A stigmatized clientele stigmatizes a programme; a stigmatized programme stigmatizes its clientele.

The greatest danger, in Titmuss's view, is that programmes targeted on a vulnerable population weaken the bonds of a society. People are divided into the worthy who do not need the programme and the less worthy who do. The splits in society widen and deepen rather than narrow. What the Welfare State could do in terms of improving the quality of society is blocked by the worsening of the divides between classes and races. Stigma and means-testing stratify a society more intensely, particularly since the non-stigmatized may begin to think that they are financially victimized by the stigmatized recipients of social benefits or that these beneficiaries are not properly grateful for all that is being done for them. The National Health Service was a great advance in Titmuss's view, because it was universal, treating all alike, providing a common experience. Universal programmes are not only more likely to be preventive but they also connect people and develop mutual interests rather than promoting competing interests of taxpayers and Welfare State beneficiaries.

The social costs of separation are becoming increasingly high in Britain, the United States and other nations as many poor people are demarcated by race or immigrant status. The divides in a society deepen when racial and ethnic differences are involved. Some notion of inferiority is likely to be attached to those who use the means-tested programmes; racism and ethnocentrism deepen. The Welfare State which could bind, now divides. While means-testing seems to save money in the short-run by narrowing eligibility, over the long-run it may add to the economic, political and social costs of a racially and ethnically divided society. Such real costs do not appear in cost-benefit calculations.

What is particularly distressing in the production of stigma is that it is not necessary. Some of the objectives of selectivity, Titmuss argued, can be attained by other approaches. For example, particular geographic areas could be designated as low income areas so that individual means-testing would not be necessary. Or, a current American proposal calls for a (taxable) family allowance to all one-parent families with the absent parent contributing to the government fund from which the allowance is paid; no means-testing would be required.

The pressure today is strongly towards increasing selectivity and the narrowing of eligibility for social programmes. Money-saving is the objective. The Titmuss analysis questions whether expenditures would be reduced in the long-run. The damage to individuals and the nation of increasing selectivity and harsh means-testing is great. Reliance on them to reduce costs is likely to be 'penny wise, pound foolish'. Statesmanship and citizenship require longer term vision.

The Conduct of Programmes

The stigma question is part of the issue of how programmes are conducted. Titmuss was the master of the detail as well as of the philosophical or social generalization. He saw that the daily life of a programme is what a policy is all about. What kind of aid is provided and secured, how people are treated, the training of programme personnel as well as their outlook are all crucial to the effects of a programme on its presumed beneficiaries.

The character of a programme is set by the details of its daily life, not only by its overall design. Titmuss loved to tell of how on his visits to local Supplementary Benefits offices around the United Kingdom he would first use the toilet. He believed that the quality of the toilet facility – its cleanliness, its paint and lights – revealed the staff's concern about the claimants. For that concern is basic to the claimant's well-being. As in many other circumstances he sought the telling incident or detail.

Again, in the touching appendix to *Social Policy* on his experience as a cancer patient with the National Health Service he emphasized that the clinic procedures assured equal, high-level treatment to all patients. Case – defined in terms of income or education – did not affect the treatment that was offered or the order in which patients were taken. The quality of care is not only exhibited in the formal aspects of the service but in the way that it is presented and the attention accorded patients.

How programmes are conducted is centrally important in their impact. Titmuss saw the importance of programme design and implementation in deeper terms than is customary. For example, he advocated that children's allowance be given to 'the mum' rather than included in the father's pay packet. If the mother directly received the allowance, it strengthened her control over the way the money was spent and increased the likelihood that the sum would aid the child. Familial structure and parental behaviour cannot be ignored in the designing of programmes.

Titmuss early understood that the Welfare State could not be understood in its impact without knowing who its recipients and beneficiaries were, the differences in their needs and changing circumstances. He recognized, as Hilary Rose has pointed out, that women were the major clientele of social programmes, a fact that is still not well understood and even less acted upon in positive, useful ways. Since women outlive men, they constitute more of old age pensioners, especially the aged (past 75) and the frail elderly. Women are involved in medical services more than men, for themselves, their children and their aged parents. Single parents who need financial aid and social supports like child care are mainly women. As women increasingly enter the paid labour force, they also require the protection of unemployment benefits and occupational safety and health regulations.

Social policies still only dimly respond to the needs of women in the design and daily conduct of programmes and ignore the fact that most Welfare State employees are women.

Reducing expenditure on a programme not only collapses its scope but also transforms its character, leading to increased pressure to bar people from gaining access to needed aid or ending rapidly such aid. Inhumanity becomes a social policy because it keeps down costs. The quality of a programme deteriorates, making it less useful to people and less sought. Tighter eligibility rules reduce people's willingness to apply for aid. Financial pressures, Titmuss realized, change programmes, shift priorities and purposes – seldom to the benefit of those in need.

Challenging reductions in programmes or advocating restorations of some cuts require more than the examination of budgets. The effects of reduced expenditures on daily functioning is the crucial issue. A social programme is what it does daily and how it does it. The political atmosphere of the 1980s is poisoning the character of programmes and eroding their contributions; the Titmuss perspective leads us to examine the delicate processes which shape the on-going experience of those who need services and benefits. The financial balance sheet has to be compared with the human balance sheet of distress, despair, isolation and stigma.

Titmuss was no rosy observer of social policy. Early on he argued that social programmes had deep problems and that the Welfare State produced inequalities and casualties. What he particularly offered is a philosophy of welfare. That perspective is missed today and makes difficult the current task – to defend and change the Welfare State. It should be defended in terms of the principles of societal responsibility and the responsibilities of building a more caring society; it should be changed to be more useful, less bureaucratic, more effective, more egalitarian. Titmuss called us to a grand vision of what a society could be and of the contributions that social policy could make toward the realization of that vision. The inroads of recent attacks on social policy make clear that this perspective is lacking today. The writings of Richard Titmuss, the premier philosopher and sociologist of the Welfare State, remain a major source of the reinvigoration of the philosophy of welfare.

Notes

1 Among the highlighted problems are: how to define what is a 'cost' and what is a 'benefit', i.e. how many side and second- and third-order effects over what time period are to be considered? (There are now experts who are called 'benefit hunters' or 'cost hunters' because of their skill in locating unrecognized benefits or costs of a policy.) Secondly, the interest rate applied to discounting the future benefits to give them a present value is somewhat arbitrary and has a marked effect on the total value of benefits. Thirdly, it is not easy to put a monetary value on all benefits and costs.

2 Titmuss, R. M., *Essays on the Welfare State*, p. 107 (Allen & Unwin, 1958).

3 Titmuss, R. M., *The Gift Relationship*, p. 72 (Allen & Unwin, 1970).

4 As above.

5 Titmuss, R. M., *Commitment to Welfare*, p. 20 (Allen & Unwin, 1968).

6 As above, p. 26.

CHAPTER

1

Introduction to the 1964 Edition of Equality by R. H. Tawney

I

When Tawney wrote his Epilogue and Preface to the 1951 edition of *Equality* the British economy had not fully recovered from the Second World War. Substantial progress had been made, more progress indeed in terms of annual rates of growth than was to occur in the 1950s, but much still remained to be done to make up for the long years when the garment of hardship had been willingly and quietly worn by the British people. Liberty, which they had prized so highly, had to be paid for not only during the war but for years afterwards.

But what was borne in the heat of a civilians' war was not so acceptable in peacetime. The right to choose between satisfying different economic and social wants became available again. And properly so. Patience lost some of its pristine virtue, especially among those who, unlike Tolstoy's creatures, had not been inured by custom and class to shuffle their feet.

For the more privileged, whose vision of Britain in the approaching 1950s bore some resemblance to the placid country-house glories of Edwardian England, it was hard to accept the merits of planning, nationalization and the 'Welfare State'. Like the trade unions, the British Medical Association and the Law Society they wanted to be left undisturbed to live out the destinies of tradition. They had not the imagination at that time to see how much benefit they would gain from using (and knowing far better

18

than others how to use) what we call the 'social services'; they had
not realized that 'classless' services (in the sense of equalizing
opportunities for people in unequal circumstances) were impossible to attain in a deeply class-divided society; nor could they
then appreciate one of the positive achievements of a socialist
administration in negatively holding at bay for six years the
predatory vulgarities of land speculators and property developers.
Finally, they had hardly begun to see that more equality in income
and wealth, education, and the enjoyment of the decencies of
social living might conceivably be a democratic precondition of
faster economic growth.

II

Tawney, with his historian's eye to the future, saw signs of
approaching reaction when he wrote in 1951. But he also saw
signs and, on balance, stronger signs, 'that a somewhat more
equalitarian social order is in progress of emerging'. Optimism
that anti-social inequalities had receded since 1938 was justified,
he thought, on the evidence then available. He looked first, as he
had always done and as socialists should continue to do, at the
two most massive pillars of indefensible disparities of income and
opportunity: inherited wealth and the educational system. He
pointed out that death duties had been steeply raised, so much so
that the state took 80 per cent from estates of £1,000,000 and
over. On the basis of the official statistics published by the Board
of Inland Revenue, he also concluded that 'disparities of pecuniary
income, if they remain surprising, are less portentous today than
in a recent past'. Heavier and more steeply graduated taxation had
been effective, and 'the herd of dinosaurs', the top, post-tax
incomes, had dwindled very considerably in size.

The development of the education and social services, which
had crept so slowly into an apologetic twentieth-century existence,
was a second reason for tempered optimism. In particular,
Tawney hoped that much would flow from the full implementation of the 1944 Education Act for the benefit of all children, and
that one-class private 'public' schools, those bastions of privilege
and snobbery (as he called them), would be radically transformed
into institutions with a civic purpose.

At the end of 1960, at the age of 80, Tawney began to think of writing a new introduction to *Equality*. Still a student, still (as he would say) 'getting over his education', he asked some of us to provide him with a reading list. He had been immersed again in Tudor and Stuart England and wanted now to understand the England of the 1950s. But the task was beyond him. Though his spirit was as lively as ever, physically he was tired; 'I sleep too much', he said, as though he should not enjoy a larger share of that desirable commodity than other and younger men.

He was daunted too by the complexities of the modern world of statistical fact. He realized that the simpler tools of measurement and analysis used by himself and others in the past were no longer adequate. Ancient inequalities had assumed subtler and more sophisticated forms; in part the product of far-reaching technological, social and economic changes. The conventional tablets of public information about the primary sources of disparities in living standards had thus become superficial, misleading, or wholly useless.

By 1960 England had become a more muffled society. The condition of its people, rich, middling and poor, was concealed by a combination of myth and computer incompetence. Inequality, as a subject of political discourse, was less in evidence everywhere, and what remained of poverty in Britain was thought to be either eradicable through the 'natural' processes of growth or as constituting a permanent residue of the unfortunate and irresponsible. The rich, it was further argued, were no longer with us; they had been taxed out of existence by the class which had formerly revered them. This was the climate of majority opinion after a decade of Conservative rule at the end of which the real value of disposable income per head had risen by less than a half. The common man, his rulers assured him in common language, 'had never had it so good'. It was high time he was led into the larger market place of choice where he could purchase for himself and his family whatever he preferred in the way of education, medical care and social security. Was this the end of equalitarian ideology?

III

I too am daunted at the thought of surveying the 1950s, however summarily, the more so since I lack the skills that Tawney had.

Introduction to the 1964 Edition of Equality *by R. H. Tawney*

The basic research, which would make possible comparisons with the past, in terms of wealth, income, inheritance, command over resources in time, health, housing and educational opportunity has been done partially or not at all. All these components must now enter any measurement of changes in inequality over time. Epidemiological research into the causes of social diseases such as lung cancer, coronary thrombosis and certain forms of mental illness has shown the importance of considering the whole complex of needs, opportunities and resources. Social and economic inequality has as many diverse and changing sources in the environment as the physical and psychological diseases of affluence.

We thus delude ourselves if we think that we can equalize the social distribution of life chances by expanding educational opportunities while millions of children live in slums without baths, decent lavatories, leisure facilities, room to explore and the space to dream. Nor do we achieve with any permanency a fairer distribution of rewards and a society less sharply divided by class and status by simply narrowing the differences in cash earnings among men during certain limited periods of their lives. During the past decade these differences, measured crudely in absolute terms, have widened substantially when calculated over the whole of a man's working life. Comparisons which take account of only a short span of time or of certain ages, though often made by those at the start of their business or professional careers, are today inappropriate and misleading. These critics of so-called teenage affluence forget that the whole complex system of incremental rewards, non-monetary as well as monetary, for professional and other classes is fundamentally different from the traditional and often primitive system in use for manual workers. This is one of the basic divisions in our society and one which is perhaps most often taken for granted.

Consider, for example, the question of the earnings of working-class boys and girls. These are often quoted today in support of the belief that Britain is a more equal society. Compared with the lot of earlier generations in the 1930s, working-class boys of 16 are undoubtedly better off in terms of real cash earnings from work, and maybe better off in weekly disposable cash than upper-middle-class boys at school or in a university today. The official statistics of earnings and income at, say, age 16 or 20 certainly

21

record them as being better off; an advantage which is recognized in the fact that they are required to pay more in taxes and social benefit charges than those who are still being subsidized educationally by the community.

Later in life, however, the latter may be twenty times or more better off than the former, measured solely in terms of annual cash income, with less disabling disease, a longer expectation of life, a lower age of retirement, more inherited wealth, a proportionately greater and more assured pension, a tax free lump sum perhaps one hundred times larger, and in receipt of substantially more non-wage income and amenities in forms that escape income tax, being neither money nor convertible into money. Which of two individuals from these classes receives more aid in absolute terms from the generality of taxpayers through 'the social services' and other redistributive mechanisms, especially during that phase of life when the foundations of earning capacity, opportunity and achievement are laid?

Such questions cannot be answered until we have considered how all the elements in 'standards of living' and 'styles of life' can be identified, measured and brought together. How do we in fact today define a 'standard of life' for purposes of estimating degrees of inequality between groups or classes of people? We have also to take account, in any realistic definition, of the period of time during which a given standard is enjoyed; of the problem of determining the unit to be counted – whether the individual or the family – and of what security and 'life chances' mean to those who plan the distribution of their wealth on a four-generation basis and those who can only command a week's resources.[1]

Whether one approves or disapproves, however, of the notion of equality as a political objective, it surely remains of supreme importance to the health of democratic societies to know the facts. Should we not continue to ask whether more or fewer of the leading positions of power and influence in society are held by those who are rich and whose fathers were rich? Whether more or fewer of the children of unskilled workers leave school at the age of 15, socially malnourished, and barely able to write a letter or read a book? Whether the total life disadvantages of leaving school at 15 and living in a slum are not becoming greater handicaps in Britain today as they are in the United States (thus leaving crime as the one remaining major form of acquisitive social mobility)?[2] Whether old age is or is not a period during which inequalities steadily widen? Whether wealth, however defined, transmitted or stored, is or is not being increasingly concentrated in the hands of a tiny minority?

There are many students of contemporary society in the United Staes and Britain who now believe that these countries have been transformed or are being transformed inexorably into non-ideological welfare states. According to them, these questions do not arise or soon will cease to arise. It is agreed that they were relevant in the past, but it is argued that industrial societies today, through the automatic processes of growth and the establishment of welfare, have largely solved their problems of redistributive social justice. Politically, all that is now left for debate are relatively minor differences between party programmes: five shillings or ten shillings more a week for old age pensioners; 5 per cent or 7 per cent of young people at universities; a 3 per cent or a 4 per cent rate of growth in the economy. Professor Lipset in his book *Political Man* (1960) spoke for many when he said (in summarizing the discussions of a world congress of intellectuals in 1955) that 'the ideological issues dividing left and right [have] been reduced to a little more or a little less government ownership and economic planning'; and there was general agreement that it really makes little difference in the West 'which political party controls the domestic policies of individual nations'.

We have had our passions; now we can leave to the sophisticated and the academic these matters of 'nicely calculated less or more'. What remains is social engineering; a mixture of art and technique in the manipulation and ordering of an existing 'good' society. It spells the end of utopian thought. Man has no longer to reach out for the politically impossible. Henceforward he must busy himself with the resurrection of utilitarian theory and cultivate the new stoicism of affluence.

The broader implications of this philosophy of history have not been examined by those who are today advancing these arguments on both sides of the Atlantic. Yet they are of profound importance to the future well-being of the democracies. The sense of freedom and self-respect, implicit in the notion of purposive control over man's secular affairs, can be diminished if it is believed that political choice has been narrowed to considerations of technique and administration. If there are no radical choices to be made

23

between conflicting social values then we have only to follow where technological change leads us. Everything becomes a matter of compromise between power groups in society. Political democracy becomes a device for choosing between different leaders but not between different social objectives. Economic growth becomes an end – not a means to serve liberty and alternative conceptions of excellence. In such circumstances, it can be presumed that the individual's sense of political freedom is diminished. He can no longer feel and no longer believe that a radically different society may or could emerge as a result of political conflict. It does not, of course, follow that the idea of social progress and the cultivation of more civilized attitudes to the deprived and the deviant necessarily come to a halt. But it is no longer possible for the deviant to be admired as a visionary, exploring the foothills of a new social order. If the path of progress is fixed and immutable, conformity becomes the supreme virtue. As Tawney remarked, 'the failures and fools – the Socrates and St Francis – of one age are the sages and saints of another'.

The logic of the argument that we have arrived – or are about to arrive – at a non-ideological destination also implies a lessening in the intensity of the search for truth about the human condition – for the basic facts about the social system and the life chances of the people in that system. If the 'good' economic society were already established it follows as a matter of course that the facts we should need to keep it in balance and repair would be of a different order from those required to support the case for radical change. Questions of a fundamental kind would seem less relevant; the technicalities of adjustment more important. The social sciences would thus be less concerned with values and with generalizations; more preoccupied with techniques and with providing the facts required by political engineers.

In this abbreviated form the discussion may not seem compelling. The reader who feels that less than justice has been done to those who now view the Western world through non-ideological spectacles should consult some of the more recent works on the subject.[3]

IV

We are thus led to ask: is Tawney's *Equality* now out of date? Is the view that equalitarian ideology is irrelevant to modern conditions supported by the evidence? Have we in Britain reached such an equalitarian position that further substantial measures of collective redistribution are not called for, economically and morally?

These are primarily questions of definition and questions of fact. The social and moral case for equality, as stated by Tawney, cannot be more persuasively argued and I make no attempt to do so here. He did not write of it in the naive sense of equality of talent or merit or personality. His concern was with fundamental equalities before the law; the removal of collectively imposed social and economic inequalities; the equalizing of opportunities for all to secure certain goods and services; the education of all children to make them capable of freedom and more capable of fulfilling their personal differences; the enlargement of personal liberties through the discovery by each individual of his own and his neighbour's endowment. Hence he stressed the critical role of education and of equality in communication between human beings. The supreme consideration was everyman's uniqueness 'without regard to the vulgar irrelevancies of class and income'. In spite of their varying characters and capacities 'it is the fact that men possess in their common humanity a quality which is worth cultivating, and that a community is most likely to make the most of that quality if it takes it into account in planning its economic organization and social institutions – if it stresses lightly differences of wealth and birth and social position, and establishes on firm foundations institutions which meet common needs and are a source of common enlightenment and common enjoyment'.

These were to Tawney the social objectives; never to be completely attained but always to be sincerely sought. As he said, 'what matters to the health of society is the objective towards which its face is set'. We are now being told that this is an old-fashioned idea in as much as we have pushed the principle of equality in policy and practice as far as it can reasonably be set. Thus, a different overriding objective must be substituted: in a word, growth – or higher standards of material living in which all

25

are promised a share by the market. Such pockets of poverty and residual distress as still prevail will in time automatically and gracefully succumb to the determinism of growth. This will be achieved by a natural process of market levitation; all classes and groups will stand expectantly on the political right as the escalator of growth moves them up.

On what basis of fact do these theories and arguments rest? The questions we need to ask are of two kinds: the first are concerned with the fabric of British society today in comparison with the recent past; the second relate to the future. What economic and technological changes are in the making which are likely to increase or diminish the case for equalitarian principles and policies?

To examine these questions seriously and to consider each and every aspect of inequality in detail would call for another book – or series of books. All we can attempt here is to cite a few of the more important studies in recent years and to draw attention to a number of relevant sources.[4]

V

Still the most striking fact about British society is the great concentration in the ownership of personal net capital. According to Professor Lydall and Mr Tipping, 1 per cent of the population owned 42 per cent in 1951–6 and 5 per cent owned 67.5 per cent.[5] Even these proportions are underestimates, for the figures exclude pension funds and trusts (which have grown enormously in recent years), and they do not take account of the increasing tendency for large owners of property to distribute their wealth among their families, to send it abroad and to transform it in other ways.[6]

This degree of concentration in the holding of wealth is nearly twice as great as it was in the United States in 1954, and far higher than in the halcyon days of American capitalism in the early 1920s.[7] Another fact of central importance has been underlined by the recent Bank of England reports on the ownership of shares and debentures. If, as the *Guardian* commented, these figures mean what they seem to say, 'institutional investors now dominate the investment scene to an extent greater than the City had hitherto imagined'.[8] On the face of it, concentration in the ownership of wealth and concentration in investment decisions would appear to be linked, though in what ways and with what consequences it is impossible to say without more information.

When we ask questions about recent trends in the distribution of wealth it is not irrelevant (in the absence of adequate British studies) to look to the United States. Since about 1949, wealth inequality has been growing in that country, the rate of increase being more than twice as fast as the rate of decline between 1922 and 1949.[9] Measured in terms of the percentage change in wealth holdings by the top 1 per cent, the growth of inequality during 1949–56 (the latest available data) was more striking than at any time during at least the past forty years. Affluence in the United States has not been accompanied by any automatic, 'built-in' equalizer. True, the thing may exist in theory, but it has not shown itself in practice.

There is little evidence to suggest that Britain has not been following in the same path since the end of the 1940s. It is even possible that inequality in the ownership of wealth (particularly in terms of family holdings) has increased more rapidly in Britain than in the United States since 1949. The British system of taxation is almost unique in the Western world in its generous treatment of wealth-holders in respect of settlements, trusts, gifts and other arrangements for redistributing and rearranging income and wealth. This is reflected in the remarkable fact that in the mid-1950s it was in the young adult age group (20–24) that the concentration of wealth in relatively few hands was most marked.

Mr Revell has recently shown that the total of personal wealth in Britain is now much larger than previous estimates have allowed for, and that the chance of possessing an estate of a given size has increased more for younger people than for older people since 1926.[10] Mr Harbury, in another recent study of inheritance, concluded that 'there was no very marked change in the relative importance of inheritance in the creation of the personal fortunes of the top wealth-leavers of the generations of the mid-twenties and the mid-fifties of this century. For either, the chance of leaving an estate valued at over £100,000, or even over £500,000 was outstandingly enhanced if one's father had been at least moderately well off.'[11]

Long years of economic depression, a civilians' war, rationing and 'fair shares for all', so-called 'penal rates' of taxation and estate duty, and the 'Welfare State' have made little impression on the holdings of great fortunes. The institution of concentrated wealth in Britain appears to be as tenacious of life as Tawney's intelligent tadpoles. Wealth still bestows power, more power than income, though it is probably exercised differently, and with more respect for public opinion than in the nineteenth century.

In contrast to what we know of life in societies of privilege, the notion and experience of social equality has had a more fragile history: 'much of its own proper beauty is locked in the hearts of unborn artists'.[12] Thirty to forty years ago political scientists and philosophers discussed these aspects of the human condition. Today, they are either passed over in silence or dismissed as irrelevant to the health of society now and in the future. Will it matter if, in ten years' time, 5 per cent of British families own 80 per cent of personal wealth in the country? Or must we assume that the continued existence of the National Health Service and somewhat more generous allowances for those on National Assistance will relieve us of the responsibility of remarking on such a stifling degree of inequality?

The statistical darkness that surrounds the distribution of income is almost as thick as that which covers the distribution of wealth. For a great many reasons, which are described elsewhere,[13] the darkest part of the income country is that inhabited by the top income groups. Their behaviour, as reported statistically by the Board of Inland Revenue, has puzzled students of income distribution during the last twenty-five years. Some of them have been forced to the conclusion that the changes in the percentage shares of various income groups between 1938 and the 1950s was due almost entirely to the behaviour of these very high incomes. The writings of tax lawyers, tax planning consultants and death duty consultants, and the publicity material issued by insurance companies show that, during this period, the behaviour patterns of the rich increased in complexity, diversity and subtlety, and the income group involved probably became more numerous. Little of this behaviour is revealed in the official statistics of work done (or tax returns examined) by the Board. The darkness has become more impenetrable; the secrecy more pervasive.

One American economist, examining critically in 1960 the

assumption of an income revolution in Britain, failed to find evidence of substantial turmoil.[14] After making various adjustments for missing investment income and undistributed company profits he concluded that the levelling of pre-tax income during the most devastating war Britain has fought in modern times had been exaggerated. After taking account of the effects of fiscal redistribution, imputed social services benefits and other factors he found that 'the 1949–55 interval shows a four per cent rise in inequality, and the over-all 1938–55 decline is more than halved. In sum, the official figures exaggerate the over-all levelling and hide a clear reversal of the trend after 1949.' Contrary to the findings of Professor Lydall and others who had reached different conclusions, he saw 'no convincing evidence of a "natural" levelling' since 1938. The income 'revolution' which did occur (attributable almost wholly to changes in the top 2 per cent of incomes) 'was a largely inadvertent or accidental by-product of the high taxes, subsidies and dividend restraint required to finance the military budget without runaway inflation' during the war; since 1949 it had been clearly reversed.

What is common ground among those who have studied these statistics of income is that the conventional annual returns do not depict the long-term gains of shareholders. Professor Lydall and Mr Tipping have estimated that the top 1 per cent of persons owned in 1954 81 per cent of stocks and shares in companies.[15] These, as Mr Douglas Jay has pointed out, are appreciating on average over a period of years by something like £1,000 million a year, without the shareholders subscribing any new money or performing any new service at all.[16] This phenomenon of long term capital gains in the hands of the minority who hold equity shares is, as he says, a relatively new force in the British economy, and has great social implications for the future. Left to itself – as it has largely been left since the end of the 1940s – it can only grind out more inequality in the distribution of income and wealth.

When we turn from trying to understand the behaviour of the top income groups to studying those at the bottom we find more light if not more sweetness. The poor have for long rendered great service to the behavioural sciences; they have helped to train countless sociologists, doctors and market researchers. Deferentially, they were conditioned in the nineteenth century; they are accustomed to answering embarrassing questions; they are more easily accessible; and their income and expenditure lives are simpler to analyse.

The studies of British poverty in the 1950s by Professor Peter Townsend, Mrs Dorothy Wedderburn and Mr Tony Lynes have produced no evidence that inequality of incomes is succumbing to economic growth. On the contrary, the very poorest families, those on National Assistance who might have been expected to benefit most as the rest of us were in a position to be more generous, are relatively worse off today than in 1948.

Mr Lynes has recently summarized these reports on poverty. Let him speak for himself.

> During the fifteen years since 1948, the poor have been hit much harder by rising prices than the rest of the population. The real improvement in the National Assistance rate for a single pensioner, even after the recent increase, is not 55 per cent [as shown by the official retail price index] but 32 per cent, compared with the average rise in incomes for the nation as a whole of about 44 per cent. The gap between National Assistance and other incomes in terms of actual purchasing power, instead of narrowing, has actually widened since 1948, relatively as well as absolutely. The poorest tenth of the population are better off then they were; but the rest of the nation has advanced more rapidly.[17]

A new analysis by Professor Townsend and Dr Abel-Smith of the national surveys of income and expenditure carried out by the Ministry of Labour in 1953–4 and 1960 shows that there has been a sharp increase in the proportion of the population living at or around the official definition of subsistence[18] – an increase which appears to have been accompanied by a rise in the incidence of malnutrition. Dr Royston Lambert, who completed at the end of 1963 a detailed and penetrating analysis of the findings of the government's National Food Survey for the period 1950–60, reached the conclusion after reworking the data by family size that 'there are now more segments of the population below the British Medical Association standard and for more nutrients than in 1950'. In terms of the proportion of the population concerned 'the indications are that at least a quarter and probably a third of the people in Britain live in households which fail to attain all the desirable levels of dietary intake. And, contrary to what is so often believed, the numbers in this situation seem to have increased since the mid-fifties.'[19]

Crude and inadequate as these data may be, both for those at the top and those at the bottom of the income distribution, there is no support here for the notion that Britain has been moving in the direction of becoming a more equal society. Moreover, in important respects the trend of taxation changes in recent years has been markedly aggressive, especially the impact on low wage-earners of higher National Insurance and Health Service charges.

What does all this portend for the future? Clearly, no 'natural' law of levelling has been at work since the 1930s either in the field of income or wealth. The first sustained period of full employment in the British economy since (at least) the end of the nineteenth century has not acted as an automatic leveller and abolished the political case for equality. What, on the other hand, we can discern are the contrary tendencies of two major forces operating in Britain today as in the mixed economies of other nations of the Western world. The first, to which we have already referred, is the phenomenon of long-term capital gains and dividend income received by the minority who hold equity shares.

The second which, if we turn again for illumination to the United States (as Tawney often did for signposts to the future), seems likely to have much the same effects is represented by automation and other technological changes in production and distribution. The social and economic consequences of these changes are beginning to show themselves in the United States; despite a steady rise in the national product, unemployment has been growing in recent years. Each wavelet in the business cycle has left a larger number of workers high and dry on the beach.

The Industrial Revolution was not a 'once and for all' affair. The consequences of automation and its technological cousins on the one hand, and more dependent needs in childhood and old age on the other, will call for a much greater investment in people and social services and a renewed search for the answers to large disparities in wealth, income and educational opportunity. Science and technology are today beginning to accomplish as thorough a revolution in social and economic theory as they are in the theory of war and international relations. The conventional doctrine that machines make work is losing its validity; machines are now replacing workers. It is already clear from American experience that some of these victims of technological displacement are no longer 'resting between engagements' (which is the theory of unemployment insurance); they are permanently out of work, permanently liberated from work. By the end of 1962, one out of every seven youngsters between the ages of 16 and 21 who were out of school was also out of work. Among young Negroes the proportion was nearly one-third.

These consequences of technology in an age of abundance are more likely to increase than to decrease differentials in income and wealth if no major corrective policies are set to work. They will contribute to the present tendency (commented on by Professor Gunnar Myrdal) for class chasms in American society to increase, and for the class structure to stiffen.[20] Without a major shift in values, an impoverishment in social living for some groups can only result from this new wave of industrialism.

VI

It would be wrong to suppose that what is happening in the United States will necessarily happen in Britain. Nevertheless, there are common structural changes at work in both economies. And while both countries are committed to economic growth it is still not realized that growth is synonymous with change and that if we value growth we must accept change as an inevitable concomitant. Many of these changes, left to themselves and to the market place, must mean more inequality, more hardship, more neglect of people and the social environment. In important respects also the British soil is less prepared to accept and resolve the social costs of change; there is a much greater degree of concentration in the ownership of wealth than in the United States; education is more deeply divided by class and privilege; and because there is less land to spare the opportunities for property to be more widely shared are substantially fewer. The problem of racial discrimination in job opportunities has begun to reappear in Britain, encouraged by the Commonwealth Immigrants Act and condoned by the Ministry of Labour.

In all these fundamental sectors of wealth, income, education, employment and the ownership of land there are no signs that Britain has been moving towards a more classless society. Mr Christopher Hollis, reviewing Mr Guttsman's new book *The*

British Political Elite, came to the conclusion that the trend has been in the opposite direction:

> We had all taken for granted immediately after the war that progress, whether it was rapid or slow, would be in the direction of classlessness – that the public schools would be either abolished or reformed, that careers would be thrown increasingly open to talents. In the last years the opposite has been happening. The structure of industry is such that it is now in many ways more difficult to rise from the ranks than it has been in the past. There are fewer *novi homines* in positions of political importance, and the most interesting question of the moment is certainly whether that process will be reversed in the next years or at the next election or not.[21]

In pondering about this question he was led to ask another: do the English really prefer to be governed by old Etonians? This was one of Tawney's favourite questions. It led him to compile Appendix I of this book, which gives figures for the schools attended by certain members of different professions in 1927. With the help of Mrs A. Hackel, we have extracted similar figures for 1961 in respect of bishops, high court judges and bank directors (we were deterred from attempting such a comparison for the other professions listed in Appendix I by the very large numbers involved). The results are given in Appendix IA. They show that what Tawney had to say in the 1930s about the strikingly high proportion educated at public schools is still true today. The influence of these schools has waned just a little among the bishops, but it has not done so for judges and bank directors. Nearly one-third of 133 directors of the five banks in 1961 received their education at one school – Eton. They are, as the Rev. Daniel Jenkins has observed in another context, 'debtors to the rest of society'.[22] Elsewhere, Mr Guttsman has told us that since the 1920s the Etonian hold over the Conservative Party has dramatically increased.[23] Nearly two-thirds of the new Conservative MPs of the post-1945 generation were public school educated, compared with 35 per cent in 1918; the proportion of those recruited from the most exclusive public schools actually doubled.

This is but one reflection of the rapidly growing popularity and prosperity of the private school sector of education since the end of the 1940s. Aided by the taxpayer and the ratepayer through a variety of indirect subsidies – even to the extent of allowing public school fees as a deductible in the calculation of University grants and of classifying Eton as a 'charity' – the whole of our educational provision has continued to be dominated by an élite-type education. Its divisive influence is felt everywhere; it nourishes class consciousness, and the concept of a narrow ladder of educational opportunity for a few 'exceptional' individuals.

The subject of this 'hereditary curse' (as Tawney put it) has become almost a national obsession – both by those who defend the system and those who criticize it for its effects on other people and on the nation in general. Contrast, for example, the lack of attention since 1950 to the needs of the C and D stream children in the secondary modern schools and our disastrous failure to reform the apprenticeship system. Until we, as a society, can rid ourselves of the dominating influences of the private sector of education we shall not have the will to embark on an immensely higher standard of provision for all those children whose education now finishes when it has hardly begun. Nor shall we have the moral conviction to search more intensively and more widely for greater equality in all spheres of our national life.

Notes

1 Some of these problems of definition and measurement are discussed in Titmuss, R. M., *Income Distribution and Social Change* (Allen and Unwin, 1962), and Wootton, B., *The Social Foundations of Wage Policy* (Unwin University Books, 1962).

2 Miller, H. P., 'Money value of an education', *Occupational Outlook Quarterly* (September, 1961), p. 4.

3 For British references see the sources quoted in Titmuss, R. M., *Income Distribution and Social Change*, esp. chap. 1; and Hartley, A., *A State of England* (1963). The chief USA references are: Bell, D., *The End of Ideology: On the Exhaustion of Political Ideas in the 50s* (rev. ed., 1961); Lipset, S. M., *Political Man* (1960); Galbraith, J. K., *The Affluent Society* (1958), and Wallich, H., *The Cost of Freedom* (1960). For a critical analysis of these American writings (to which the present author is much indebted) see Rousseas, S. W., and Farganis, J., 'American politics and the end of ideology', *British Journal of Sociology* (December, 1963).

4 See, for example, the Rev. Daniel Jenkins's critical analysis *Equality and Excellence*, published for the Christian Frontier Council (1961); Williams, Bernard, on 'The idea of equality' in *Philosophy, Politics and Society*, eds

Introduction to the 1964 Edition of Equality *by R. H. Tawney*

Laslett, P., and Runciman, W. G. (1962); and Crosland, C. A. R., *The Conservative Enemy* (1962).

5 Lydall, H. F., and Tipping, D. G., *Bulletin of the Oxford Institute of Statistics*, vol. 23, no. 1 (February, 1961).

6 For some discussion of these trends see Titmuss, R. M., *Income Distribution*.

7 Lampman, R. J., *The Share of the Top Wealth-Holders in National Wealth, 1922–1956* (1962).

8 Bank of England, *Quarterly Bulletin* (September, 1963), and *The Guardian*, 13 September, 1963.

9 There is also evidence that income distribution has become more unequal in the last few years (Conference Report on Economic Progress, *Poverty and Deprivation in the U.S.* (1961), known as the 'Keyserling Report').

10 Revell, J. R. S., *British Tax Review* (May–June 1961), p. 177, and *The Times*, 11 July, 1961.

11 Harbury, C. D., *The Economic Journal*, vol. 72, no. 288 (1962), pp. 866–7.

12 Myers, H. A., *Are Men Equal?* (New York, 1955), p. 20.

13 Titmuss, R. M., *Income Distribution*.

14 Brittain, J. A., *American Economic Review*, vol. 50, no. 2 (1960).

15 Lydall, H. F., and Tipping, D. G., *Bulletin of the Oxford Institute*, p. 90.

16 Jay, Douglas, *Socialism and the New Society* (1962).

17 Lynes, T., 'Poverty in the Welfare State', *Aspect*, no. 7 (August, 1963).

18 Townsend, P., 'The meaning of poverty', *British Journal of Sociology*, vol. 13, no. 3 (1962), p. 210. See also Lambert, Royston, *Nutrition in Britain: 1950–60. A Critical Discussion of the National Food Survey and its Findings* (Occasional Papers in Social Administration, 1964).

19 Myrdal, G., *The Role of Government in the Economy* (Paper prepared for the Tenth Anniversary Convocation of the Fund for the Republic, Jan. 1963).

20 Hollis, C., *Observer*, 21 July, 1963.

21 Jenkins, D., *Equality and Excellence*, p. 174.

22 Guttsman, W. L., *The British Political Élite* (1963).

23 See Holbrook, D., *English for the Rejected* (1963).

Appendix I Schools Attended by Certain Members of Different Professions

The following figures are compiled from *Whitaker's Almanack* for 1927 (for 1926 as regards Governors of Dominions), the *Stock Exchange Year Book* for 1927 (for Directors of Banks and Railways), and *Who's Who*.

Professions*	Number for whom information is available	Educated at								
		English public schools†			English schools other than public schools	Welsh, Scottish, and Irish Schools.				Privately or abroad
		One of the fourteen principal schools	Others	Total		Welsh	Scottish	Irish	Total	
Bishops (68)	56	38	14	52	4	–	–	–	–	–
Deans (30)	24	13	6	19	4	–	–	–	–	1
Lords of Appeal, Justices of Court of Appeal and High Court (39)	25	11	6	17	1	1	4	–	5	2
County Court Judges, Recorders, Metropolitan Magistrates, Stipendiary Magistrates (215)	156	75	47	122	20	1	1	3	5	9

Home Civil Servants (Members of 20 Departments receiving £1,000 a year and upwards (455))	210	70	82	152	29	1	10	4	15	14
Members of Indian Civil Service (English names only) (105)	41	17	16	33	1	–	5	–	5	2
Governors of Dominions (65)	47	21	9	30	14	–	–	–	–	3
Directors of 5 Banks (165)	82	53	9	62	5	–	7	–	7	8
Directors of 4 Railway Companies (91)	50	32	5	37	2	–	7	–	7	4
Total	691	330	194	524	80	3	34	7	44	43

* The figures added in brackets in this column indicate the total number in each category.
† i.e. the 135 English schools represented at the Headmasters' Conference.

Appendix IA Comparison of selected groups from Appendix I for 1927 and 1961

Profession	1927		Educated at		1961 [1]		Educated at	
	Total number	Number for whom information is available	English public schools [2]	Other schools or privately	Total number	Number for whom information is available	English public schools [2,3]	Other schools or privately
Bishops	68	56	52(38)	4	87	74	50(19)	24
Lords of Appeal, Justices of Court of Appeal and High Court	39	25	17(11)	8	63	59	45(28)	14
Directors of five Banks	165	82	62(53)	20	149	133	94(83)[4]	39

(1) Sources of 1961 figures: *Whitaker's Almanack* for 1962, the *Stock Exchange Year Book* for 1961, and *Who's Who*.
(2) Figures in brackets indicate, for 1927, numbers educated at 14 principal schools and, for 1961, at 15 schools attended by 3 or more individuals.
(3) The 182 schools represented at the Headmasters' Conference in 1943 (listed in the *Report of the Committee on Public Schools*, HMSO, 1944).
(4) Includes: Eton, 38; Harrow, 7; Winchester, 8.

CHAPTER

2

The Social Division of Welfare: Some Reflections on the Search for Equity

I

Some students of social policy see the development of the 'Welfare State' in historical perspective as part of a broad, ascending road of social betterment provided for the working classes since the nineteenth century and achieving its goal in our time. This interpretation of change as a process of unilinear progression in collective benevolence for these classes led to the belief that in the year 1948 the 'Welfare State' was established. Since then, successive governments, Conservative and Labour, have busied themselves with the more effective operation of the various services, with extensions here and adjustments there and both parties, in and out of office, have claimed the maintenance of the 'Welfare State' as an article of faith.

On this view it could be supposed that, speaking generally, Britain is approaching the end of the road of social reform; the road down which Eleanor Rathbone and other reformers and rebels laboured with vision and effect. This would seem to be the principal implication of much public comment on the social services during the past few years, and one which has received endorsement in policy statements of the Conservative and Labour parties.[1] An analysis of the more important writings on the subject since 1948 lends support, for the dominant note, far from suggesting that social needs have been neglected, has been that the 'Welfare State' was 'established' too quickly and on too broad a scale. The consequences, it was argued, have been harmful to the economic health of the nation and its 'moral fibre'.

Against this background, compounded of uneasiness and complacency, criticism has mainly focused on the supposedly equalitarian aims or effects of the social services. It is said that the relief of poverty or the maintenance of a national minimum as an objective of social policy should not mean the pursuit of equality; 'a fascinating and modern development' for the social services according to Hagenbuch.[2] The Beveridge 'revolution' did not, it is argued, imply an equalitarian approach to the solution of social problems. The error of Welfare State policies since 1948 has been, according to this diagnosis, to confuse ends and means and to pursue equalitarian aims with the result that the 'burden' of redistribution from rich to poor has been pushed too far and is now excessive. Thus, the upper and middle classes have been impoverished, in part a consequence of providing benefits for those workers who do not really need them. 'Why', ask Macleod and Powell, 'should any social service be provided *without* test of need?' (italics in original)[3] Their conclusion, like that of Hagenbuch in his analysis of 'The rationale of the social services'[4] and other writers, is that there should be a closer relationship between what people pay in and what they take out. Social security should be based on 'more genuine' actuarial principles, while the ultimate objective for other social services should be 'self-liquidation' as more and more people are raised above a minimum standard of living to a position of freedom in which they may purchase whatever medical care, education, training and other services they require. The mass of the people would thus, in time, come to behave like, if they do not resemble, the middle classes (who at present are presumed to derive little benefit from the social services). Pursued to its logical conclusion then, the 'Welfare State' would eventually be transformed into the 'Middle Class State'. Meanwhile, social legislation and its application should recognize much more clearly than it does at present that (as Macleod and Powell put it) 'the social services only exist for a portion of the population',[5] namely, that portion which takes out more than it puts in.

These views were tersely summed up by *The Economist* in June 1954, when it affirmed, as a guiding principle for social policy, that 'no one should live on the taxpayer unless he needs to'.[6] Already, 'the social well-being of the nation had been endangered by the redistribution of wealth'[7] a phrase which, according to a variety of social theorists, embraced more deeply felt anxieties than a simple material concern about economic and fiscal trends. De Jouvenel, for example, drew attention to the 'sordid utilitarianism' of redistributionist social services; to a 'precipitous decline' in voluntary, unrewarded services upon which culture and civilization depend, and to a 'tremendous growth' in the power of the State as a consequence of the rising cost of the social services.[8] At the same time, two popular books by Lewis and Maude rounded out the picture of a decaying, overworked and anxious middle class.[9] Finally, we may note the specific counter-proposals of two other critics. Ffrangcon Roberts has entered a vigorous plea for state medicine to return a business profit, and for the benefits of the National Health Service to be reserved for economically productive workers.[10] Colin Clark, foreseeing a totalitarian threat in the continued existence of the social services, would 'denationalize' them and entrust some remnant of their functions to the churches, local friendly societies and voluntary organizations.[11]

II

Whatever their validity in fact or theory, these views have had an important influence in shaping opinion since 1948 about the future of the social services. They have helped, no doubt unwittingly, to produce in the public eye something akin to a stereotype or image of an all-pervasive Welfare State for the Working Classes. Such is the tyranny of stereotypes today that this idea of a welfare society, born as a reaction against the social discrimination of the poor law may, paradoxically, widen rather than narrow class relationships. As Gerth and Mills have pointed out 'if the upper classes monopolize the means of communication and fill the several mass media with the idea that all those at the bottom are there because they are lazy, unintelligent, and in general inferior, then these appraisals may be taken over by the poor and used in the building of an image of their selves'.[12] That is one danger in the spread of the 'Welfare State' stereotype. A second emanates from the vague but often powerful fears that calamity will follow the relaxation of discipline and the mitigation of hardship which, in the eyes of the beholders, seems implicit in this notion of collective benevolence. Such fears inevitably conjure up a demand for punishment and reprisal; the history of public opinion in recent years on the subject of juvenile delinquency (to take one example) is suggestive of the operation of what Flugel called the 'Polycrates complex'.[13]

These brief observations on contemporary thinking about social policy are essential to the argument that follows; they constitute the political frame of reference. Nevertheless, they are a poor substitute for a close and detailed analysis of the critical views so summarily mentioned. Such an analysis would require many more words than one essay allows and must, therefore, be deferred. However, having set the stage in this general way, it is now proper to state the main purposes of this paper: first, to examine certain assumptions underlying these views, secondly, to outline the development of three major categories of social welfare and, thirdly, to relate these developments to trends in the division of labour and the search for social equity. At the end, in drawing together these different threads, it emerges that much of the criticism and all the complacency about the 'Welfare State' is either irrelevant or unbalanced and that we need to re-examine, by returning to first principles, current notions of what constitutes a social service.

First, however, it is necessary to bring into view certain assumptions, seldom made explicit, which run through practically all the recent critical writings on social policy. It is assumed:

First, that the intended or declared aims of social policy since the Beveridge Report of 1942 have been wholly or largely achieved in the translation of legislation into action. In other words, that the performance of welfare has more or less fulfilled the promise of welfare.

Secondly, that the aggregate redistributive effects of social service activity since 1948 have wholly or largely represented a transfer of resources from rich to poor.

Thirdly, that in the present inadequate state of knowledge about the working of social institutions it is possible to define what is a 'social service' and to identify, in each sector of state intervention, who has benefited and who has paid.

Fourthly, that it is practicable, desirable and has any meaning in a complex society undergoing rapid and widespread change to abstract a 'social service world' from the Greater Society, and to consider the functions and effects of the part without reference to the life of the whole.

The first and second assumptions call, I would suggest, for a detailed study of the 'unintended consequences' of social policy over the past decade. This cannot be attempted here.[14] I must content myself with making explicit the nature of these assumptions. In the following section, however, I examine certain facts relevant to the third and fourth assumptions.

III

All collectively provided services are deliberately designed to meet certain socially recognized 'needs'; they are manifestations, first, of society's will to survive as an organic whole and, secondly, of the expressed wish of all the people to assist the survival of some people. 'Needs' may therefore be thought of as 'social' and 'individual'; as interdependent, mutually related essentials for the continued existence of the parts and the whole. No complete division between the two is conceptually possible; the shading of one into the other changes with time over the life of all societies; it changes with time over the cycle of needs of the individual and the family; and it depends on prevailing notions of what constitutes a 'need' and in what circumstances; and to what extent, if at all, such needs, when recognized, should be met in the interests of the individual and/or of society.

When we apply these formulations to modern society we note the importance of definition. What is a 'need'? What is a 'service'? What was yesterday's conception of 'need' and 'service'? Of one thing at least we can be certain when all else is uncertain; the situation in which different kinds of need arise and are recognized as 'needs' has changed and will continue to do so. The Britain of the 1950s is a very different society from the Britain of the 1900s. Not only are the 'needs' and 'situations' different but they are differently seen. The social–individual equation of need is a different equation and, again, it is differently seen. Freud for one, in undermining our psychological innocence, and Marx for another, in opening our eyes to economic realities, contributed to changing our perception of the equation. So have the infinite and cumulative processes of social and technological change since the end of the nineteenth century.

It is this period I want to consider particularly, for it is this period of roughly fifty years – the era of rising expectations – that has witnessed the emergence and growth of those forms of state intervention which, by custom and common approval, have come to be called 'the social services'. The development of these services from the welfare revolution of 1905–14 under a reformist Liberal government, through the experience of two world wars and mass unemployment, to the Beveridge 'insurance revolution' and its aftermath has been amply documented in legislative detail. At the same time as the services themselves developed in scope and range, the term 'social service' has come to be applied to more and more areas of collective provision for certain 'needs'. It has indeed acquired a most elastic quality; its expanding frontiers, formerly enclosing little besides poor relief, sanitation and public nuisances, now embrace a multitude of heterogeneous activities. For example, Boer War pensions and disablement benefits were officially classified as social services in 1920; the universities and public museums were added after the Second World War. And so on. No consistent principle seems to obtain in the definition of what is a 'social service'.

The following simple examples, taken from the present Treasury classification,[15] give some indication of the area of confusion concealed by the assumptions of the critics of social policy,[16] and warn us of the dangers in any conception of a self-contained social service system expressly designed for the transmission of benefits from one income group of the population to another.

(1) Approved schools and remand homes are social services. The probation service is not.
(2) Further education and training for ex-members of the Defence Forces is a social service. The Youth Employment Service is not.

(3) The training of doctors is a social service. Marriage guidance services are not.

(4) Pensions and allowances attributable to the Boer War and First World War are social services. Industrial health services are not.

(5) The family allowance is a social service. The child allowance as remission of tax is not.

(6) The investigation of legal aid applications is a social service. Legal aid grants are not.

(7) Village halls and playing fields are social services. Cheap tobacco for old age pensioners is not.

(8) Technological training and further education is a social service. Subsidized housing for miners is not.

(9) Compensation to doctors for loss of right to sell medical practices is a social service. Non-contributory pensions and superannuation under occupational pension schemes are not.

(10) University education is a social service. The training of domestic workers is not.

When so much confusion exists (and these examples are but a selection from a large body of data) it is difficult to know precisely what it is that the critics are criticizing. The assumptions concealed behind such vague generalities as 'the social services' and the 'Welfare State' thus seem to be largely irrelevant. This becomes clearer when it is understood that those acts of state intervention which have somehow or other acquired the connotation of 'social' have developed alongside a much broader area of intervention not thought of in such terms but having in common similar objectives. It is this differential development I want to emphasize: the growth in the social division of welfare in response to changing situations and conceptions of 'need'.

Considered as a whole, all collective interventions to meet certain needs of the individual and/or to serve the wider interests of society may now be broadly grouped into three major categories of welfare: social welfare, fiscal welfare, and occupational welfare. When we examine them in turn, it emerges that this division is not based on any fundamental difference in the functions of the three systems (if they may be so described) or their declared aims. It arises from an organizational division of method, which, in the main, is related to the division of labour in complex, in-dividuated societies. So far as the ultimate aims of these systems are concerned, it is argued that their similarities are more important than their dissimilarities. The definition, for most purposes, of what is a 'social service' should take its stand on aims; not on the administrative methods and institutional devices employed to achieve them.

The development in this century of our first category of welfare – that which commonly goes by the term 'social service' – has already been mentioned. A major factor in this development should now be noted, for it has played a similarly important role in the growth of our two other categories of welfare.

With the gradual break-up of the old poor law, more 'states of dependency' have been defined and recognized as collective responsibilities, and more differential provision has been made in respect of them. These 'states of dependency' arise for the vast majority of the population whenever they are not in a position to 'earn life' for themselves and their families; they are then dependent people. In industrialized societies there are many causes of dependency; they may be 'natural' dependencies as in childhood, extreme old age and child-bearing. They may be caused by physical and psychological ill-health and incapacity; in part, these are culturally determined dependencies. Or they may be wholly or predominantly determined by social and cultural factors. These, it may be said, are the 'man-made' dependencies. Apart from injury, disease and innate incapacity, they now constitute the major source of instability in the satisfaction of basic needs. They include unemployment and under-employment, protective and preventive legislation, compulsory retirement from work, the delayed entry of young people into the labour market, and an infinite variety of subtle cultural factors ranging from the 'right' trade union ticket to the possession of an assortment of status symbols. All may involve to some degree the destruction, curtailment, interruption or frustration of earning power in the individual, and more pronounced secondary dependencies when they further involve the wives, children and other relatives.

In general, many of these culturally determined dependencies have grown in range and significance over the past century, partly as a result of a process of cumulative survivorship, for those who experience such states of dependency do not now die as others did before the twentieth century. The total of current needs may be

higher because of a proportionately higher representation of survivors of past dependency-creating experiences – wars, unemploy-
ments, injuries, enforced family separations and so forth. Apart,
however, from the effects of this process, the dominating operative
factor has been the increasing division of labour in society and,
simultaneously, a great increase in labour specificity. This is
perhaps one of the outstanding social characteristics of the
twentieth century: the fact that more and more people consciously
experience at one or more stages in their lives the process of
selection and rejection; for education, for work, for vocational
training, for professional status, for promotion, for opportunities
of access to pension schemes, for collective social benefits, for
symbols of prestige and success, and in undergoing tests of mental
and physical fitness, personality, skill and functional performance.[17] In some senses at least, the arbiters of opportunity and
of dependency have become, in their effects, more directly
personal, more culturally demanding, more psychologically threatening. There are more roles for the super-ego to play as one's
appreciation of reality becomes more accurate.

We cannot, however, pursue here the deeper psychological
implications of this trend, implied but not described in detail by
Durkheim when he observed that as man becomes more individual
and more specialized he becomes more socially dependent.[18] This
is of primary importance in understanding the development of
systems of welfare; this and the fact that, simultaneously, man
becomes more aware of what has caused his dependency, and thus
more exposed to uncertainty and conflict about the purposes and
roles he himself is expected to fulfil. More self-knowledge of the
'man-made' causes of dependency has been reflected in social
policies through the greater recognition accorded to individual
dependencies and their social origins and effects. It has also
influenced the growth of our other categories of welfare.

I now turn, therefore, to consider these notions in relation to
the development of fiscal welfare and occupational welfare.

IV

Under separately administered social security systems, like family
allowances and retirement pensions, direct cash payments are

made in discharging collective responsibilities for particular dependencies. In the relevant accounts, these are treated as 'social service' expenditure since they represent flows of payments through the central government account. Allowances and reliefs from income tax, though providing similar benefits and expressing a similar social purpose in the recognition of dependent needs, are not, however, treated as social service expenditure. The first is a cash transaction; the second an accounting convenience. Despite this difference in administrative method, the tax saving that accrues to the individual is, in effect, a transfer payment.[19] In their primary objectives and their effects on individual purchasing power there are no differences in these two ways by which collective provision is made for dependencies.[20] Both are manifestations of social policies in favour of identified groups in the population and both reflect changes in public opinion in regard to the relationship between the state, the individual and the family.

Since the introduction of progressive taxation in 1907 there has been a remarkable development of social policy operating through the medium of the fiscal system. This has chiefly taken the form of increasing support for the family through the recognition of more types of dependencies and substantial additions to the value of the benefits provided. Another important aspect of this development is that, originally, these dependants' benefits were deliberately restricted to the lowest paid sections of the income tax population; in the course of time these restrictions have disappeared. The Royal Commission on Taxation now proposes that such benefits should be allowed in the calculation of liability to surtax.[21]

A brief historical sketch of the main features of fiscal welfare shows the growth in public concern and responsibility for 'states of dependency', family and kinship relationships, individual 'self-improvement' and standards of 'minimum subsistence' among income taxpayers. It shows too, as W. Friedmann has pointed out, the extent to which Taxation Acts are now regarded as social purpose Acts;[22] that taxation has more or less ceased to be regarded as an impertinent intrusion into the sacred rights of private property and that, for the purposes of social policy, it can no longer be thought of simply as a means of benefiting the poor at the expense of the rich.[23]

A child allowance of £10 for all children aged under 16 for those – as a 'special consideration' – whose incomes were under

£500 was introduced in 1909; thus ante-dating by thirty-seven years family allowances for second and subsequent children.[25] This has gradually risen (through thirteen changes) to £100 in 1955.[26] The income qualification was raised in 1916, 1918 and 1919 and finally extended to all taxpayers in 1920. The allowance has been further developed to include children receiving full time education at a university or other educational establishment for the reason that, in the words of the Royal Commission, 'the child's immediate earning capacity has been foregone in order that he should qualify himself for work on a higher level in the future'.[27] Social policy has thus been extended beyond the confines of support for childhood dependency to the support of individual 'self-improvement'. These allowances are given regardless of education and scholarship awards.[28] The Royal Commission now proposes a further major development, namely, that the allowance should vary with the size of the taxpayer's income up to a limit of £160 for all income and surtax payers, and that such allowance should continue to the age of 21 for all 'incapacitated' children.[29] The estimated cost of the existing allowances in 1955–6 was £200 m.,[30] covering broadly about half the child population. We may illustrate these differences in social policy by considering the respective awards to two married men, one earning £2,000 a year and one earning £400 a year. Both have two children aged under 15. The first father now receives an annual net bounty of £97; the second one of £28.[31] Over the lives of the two families the former will receive a total of £1,455 and the latter a total of £422. If the Royal Commission's proposal is adopted the bounty for the first father will rise to over £2,200. The fact that already the child bounty rises steeply with increasing income appears to have been overlooked by Professor Robbins in his plea that, 'to eliminate some of the injustices of progression', these allowances should be provided 'in some measure proportionate to the expenses of the income group into which they are born'.[33]

Equally fascinating to the sociologist is the story of when and why wives were recognized in this system of social welfare (significantly enough in 1918); aged, incapacitated and infirm kinship dependants; housekeepers according to particular situations of family need; widowed mothers; incapacitated wives; unmarried daughters assisting infirm taxpayers; 'unmarried wives' and children of deceased members of the Forces; mourning costs (under estate duty); old age; professional 'self-improvement';[34] divorced wives,[35] unemployed taxpayers (loss of office compensation); married women at work (first introduced in 1920 in recognition of 'extra household expenses');[36] housekeepers for professional women on full time work and, as a 'special indulgence' for poorer taxpayers and those with precarious incomes finding it difficult to save for their dependants and for old age,[37] life assurance and superannuation allowances.[38] The latter benefit, though partly attributable to developments in fiscal policy, would seem to be more logically classified under 'occupational welfare'. It is, therefore, discussed under this head.

Underlying all these individual stories of the growth in fiscal welfare policies is a continuous search for a reasonable 'subsistence minimum' for income tax payers.[39] It was needed as a basis for the various benefits, for fixing exemption limits and for determining the extent to which a taxpayer's kinship relationships and particular states of need should be recognized. This problem is, however, part of a much more fundamental one which has plagued the Royal Commissions after both world wars of reconciling, on the one hand, the imperious demands of preferential social policies with, on the other, 'a general equitable principle' of fairness and progression in assessing individual taxable capacity.[40] This duality of roles is the major source of conflict and confusion. The more that the uniqueness of individual needs and dependencies is recognized and relieved in an occupational society based on individual rewards the more may principles of individual equity fall into disrepute. Since 1920, the concept of individualism in direct taxation has increasingly become more tenuous. For both Royal Commissions, the claims of social policy have overruled the claims of individual equity.[41] As a result, the cost of dependants' benefits has risen from a negligible figure in the early 1920s to over £425 m. today.[42] This compares with a total net cost to the Exchequer in 1954–5 of £770 m. for all direct cash payments under national insurance, industrial injuries, family allowances, national assistance and non-contributory pensions.[43]

V

During the period that has witnessed these far-reaching developments in social and fiscal welfare benefits there has also occurred a great expansion in occupational welfare benefits in cash and in kind. They have now reached formidable and widespread proportions as the Final Report of the Royal Commission recognized.[44] Their ultimate cost falls in large measure on the Exchequer. They include pensions for employees, wives and dependants; child allowances; death benefits; health and welfare services; personal expenses for travel, entertainment, dress and equipment; meal vouchers, motor cars and season tickets; residential accommodation; holiday expenses; children's school fees; sickness benefits; medical expenses; education and training grants; cheap meals; unemployment benefit; medical bills[45] and an incalculable variety of benefits in kind ranging from 'obvious forms of realizable goods to the most intangible forms of amenity'.[46] The implications of this trend are cautiously noted by the Royal Commission: 'Modern improvements in the conditions of employment and the recognition by employers of a wide range of obligations towards the health, comfort and amenities of their staff may well lead to a greater proportion of an employee's true remuneration being expressed in a form that is neither money nor convertible into money.'[47]

A substantial part of all these multifarious benefits can be interpreted as the recognition of dependencies; the dependencies of old age, of sickness and incapacity, of childhood, widowhood and so forth. They are in effect, if not in administrative method, 'social services', duplicating and overlapping social and fiscal welfare benefits. The rapidity of their growth in recent years has increasingly diminished the value and relevance of salary, wage and income statistics. Occupational pension schemes, to give one example of the present order of provision, may now cover one-half of the total male labour force (excluding agriculture).[48] Their cost to the Exchequer (including tax free deferred salaries) already runs to £100 m. a year,[49] a figure substantially in excess of the present Exchequer cost of national insurance pensions.[50] Contrary to the apparent intentions of the 1920 Royal Commission, which considered tax relief for such schemes appropriate for poorer taxpayers, the benefits have increasingly favoured wealthier taxpayers, through the medium of tax free lump sums and other devices.[51] In this sense, they function as concealed multipliers of occupational success. Sick pay and other 'social service' benefits have followed a similar upward trend. A recent official sample inquiry tentatively suggested that about half the claimants for national insurance sickness benefit were also covered by employer's sick pay schemes, the proportion ranging from one-third among manual workers to 90 per cent for administrators.[52] Adding these benefits together, sickness is now a better financial proposition for many people than health.

No doubt many of these forms of occupational social services express the desire for 'good human relations' in industry. Their provision is part of the model of the 'good' employer.[53] But as they grow and multiply they come into conflict with the aims and unity of social policy; for in effect (whatever their aims might be) their whole tendency at present is to divide loyalties, to nourish privilege, and to narrow the social conscience as they have already done in the United States, in France and in Western Germany.[54] One fundamental question of equity that they raise (which is analogous to that raised by the dual roles of fiscal policy) is whether and to what extent social service dependency benefits should be proportionately related to occupational and income achievement. That is a question which, along with others, must be left unexamined in this paper.

VI

Three different systems of 'social services' have been briefly surveyed in this paper. Considered as a whole, their development shows how narrowly conceived and unbalanced are the criticisms so frequently levelled at the one system traditionally known as 'the social services' or, more recently and more ambiguously, as the 'Welfare State'. The latent assumptions which commonly underlie these criticisms can, therefore, have little relevance while they remain attached to a stereotype of social welfare which represents only the more visible part of the real world of welfare. The social history of our times inevitably becomes, in the process, sadly distorted.

At present, these three systems are seen to operate as virtually distinct stratified systems. What goes on within and as a result of one system is ignored by the others. They are appraised, criticized or applauded as abstracted, independent, entities.[55] Yet, despite this division, they all in varying degrees signify that man can no longer be regarded simply as a 'unit of labour power'; they all reflect contemporary opinion that man is not wholly responsible for his dependency, and they all accept obligations for meeting certain dependent needs of the individual and the family. Nevertheless, despite these common social purposes, the search for equity between taxpayers – that like cases should be treated in like manner – proceeds regardless of the need for equity between citizens. The drive to 'buy' good human relations in industry widens class and vocational divisions through the provision of differential welfare benefits based on occupational achievement. The lack of any precise thinking about what is and what is not a 'social service' confuses and constrains the social conscience, and allows the development of distinctive social policies based on different principles for arbitrarily differentiated groups in the population.

Behind the facts of this development we can see the play of powerful economic and political forces; the strength and tenacity of privilege; the continuing search for equity in a rapidly changing society. Conceptions of 'need' and 'dependency' have simultaneously been profoundly affected by technological, industrial and social change – 'the gales of creative destruction' to use Schumpeter's striking phrase.[56] The problems of equity in social policy have thus become more complex as a result of the accumulation of long-lived 'disservices';[57] the increasing division of labour; higher standards of labour specificity; the lengthening of the 'natural' dependencies of childhood and old age; the diversification, creation and decay of functional skills and roles; and the growth of sectional solidarities which, in turn, have tended to enlarge the area and significance of social differentiation. More social differentiation – whether by age, class, education, personality, physical standards, intelligence quotient or professional qualification – may result, as G. Friedmann has observed, in more social inequalities.[58] Failure, ineffectiveness and social inferiority thus acquire a deeper significance. External inequalities – those which do not express natural inequalities – become 'more insupportable as labour becomes more divided'.[59] More insight into the complexities of human stress allied to the tendency of special groups to become more self-conscious leads to the search for sectional equalities. In so far as they are achieved, the interests of society as a whole at one extreme, and of the 'unattached' and dependent individual at the other, are subordinated to the interests of the group or class. The aims of equity, ostensibly set for society as a whole, become sectional aims, invariably rewarding the most favoured in proportion to the distribution of power and occupational success.

At the centre of this process of division based on the specialized content of individual occupational performance, man becomes more dependent; he also becomes, in the pursuit of individual life goals, more aware of his dependency, more viable to failure, more exposed to pain.[60] The corollary for any society which invests more of its values and virtues in the promotion of the individual is individual failure and individual consciousness of failure.

Within this theoretical framework it becomes possible to interpret the development of these three systems of social service as separate and distinctive attempts to counter and to compensate for the growth of dependency in modern society. Yet, as at present organized, they are simultaneously enlarging and consolidating the area of social inequality. That is the paradox: the new division of equity which is arising from these separate responses to social change. And that, today, is the real challenge to social policy and to those who, mistakingly, still look to the past for a solution.

Notes

The Sixth Eleanor Rathbone Memorial Lecture, given at the University of Birmingham on 1 December 1955, and published by Liverpool University Press in 1956.

1 See, for example, *One Nation*, Conservative Political Centre (1950), and *The Welfare State*, Labour Party Political Discussion Pamphlet (1952).
2 Hagenbuch, W., *Lloyds Bank Review* (July 1953), p. 5.
3 Macleod, I., and Powell, J. E., *The Social Services – Needs and Means* (1949)
4 Hagenbuch, W., *Lloyds Bank Review*.
5 Macleod, I., and Powell, J. E., *The Social Services*, p. 4.
6 *The Economist* (5 June, 1954), p. 783.
7 This statement, expressing a widely held view of the effects of social policy, appeared in *One Nation*, published by the Conservative Political Centre in 1950.
8 De Jouvenel, B., *The Ethics of Redistribution* (1951).
9 The authors illustrate their theme by describing how middle-class leisure has been drastically reduced while that enjoyed by the working class has increased (*The English Middle Classes*, 1949, p. 214 and *Professional People*, 1952,

Lewis, R. and Maude, A.). This apparently undesirable happening (if it has happened) is not peculiar to this country. In the United States 'there is a tendency among social scientists today, not mitigated by Kinsey, to think that the lower classes have all the fun, the middle classes all the miseries and inhibitions' (Denney, R. and Riesman, D. in *Creating an Industrial Civilization*, ed. E. Staley, 1952).

10 Roberts, F., *The Cost of Health* (1952), pp. 134–7.

11 Clark, C., *Welfare and Taxation* (1954).

12 Gerth, H., and Mills, C. W., *Character and Social Structure* (1953), pp. 88–9.

13 Flugel, J. C., *Man, Morals and Society* (1945), especially chs 11 and 18.

14 A critical examination of the primary data used by A. M. Cartter (to quote only one recent attempt to measure the redistributionist effects of the social services) would serve to show how tenuous are the conclusions, commonly drawn, about the fiscal consequences of the 'Welfare State' (Cartter, A. M., *The Redistribution of Income in Post-War Britain*, 1955).

15 This classification relates to 'social service' expenditure (*Monthly Digest of Statistics*, Central Statistical Office, May 1955).

16 It should also be noted that all the definitions employed by the various authorities mentioned in this essay differ very substantially, namely, those used by *The Economist*, Macleod and Powell, Hagenbuch, Cartter, De Jouvenel and Clark.

17 The assessment of specific labour skills now includes, in addition to the standard intelligence tests which attempt to measure verbal ability, visualization and numerical skill, such concepts as tone discrimination, accident proneness, taste sensitivity, colour blindness, digital dexterity, analogizing power, mechanical and clerical aptitude and mental maturity (see Caplow, T., *The Sociology of Work*, 1954).

18 Durkheim, E., *The Division of Labour in Society*, trans. G. Simpson (1933), p. 131.

19 As Cartter observed: 'By reducing the tax liability of a person with dependants the State is sharing in the responsibility of caring for each taxpayer's family just as certainly as if it were paying cash allowances in each case.' (Cartter, A. M., 'Income-tax allowances and the family in Great Britain', *Population Studies*, vol. 6, no. 3, 1953, p. 219). Other authorities also take the view that no distinction can be made between implicit and explicit transfer payments; see, for example, United Nations, *Economic Bulletin for Europe*, vol. 4, no. 2 (1952); Haynes, A. T., and Kirton, R. J., 'Income tax in relation to social security', *Journal of the Institute of Actuaries*, vol. 72, pt 1, no. 333 (1944), pp. 83–5; and *Samordning Af De Nordiske Landes Statistik Vedrorende den Sociale Lovgivning*, Copenhagen (1955), reporting the agreement of the five Northern Countries that 'tax deductions are quite analogous to . . . allowances in cash'). Though the Royal Commission on the Taxation of Profits and Income did not address itself directly to this question there are innumerable references in the 612 pages of its Second and Final Reports which support this approach. Thus, in discussing relief for charities costing around £35m. a year, the Commission observes that this 'does amount in effect to a grant of public moneys'. (*Final Report* Cmd 9474, 1955, p. 55; also *Second Report*, Cmd 9105, 1954).

20 Pigou recognized this in his *The Economics of Welfare* (4th ed., 1932, p. 98) when he wrote of tax relief for children as 'deliberate and overt bounties' for large families. Curiously, however, the similarity of these reliefs to family allowances seems to have escaped Eleanor Rathbone.

21 *Second Report*, Cmd 9105 (1954), p. 56.

22 Friedmann, W., *Law and Social Change in Contemporary Britain*, 1954, p. 262.

23 This would seem to be the implication of Professor Lewis's article 'A socialist economic policy', in *Socialist Commentary* (June 1955, p. 171), and of Professor Robbins's criticisms of progressive taxation ('Notes on public finance', *Lloyds Bank Review*, October 1955).

24 The chancellor of the exchequer in his Budget Speech, 1909, *Hansard*, vol. 4, cols. 507–8.

25 Thus, fiscal policy supports the first child in all circumstances; social welfare policy does so only when the parents are sick or unemployed.

26 The 1909 benefit represented, at the maximum, an annual tax saving of 7s 6d per child. The corresponding figure for 1955 (earned income £2,000) is approximately £48.

27 *Second Report*, p. 55. Or as Talcott Parsons puts it: 'The development of adaptive socialized anxiety in middle-status life is all the more essential because the social and prestige rewards of this status must necessarily be postponed during the prolonged training of the child and adolescent for high skills and complex responsibilities.' (Parsons, T., cited in T. Caplow, *The Sociology of Work*, 1954).

28 The scale of assessing parents' contributions for state scholarships laid down by the Ministry of Education further increases the total benefit for taxpayers. Its does so by allowing deductions from income, superannuation contributions and life assurance payments up to a specified proportion of income. National Insurance contributions are not allowable (see *Report of Working Party on Grants to Training College Students*, 1955, p. 21).

29 Pp. 56–61.

30 Information supplied by the Treasury (letter 9 November, 1955).

31 The basis of this calculation is a comparison, in both cases, with a married man without children. It assumes earned income, and takes account of family allowances, National Insurance contributions (including tax treatment), earned income allowance and personal allowances. The rates used are for 1955–6.

32 If the first father happens to be a university don or eligible for an employer's child allowance scheme of £50 per child per year his total bounty is further increased.

33 Robbins, L., 'Notes on public finance', *Lloyds Bank Review* (October 1955), p. 12.

34 Partly through benefits up to age 21; partly through relief for professional training expenses, and partly through the provision of 'added years' in increased superannuation benefits. These 'added years' are intended to cover years of professional training during which superannuation contributions were not paid (see, for example, *Local Government Superannuation (Benefits) Regulations*, 1954, Reg. 12).

35 'A super-taxpayer may and quite frequently nowadays does have a number of wives living at the same time since after divorce his ex-wives are not treated as one with him for tax purposes he can manage quite nicely since he is permitted to deduct all his wives' maintenance allowances from his gross income for tax purposes leaving his net income comparatively slightly affected.' (Memorandum by Lord Justice Hodson to the Royal Commission on Marriage and Divorce, MDP/1952/-337).

36 *Second Report*, pp. 39–40. The allowance rose from a maximum of £45 in 1920 to, in effect, £172 in 1954. On grounds of social policy, apparently, the Royal Commission thought the present figure excessive.

37 *Report of the Royal Commission on the Income Tax*, Cmd 615 (1920), para. 296.

38 The conditions laid down for the right to these various fiscal benefits are mostly far more generous and pay more regard to the social realities of kinship relationships than those specified in the National Insurance Scheme. They merit an anthropological analysis. Under the former, for instance, widows can claim a housekeeper's benefit while, under the latter, elderly widows found by the Ministry to be 'cohabiting' with elderly men have their pensions withdrawn. The fiscal benefit for adult dependants does not stipulate residence with the claimant; the corresponding National Insurance benefit does. Dependent relatives by marriage are covered for fiscal benefits; they are not prescribed under the Unemployment and Sickness Regulations (see also Section 24 of the National Insurance Act, 1946). There is no limit to the number of dependent relatives for whom fiscal benefits can be claimed; under the National Insurance Scheme claimants are allowed only one dependent relative. If, however, payment is made for a dependent wife even one dependent relative is not admissible. The definition of a dependent relative for whom fiscal benefits can be claimed is wide enough to include almost any relative; for National Insurance purposes there is a narrowly prescribed list of kinship relationships. Moreover, male relatives must prove incapacity. This means that benefits can be claimed for a daughter at a university (though she must not earn more than 20s a week in the vacations or at any other time) but not for a son.

39 Not the least remarkable aspect of this search is the complete absence of any reference in all the relevant reports to the simultaneous search for a 'subsistence minimum' as a basis for social welfare policies from 1920 to the Beveridge Report and subsequently (see, for example, *Second Report*, p. 50, and Shehab, F., *Progressive Taxation*, 1953, especially pp. 260–6).

40 Cmd 9474, p. 21.

41 The 1920 commission concluded 'that in all ranges of income some regard should be had to the taxpayer's marital and family responsibilities'. (pt 2, p. 29). The 1954 commission went further in their recommendations: 'their general tendency is to advocate that the tax scheme should recognize variations of individual circumstance more fully than it does at present' (*Second Report*, p. 25). It therefore proposed, *inter alia*, a substantial disability benefit without test of means; an automatic infirmity benefit for all taxpayers at age 75 again without any test; a dependent relatives' allowance for deserted wives and mothers without proof of incapacity; an extension of the housekeeper

allowance to cover non-resident child care services; universal superannuation benefits and so forth (p. 70).

42 Including only child allowance, dependent relative allowance, age relief, housekeeper allowance, life assurance relief and wife's earned income relief (Letter from Treasury, 9 November, 1955).

43 Central Statistical Office, *National Income and Expenditure* (1955), Table 37.

44 Pp. 67–75 and 410–12. In the 1955 Chance Memorial Lecture on 'Welfare in industry', Mr H. V. Potter gave estimates of the total cost to industry in Britain of what he called the 'social indirect services'. These estimates, for 22 million employees, ranged from £550 m. to £880 m. a year (excluding National Insurance contributions and statutory holiday payments). They also appear to exclude many of the items listed below involving individual benefits such as personal expenses, car allowances and so forth (Potter, H. V., *Chemistry and Industry*, September 1955, pp. 5–7).

45 To give evidence on one point: according to a statement in the *British Medical Journal*, 25 per cent of all medical bills at one 'leading nursing-home' are paid for their employees by firms (*Journal Supplement*, 8 October 1955, p. 81).

46 P. 68.

47 P. 72.

48 For more details see *Essays on 'The Welfare State'*, 3rd edn (1976), ch. 3. See also *Report of the Committee on the Economic and Financial Problems of the Provision for Old Age* (Cmd 9333, 1954) and Abel-Smith, B., and Townsend, P., *New Pensions for the Old* (1955).

49 In addition, life assurance relief was costing the Exchequer £35 m. in 1955–6. (Letter from Treasury, 9 November 1955).

50 See *Essays on 'The Welfare State'*, ch. 3, p. 69.

51 If the far-reaching proposals for extended benefits of the Millard Tucker Report are accepted – a State Paper which ranks in importance with the Beveridge Report – the cost of these benefits might well double in a few years, particularly as the Report insists that they 'should not depend on a "means test" ' (*Report of the Committee on the Taxation Treatment of Provisions for Retirement*, Cmd 9063, 1954, p. 101).

52 The great majority of these schemes were non-contributory. The inquiry was made by the Ministry of Pensions and National Insurance into a 5 per cent sample of new claims for benefit in September 1953. The results are probably subject to a substantial margin of error (*Report of the National Insurance Advisory Committee on the Question of Benefit for Short Spells of Unemployment or Sickness*, 1955, paras. 73–5).

53 The Conservative Party advocates a wide extension in these schemes (*The Industrial Charter. A Statement of Conservative Industrial Policy*, 1947, p. 30).

54 See United States Chamber of Commerce, *Fringe Benefits, 1953*, and United Nations, *Economic Bulletin for Europe*, vol. 4, no. 2 (1952).

55 The Beveridge Report paid no particular regard to fiscal welfare benefits; the Reports of the Royal Commission on Taxation in discussing social policies virtually ignore the commonly termed 'social services', and the Phillips Committee disregard fiscal benefits even to the extent of suggesting that the

development of occupational pension schemes might reduce pension costs falling on the Exchequer (Cmd 9333, p. 64).

56 Schumpeter, J. A., *Capitalism, Socialism and Democracy* (1954), p. 84.

57 Pigou developed systematically the notion of 'uncharged disservices' and 'uncompensated services' in his *The Economics of Welfare* (4th ed., 1932). For a discussion on trends and a more detailed treatment generally see Kapp, K. W., *The Social Costs of Private Enterprise* (1950).

58 Friedmann, G., 'The social consequences of technical progress', *International Social Science Bulletin*, vol. 4, no. 2 (1952), p. 254.

59 Durkheim, *The Division of Labour*, pp. 384–5.

60 For extended theoretical treatment see Durkheim, E., *The Division of Labour*.

CHAPTER

— 3 —

The Irresponsible Society

I

One of the most important tasks of socialists in the 1960s will be to re-define and re-state the inherent illogicalities and contradictions in the managerial capitalist system as it is developing within the social structure of contemporary Britain. Much of the doctrine of Victorian Marxism is no longer applicable to a different set of fundamental illogicalities in a different age. The future roles and functions of public ownership and social policy will be more clearly seen if they are analysed in terms of the problems of today and tomorrow.

Not least in importance in this approach to the future will be the study of the changing concentrations of economic and financial power. Who behind the 'decorous drapery of political democracy'[1] (in Professor Tawney's phrase) has power, who really governs, who is and will be making the critical decisions that will influence the design and texture of social and economic life in the 1960s? It is part of the purpose of this essay to indicate something of the nature of these problems in one sector of the economy. As an illustration, the private insurance sector is examined in a limited fashion. Similar and more far-reaching questions need to be asked in other sectors where combination and concentration may threaten the rights and liberties of the subject to choose the values and decide the social priorities that will shape his society.

Irresponsible Power

Five years ago Mr R. H. S Crossman, in a notable Fabian pamphlet,[2] examined the problem of monopolistic privilege and restated the need to expose the growth of irresponsible power, private and public. Since then, rising standards of living, the accumulation of the great tax free fortunes of the 1950s, the growth of monopoly and other factors, have all served to endorse the need to scrutinize these threatening concentrations of power and privilege.

It is one of the arguments of this essay that as the power of the insurance interests (in combination with other financial and commercial interests) continues to grow they will, whether they consciously welcome it or no, increasingly become the arbiters of welfare and amenity for larger sections of the community. Their directors, managers and professionally trained advisers will be making, in their own eyes and in the eyes of many other people, sober, profitable and responsible decisions. But ultimately and in the aggregate they will not lead to a more rational and balanced disposition of social resources in relation to the needs of the nation and the problems of social organization in a new age. These office-holders of power will not see – for it is not, after all, their purpose or business to see – that one of the most important problems of the future will centre round the socially effective use of rising national incomes and not the technical running of this or that part of the economic system. A wrong sense of proportion in attitudes to the 'economic surplus' – to the savings of the community – for example, may well be one of the more serious dangers to public morality in the 1960s.

Nevertheless, these men will be driven, not as wicked men but as sober, responsible decision-makers, to intensify the contradictions which are distorting the economy and blurring the moral values of society. Social policies will be imposed without democratic discussion; without consideration of the moral consequences which may result from them. In this sense they will be irresponsible decisions.

I attempt to illustrate, later in this chapter, the nature of some of these contradictions which are developing in contemporary Britain. Some concern the welfare of the politically obscure minorities; the powerless groups; the dependent poor, the disabled, the deprived and the rejected. There is, I suggest, a direct relationship between the shifting concentration of economic power in a more prosperous society and the future of the public services whose avowed purpose it is to assist, without discrimination, these powerless groups. There is little evidence from the history of the last ten years that society is any nearer to the solution of these problems of dependent poverty, inequality and unfreedom. By any objective criteria of wealth and opportunity it is in some respects further away.

Private and Public Spending

Expenditure by local authorities on welfare services for the aged, the handicapped and the homeless, for example, recognized as one of the most under-staffed and impoverished services in 1949, has risen at a slower rate than almost all categories of private and public expenditure.[3] Nor is there much hope for a better future for these minority groups from the enhanced power of insurance and financial interests. By their very nature, by their own rules of selection and rejection without right of appeal, they cannot help those they reject.[4] Though not taken on any grounds of intolerance, these decisions can nevertheless easily be interpreted as intended discrimination. Thus, they deepen the sense of powerlessness and rejection among these minorities struggling to make something of their lives in a more affluent and seemingly arrogant society. Social manifestations of frustration are more likely to flourish in Britain (as they have and are doing in the United States) as these forces develop. More prosperity and more violence may be one of the contradictions in a system of unfettered private enterprise and financial power oblivious to moral values and social objectives.

II

The subject of power has not been fashionable in recent years either in the world of political action or in those places where questions of freedom and justice are reputedly discussed. Sociologists have left it to economists who, in turn, have left it to philosophers. And they are not interested: so we are told by Mr

Ernest Gellner in his new book.[5] Perhaps it is that rising standards of living have hidden from sight the less obvious manifestations of arbitrary power. The iniquities of public bureaucrats have been repeatedly exposed to the greater glory of private bureaucrats. The makers of public policies have been decried to the advantage of the makers of private fortunes. A national press which, as a whole, has steadily taught the public for fifteen years to sneer at public order and public service and to admire cupidity and acquisitiveness has no doubt had some effect. Facts themselves matter less; all that matters is how the thing is put. Values matter less; what does matter is the kind of show that people put on. The Minister of Transport may now plead for more social discipline, order and collective planning to overcome the problems of urban congestion and road chaos, but the tide is running against him.[6] He and other ministers concerned with social amenity, town planning and a civilized design for living are now the prisoners of their own propaganda.

The 'Welfare State' Myth

The last decade has also witnessed a demonstration of the effectiveness of the myth as a motive force in British political beliefs and behaviour. Chief amongst these has been the myth of the 'Welfare State for the Working Classes'. This has had a number of consequences. Reinforced by the ideologies of enterprise and opportunity, it has led to the assumption that most – if not all – of our social problems have been – or soon will be – solved. Those few that remain will, it is thought, be automatically remedied by rising incomes and minor adjustments of one kind or another. In short, it is coming to be assumed that there is little to divide the nation on home affairs except the dreary minutiae of social reform, the patronage of the arts, the parking of cars and the effectiveness of corporal punishment.

Exaggerated though all this may be for the sake of brevity, I want to examine some of the implications which flow from these assumptions. To do so may throw a little light on the context in which monopolistic power is likely to operate in the future. And my purpose in stating these general propositions is to show a little more clearly the real nature of the choices that lie before us in the 1960s.

III

In highly complex and wealthy societies like our own almost all social forces tend to encourage the growth of conformism unless checked by strong, continuing and effective movements of protest and criticism. If these do not come from socialists and if they are not stated in terms of power they will not come at all. To assume that there is now little to remedy in the social affairs of the nation further strengthens this trend towards conformism and political consensus. It makes political atheism and professional neutralism more respectable, especially among the young. It avoids the raising of new questions about the changing concentrations of economic and social power. It accepts, with growing affluence, the legitimation of a class structure. It implies, not just a truce about equality, but virtually a permanent settlement in the struggle for social justice.

This movement of opinion constitutes a threat to the democratic process. If it is thought that less divides us, there is less to argue about. That is the point of view of many university students today. The Keynesian Revolution, the acceptance of the 'Welfare State', the upsurge and growth of professional power, and the doctrine of Rostow[7] all combine to provide a justification for the absence of social protest in our society. Material success and the pursuit of professional and class symbols of success are taken to be the basis of all success.

This seems a long way from the 1930s. But can it really be true that within two decades − so short a period in the struggle to make democracy a cultural and social reality − we have made so much moral progress?

What We Believed in

When I was young what some of us argued about was the democratic process. We wanted to know in our academically illiterate way whether more dialogue, more democracy, was possible. We thought it a dreadful crime to prevent other people from speaking up. We realized that the poor (whether they numbered 2 million or 10 million), the mentally ill, the disabled and other casualties or failures in our society were penalized, not only by their poverty, but because they were denied the social rights of protest and full membership of society. We believed in the possibility of an alternative government. We did not understand that government by the people could mean that power in government, the Cabinet and the City, could lie almost permanently in the hands of those educated at Eton and other public schools.

Thinking then that we could change our representatives, and helped by a popular press that was radical and outspoken compared with the acquisitiveness of Fleet Street today, we rebelled against the impersonal agents of injustice and inequality. We rebelled too against the personal ones; the bureaucratic despotism of large scale private as well as public agencies; the social discrimination that operated in all the processes of selection and rejection for education, work, professional and trade union associations, welfare benefits, pension rights, medical care, tax concessions and so forth. We began to see, in terms of the individual, the demoralizing effects of cumulative social rejection. But in those days there was some safety in numbers for the rejected; some compensation in the company of many others in similar situations of unemployment and poverty and with similar life experiences. The social system could still be blamed for its failure to give men the right to *any* sort of work. Now it cannot.

What Do We Offer?

Today, rebellion among the young seems to express itself in different forms. It is less concerned wtih political and democratic ideas. Yet if we are honest we must admit that the fault is not entirely theirs. Consider the state of political philosophy in Britain today. Or economics. Or sociology. Or law. Consider the growing substitution of specialization for general education. What education for democracy is there in much of the professionalized, sectionalized diet served up today to students in most universities, technical colleges, teachers' training courses, and other places of instruction? Are we not, indeed, witnessing a triumph of technique over purpose? What, in fact, are we offering to a majority of the young beside material success, the social graces, vocational techniques and, in particular, professional salvation? And what are we offering to women who, as voters, now outnumber men by more than 2 million?

Changes in the family, in the roles and relationships of husbands and wives, younger marriage and more marriage, and the fact that in the last few years some 4 to 5 million married women have become in many homes the main agents of relative prosperity are matters of great political significance. We must not and should not expect them to vote as their husbands do or their fathers did. Their great and abiding loyalty is not to their fellow workers, to associations of workers, to concepts of justice in systems of social security, to abstract ideas about democracy, but to the material advancement of their families.

Social and economic changes of a far-reaching character in these and other spheres now face us with a new set of democratic problems. They represent a challenge to our whole educational system. Yet the current obsession which sees education as capital investment for the purpose of 'keeping up in the economic race' suggests that our values are being distorted. 'The fact that politics are controversial – that honest men disagree – makes preparation for citizenship a difficult matter for schools.'[8] This is the comment of the Crowther Report. It went on to say: 'But it ought to be tackled, and not least for the ordinary boys and girls who now leave school at 15 and often do not find it easy to see any argument except in personal terms.'

Moral Leadership

The essential point is that we are now, as a nation, better able to teach our young people about democracy. More of us, as individuals, can now afford to be moral in our attitudes to the great problems of world inequality and racial intolerance. But for this to happen it surely means that those who hold positions of power and influence in our society should set examples for the younger generation in moral leadership and higher standards of social responsibility. If we cannot put our own moral houses in order it is difficult to see how we can give disinterested help to the poorer nations. To give – to be taxed – has never been a simple matter in human history; for our neighbours, fellow workers, the poor, the sick, the ignorant and the feckless. In the decades ahead, we shall need all the social inventiveness, democratic skills, and sense of responsibility which we can mobilize if we are to begin to close the gap of national inequalities.

The record of the 1950s does not, however, yield much evidence of moral progress in these respects. Economic growth, rising standards of living, and a great outburst of scientific, technical and professional training all over the Western world has, along with other forces, installed and strengthened governments wedded to inequality, secretiveness in administration, monopolistic privilege, and intolerance of nonconformity. More ominous still is the fact that these trends have been accompanied by a disenchantment with democracy which, as Mr Robert Hutchins puts it, has little or nothing to do with the seductions of the Kremlin.[9]

It is not only the Labour Party which should be thinking about these issues. To advance and widen democracy through education, by breaking down the barriers of social discrimination in all our public services, and by civilizing not only government but the great private bureaucracies and professional associations whose decisions so vitally affect our lives, is also a responsibility of government.

Scale of Values

What may we expect? Are we likely to see these anti-democratic trends arrested and reversed in the 1960s? Consider what Lord Hailsham, formerly Minister of Education and Chairman of the Conservative Party, now Minister of Science, has to say in his measured statement of *The Conservative Case*:

> Conservatives do not believe that political struggle is the most important thing in life. In this they differ from Communists, Socialists, Nazis, Fascists, Social Creditors, and most members of the British Labour Party. The simplest among them prefer fox-hunting – the wisest religion.[10]

Such a statement would have been unthinkable in the context of 1940 or 1945. Yet its author was, last month, elected rector of Glasgow University by its 6,000 students with a great majority over the Rev. Michael Scott. Only Mr Butlin came within measurable distance of challenging Lord Hailsham.[11]

These are social facts of importance; there are lessons here for all political parties. During the recent general election, one of the popular daily newspapers with an immense circulation warned its readers not to vote for the Labour Party because that party, if returned to office, would stop tax evasion and all those practices which go by the name of 'fiddling' in one income group and 'fixing' in another.[12]

Facts such as these cannot be ignored. Along with other evidence, they suggest the growth of irresponsibility in public affairs and in the formation, by precept and example, of public opinion.

This is the context, briefly outlined, in which I now want to consider, first, the position of the dependent poor and other minority groups in relation to the future role of social policy and, secondly, the social control of economic and financial power, taking as an example the power of the private insurance market. Different aspects of social responsibility, of altruism in public affairs, are expressed and reflected in both these spheres. It is necessary, however, to be very selective, particularly as I want to offer some facts in place of generalities. It will not, therefore, be possible to discuss other important aspects of monopolistic power or each branch of social policy.

IV

I have written in this book about what I called 'The social division of welfare'. Instead of thinking about the 'Welfare State' as an abstraction I suggested that we should consider the development of social rights and benefits in three categories or systems; occupational (employee welfare) benefits, fiscal benefits and social service benefits. All are concerned in some measure and in different ways with increasing or decreasing inequalities in the distribution of income and wealth. All attempt in some degree, and for different sections of the population, to resolve or alleviate the inequalities of dependency; the economically dependent states of old age, widowhood, childhood, sickness and infirmity.

While it seems that we have, to a large extent, reduced the more serious problems of economic dependency arising from unemployment, far less progress has been made in removing other causes of poverty, inequality and chronic ill-health. As Mr Peter Townsend has shown, there may be some seven to eight million people today living precariously close to the margins of poverty.[13] Many are old, disabled and handicapped. Britain is not alone among the more prosperous societies in finding this problem of the poverty of dependency an intractable one. A few months ago in a newly appointed Senate Committee on 'The aged in the United States', it was asked: 'Why is it that despite the substantial liberalization of our old-age income maintenance programs ... we still find that the average income of elderly people is so low?'[14] In 1957 more than a sixth of all persons aged 65 and over in the United States had no income of their own,[15] and about three-fifths had incomes of less than the equivalent of about £4 a week.[16]

Finding the Facts

However unsuccessful they may be in solving this great moral contradiction, at least it can be said that in the United States some attempt is made to find out the hard facts of poverty and dependency.[17] In Britain, we simply do not know. No effort has been made by government to discover the real incidence of poverty and levels of living among the old and other dependent groups. This to me is one of the more striking signs of irresponsibility of the 1950s. In so far as a society fails to identify, by fact and not by inference, its contemporary and changing social problems it must expect its social conscience and its democratic values to languish.

All one can say with assurance is that, in terms of the relationship of national insurance benefits and allowances to average industrial earnings, most beneficiaries are relatively worse off today than they would have been in 1948.[18] The fall in standards for them is a greater fall into poverty. The objective of social policy during the 1950s, it has been said repeatedly, is to concentrate resources on those who most need help. But what are the facts? The new National Insurance Scheme of graded pensions, which adds a few shillings to 50s. in ten years' time, omits everyone earning less than £9 a week, yet the Minister has stated quite emphatically in the House 'we do not want to encourage more people to rely on Assistance'.[19] This policy has been made effective substantially through the operation of 'disregards' in the means test (capital assets, war savings, sick pay, voluntary gifts from relatives and friends and charitable payments). In important respects these tests are relatively harsher today than in the middle of the war when the Determination of Needs Act was insisted on by Ernest Bevin; harsher in some respects than at the height of the slump in 1932; and even harsher in allowing relatively smaller payments for sick pay than in 1904 under the poor law.[20] Yet they were attacked in 1951 by *The Economist* as 'too generous for a nation which, in one way or another, is going to be forced to curtail its social services'.[21]

The improvements which were hurriedly made before the election to the scales of National Assistance[22] are of no help to those who are discouraged or deterred from applying. In any case, an administrative agency – like the Assistance Board – which finds it necessary to be severe in its handling of the feckless, the 'work-shy', and the coloured immigrant is not likely to be attractive to the 'respectable poor'. And for those who are on Assistance – nearly 2,500,000 people – these belated improvements have to be weighed against a host of incalculables; the removal of food and general housing subsidies, the loss of tobacco coupons, higher prescription charges, a more expensive and poorer transport system, and the fact that many old people, relative to the standards of the rest of the population, are probably worse off today than they were in 1951 in terms of housing conditions and domestic equipment.

'No one whom I marry', said the Vicar of St George's, Camberwell, 'now has a chance of getting their own place through the housing list for at least four and a half years.'[23] If this is the situation for young married couples today in such areas, it is likely to be far worse for the elderly and those on National Assistance. Yet *The Economist* could suggest after the Notting Hill 'race riots' in 1958 that coloured immigrants should be given 'special privileges' on council waiting lists.[24] Coloured workers, it was argued, were 'definitely a net gain to the British economy'; they are more 'mobile', and more likely to provide a pool of unemployed to keep 'the economy functioning smoothly'.[25] A 'liberal' immigration policy was therefore necessary to provide a pool of unemployed. Any housing difficulties could be met by giving coloured immigrants 'special privileges' on waiting lists. Meanwhile, public housing activities should be ruthlessly pruned. It is sad to see such arguments advanced in the name of liberalism.

They are unlikely to appeal to many Commonwealth citizens looking to Britain for moral leadership.

In Greatest Need

There is little here to suggest that much progress has been made, during the last nine years in which great fortunes have been accumulated,[26] to concentrate help through the public services on those whose need is greatest. For all we know this conclusion may hold for other branches of the social services; medical care, education, housing and other welfare provisions. In terms of the quality and effectiveness of medical care (for the physically and mentally ill), who are the major beneficiaries of the National Health Service? We do not know; no official attempt has been made to find out who utilizes the Service, how often, in what sectors of cost and quality, and with what results. In the field of housing, social workers could, ten years ago, quite hopefully put their more serious cases of hardship on council waiting lists. Now it is quite hopeless in many areas; waiting lists have either been abolished or remain as a polite administrative fiction. And many people believe that, without a revolution in local government and its financial resources, the new Mental Health provisions for community care will remain virtually a dead letter.

These illustrations of the retreat from government in the field of the traditional social services are indicative of what we may expect in the 1960s. Secretiveness in administration, an appalling lack of facts, the decline in quality of Royal Commissions and committees of inquiry have all combined to maintain much of the mythology of the 'Welfare State'. Many of us must also now admit that we put too much faith in the 1940s in the concept of universality as applied to social security. Mistakenly, it was linked with economic egalitarianism. Those who have benefited most are those who have needed it least. We are only just beginning to see that the problems of raising the level of living, the quality of education, housing, and medical care of the poorest third of the nation calls for an immense amount of social inventiveness; for new institutional devices, new forms of co-operation, social control, ownership and administration, and new ways of relating the citizen and consumer to services that intimately concern him. Social ideas may well be as important in Britain in the next half-century as technological innovation.

Welfare for the Better Off

These problems will not and cannot be solved by the private insurance market, by property speculators, by forcing land values to insanely prohibitive levels, or by any criteria of profits and tax free gains. Private enterprise is only building about 1,000 new dwellings a year in the county of London, for example, and most of these are luxury flats for the rich.[27] Nor will they be solved by the growth of the 'social welfare firm' and the provision of more occupational and fiscal benefits. Such developments in the last ten years have nearly all been concentrated on the better off third of the population, particularly in regard to pensions, tax free lump sums, compensation for loss of office, life assurance, sick pay, school fees, higher education, housing, free clothing, travel and an immense variety of benefits and amenity in kind. Fringe welfare, as it is so charmingly called, rises very steeply with income. The cost per employee for staff pension schemes, for example, exceeds that for works pension schemes by about 700 per cent.[28] Tax free lump sums on retirement run from £100 at the bottom to £40,000 or more at the top.[29] Such ratios would seem high in the USSR. What is now developing rapidly is the provision of private medical care and sickness insurance as a fringe benefit, aided by tax concessions and other devices.[30]

The annual value of fringe welfare today, including cheap stock options, may well exceed, if spread over working life, the salaries paid to the managerial, executive and other classes. Their standard of living is doubled – or more than doubled. But it is mostly contingent welfare; the undivided loyalty tranquillizer of the corporation; the basis of a new monolithic society which, as Mr Theodore Levitt has said of the American corporation, is on the way to becoming 'a twentieth century equivalent of the medieval church.'[31]

To encourage this development, and to bind employers and employees more closely together, the present government has insisted on the unilateral right of the employer to contract his employees out of the new National Insurance Scheme. More fringe welfare for the better off will then provide the argument that Britain should lead the world in abolishing a state system of social security.[32]

We have indeed almost reached a stage when it would be more

appropriate in this world of fringe welfare to speak of 'The Pressure Group State'; expressing a shift from contract to status; from open social rights to concealed professional syndicalism; from a multiplicity of allegiances to an undivided loyalty.

Much of this was foreseen in America nearly thirty years ago by Roscoe Pound when he wrote of the distribution of stock and company welfare 'as the great feudal lords distributed estates in the Middle Ages'.[33] Whatever their wider implications for the future in terms of liberty and justice we can see here the connections between social policy, fiscal policy and the distribution of economic and social power in society. Here it is that inequality has a dynamic of its own.

These propositions about trends in our society now lead me into another area even less charted with facts. But we have to enter it if only to understand some of the problems of economic freedom in relation to the growth of irresponsible power.

V

It was no fortuitous event or sudden fever in crowd behaviour which led the London Stock Exchange, in the words of *The Times*, to 'blaze into glory' on 9 October.[34] Coats were torn and millions were made to signal, in the affairs of the nation, a further extension in the almost unfettered reign of the City – of what Sir Roy Harrod has described as 'the wonderful recipe of the market mechanism'.[35] It is not surprising therefore that certain codes of behaviour, presumably to protect the powerful Guilds, are now to be drawn up, not by Parliament, but by the Institute of Directors, the Banks and the Investment Protection Committee of the British Insurance Association.

As government retreats, and the management of our economic affairs is increasingly delegated to the anonymous authority of the City, we must expect that other of our institutions will also be affected in a variety of ways. At the universities, as we attempt to 'declassify' students in terms of their social origins and then 'reclassify' them in professional ways with professional values,[36] we must expect that more professors and teachers will become directors of commercial concerns.[37] There will be other teachers too who will increasingly share their values with market consultants, persuaders, the pharmaceutical industry,[38] and promotional men. Some will get caught up in the process described by one indignant writer as 'our new way of getting rich which is to buy things from one another that we do not want at prices we cannot pay on terms we cannot meet because of advertising we do not believe'.[39]

The Power of Insurance Companies

The great insurance corporations and pension funds, now taking up securities in public companies at a rate which exceeds in value the total capital issue in the year by those same companies,[40] will recruit to their interlocking directorates and consultant ranks able men from the universities, the civil service and other walks of life. Already, since 1946, of four retiring permanent secretaries of the Ministries of Pensions and National Insurance two have entered the private insurance world; one as director of one of the large combines;[41] the other as executive chairman of the Society of Pension Consultants formed in 1958 to represent the views of brokers and pension consultants to the government about unnecessary developments in social insurance schemes.[42] Other staff have been recruited from the Board of Inland Revenue and various departments to senior posts as 'taxation controllers', directors and consultants.[43]

The last decade has witnessed something of an explosion in the accumulation of immense funds in the hands of private insurance companies and pension trusts. The rate of growth in this control over the 'economic surplus' may be even more dramatic in the next ten years. Though there are many causes, it is the relatively sudden impact and union of two major forces in Western society which has led to this explosion: demographic change and economic growth. No one who attempts to foresee the future of the public social services (to say nothing of economic freedom) in Britain, the USA, and other countries can now ignore this development.

Although only meagre information has been published, it would seem, comparing New York and London Stock Exchange lists, that the percentage holding of equities by British insurance companies and pension funds was in 1957 already more than double the percentage holding of common stock by their opposite numbers in the USA.[44] In other words, these institutions are twice as powerful in Britain as in America in terms of the ownership of industrial assets.

More significant still is the rate of growth of these funds as a source of new capital. In an important report just published by Mr Robert Tilove for the American Foundation, the Fund for the Republic, the author (as well as a Senate Committee on Banking and Currency) is concerned about the implications of the fact that pension funds (considered alone) are 'the most rapidly growing sector'.[45] It is said that they may soon become 'the biggest of the institutional investors in equities'.[46]

Source of New Capital

This position appears to have been reached several years ago in Britain in respect of insurance companies. According to the Radcliffe Report, the insurance companies and pension funds now 'constitute by far the largest single source of new capital, the net rate of accumulation of the funds of the two groups of institutions being now some £600 million per annum'.[47] As investors, they now dominate the City.

The significance of the Finance Act of 1956, which gave substantial tax concessions for pensions for the better off self-employed, now falls into place. Equally significant in this context are the five great insurance mergers which took place in 1959 to reduce still further what little competition remains between these large scale bureaucracies.[48] So also is the new National Insurance Act which has been deliberately framed to encourage the further growth of private insurance power.[49]

Here are some of Mr Tilove's conclusions in the report I have quoted:

> In terms of sheer total of common-stock holdings, there is a vast potential for these institutions to exercise corporate control and influence.

And further:

> It is still startling to realise that pension funds may accumulate sufficient assets to be able to buy a significant part in the ownership of corporations.[50]

This *potential* for control and influence is greater in Britain. Yet we know nothing about how this responsibility is exercised. The insurance companies even refused to disclose to the Radcliffe Committee the market value of their assets.[51] They publish practically nothing about their purchases and sales of financial assets; they are allowed to maintain hidden reserves which are allocated among the different classes of assets as the directors think fit; their balance sheets 'materially under-state the current value of equity assets';[52] no precise and comprehensive statistics have ever been published for the insurance market's foreign income and expenditure;[53] it is not known whether the funds accumulated by the companies from income from colonial and underdeveloped areas are invested there; they never report the number of people who lose their pension expectations through unemployment, change of job and other reasons. Nothing is known as to the number of individual 'top hat' pension policies issued with a capital value exceeding £100,000, or of the total cost to the taxpayer during the last ten years of non-contributory back service pension rights for directors and executives.[54] Nor do the insurance companies or pension consultants tell us anything about the psychological and social harm they do to people in rejecting them or rating them sub-standard for life and pension purposes.[55] We do not even know who is responsible for making some of the important decisions in the shaping and administration of private pension plans – employers, insurance companies, or pension consultants. One such firm of consultants claims to have devised and to be administering the pension schemes of one in four of the major British industrial and commercial firms.[56] What we do know is that there is no appeal machinery in this complex and costly bureaucratic system; no opportunity to speak up as there is in the National Insurance system.

Increasing the Problems

What Mr Tilove's and other American studies have to say about freedom to change one's work, about the difficulties of middle-aged and elderly men and women in getting work and continuing in work after certain ages, is relevant to the many similar problems we face here.[57] It is clear from American experience (the British insurance companies having published no facts) that these problems are gravely accentuated by the growth of private insurance plans.[58] In 1958, it should be noted, the British government disbanded its National Advisory Committee on the Employment of Older Men and Women. It was beginning to ask awkward questions about freedom to work in old age, and about the growth of unregistered unemployment among the elderly.

In addressing the International Congress of Actuaries in New York in 1957, one of the vice presidents of the Prudential Insurance Company of America estimated that within ten to twenty years at the most all forms of welfare benefits would be paid for by employers – with the continued help of tax concessions.[59] This means not only provisions for pensions, widows and dependants, but also for medical care for the family, sickness insurance, professional training, higher education, and other forms of 'fringe welfare'. Ever since the Prudential and other companies entered this field they have done everything (so Vice President Whittaker claimed) 'to make national health insurance unnecessary' in the USA.[60]

That their invasion of the field of welfare has already been extensive is something of a feat because American insurance companies are subject to a far greater degree of public supervision, control over equity investment, inspection and statistical study than their opposite numbers in Britain.[61] Similarly, in Sweden and other countries public control is wider and deeper.[62] Under the regime of a 'Welfare State' in Britain, bitterly attacked on numerous occasions at the annual meetings of insurance companies since 1945,[63] their directors and investment managers, like the medical profession in another context, have enjoyed more freedom to do as they like than in most countries of the Western World. They are, it was remarked at the 1957 Actuarial Congress, 'the envy of insurers in the stronghold of private enterprise'.[64]

VI

I have devoted space to these matters because they constitute a major shift in economic power in our society. It is a power, a potential power, to affect many important aspects of our economic life and our social values in the 1960s. It is power concentrated in relatively few hands, working at the apex of a handful of giant bureaucracies, technically supported by a group of professional experts, and accountable, in practice, to virtually no one.

From other points of view, it is a force making for greater centralization of decision-making power reminding us again, as the Conservative Party has recently done, of Disraeli's warning, 'centralization is the death-blow of public freedom'.[65]

We do not know how this power is being used in terms of social welfare priorities or how far these massive investment funds are being or will be used to restore the outworn, mid-Victorian social capital of Britain. What we can only call 'social policy decisions' are, however, continually being made, without any proper awareness or public discussion of what is involved in terms of the common good, and what consequences may flow from the choices made. It all goes on in what Weber described as 'the secret sessions' of private bureaucratic power. 'The "secret" ', he added, 'as a means of power, is, after all, more safely hidden in the books of an enterpriser than it is in the files of public authorities.'[66]

The insurance companies claim that the financial resources they control are used only for 'pure' investment in profitable enterprises.[67] This is the general view, and it was accepted by the Radcliffe Committee.[68] At the same time, however, it seems somewhat inconsistent to demand, as the insurance companies do, the abolition of what is called 'the anachronism of the non-voting share'.[69] Moreover, is it so certain that this position will continue to hold good in the future as the funds continue to increase in size?

In any event there are no published facts apart from what one can learn from an examination of the interlocking characteristics of insurance directorates. Of 126 directors of 10 leading British companies in 1956, one-half went to Eton and 6 other public schools; most of them belong to a small circle of clubs among which the Carlton is the most popular; a high proportion are titled; and most have extensive connections with industry, finance and commerce.[70] Democratic pleas from such quarters on behalf of voteless shareholders remind one of La Rochefoucauld's maxim that 'hypocrisy is the tribute which vice pays to virtue'.

Relieving Squalor

Looking to the future, there can be little doubt that what is needed is the direction of an increasing flow of savings into the British domestic areas of public squalor. They are easily identified: the slums of Lancashire and the North; the dying coalfields of south Wales and Scotland; and the ugly and ancient hospitals, schools and other public institutions which Dr Abel-Smith so vividly described in his essay in *Conviction*.[71] But if recent experience and the concept of profitability is any guide this will not happen. In the last few years insurance companies have become increasingly interested in the London and South-East property market – Britain's area of private opulence. They have preferred to finance large blocks of office buildings and luxury flats – London's new architectural indignities. One company, Town and City Properties, announced in November 1959, that it had entered into an understanding with the Prudential 'to facilitate the provision for finance for such property development as may be approved by the Prudential'.[73] Other insurance companies, among which are the Pearl, the Norwich Union and the Legal and General, are now playing a major role in changing the face of London and the South-East[74] – not least in Piccadilly Circus.[75]

To raise the quality of environment for all our people should be at the very centre of social policy. Yet, over the same period of time in which we have remarked this shift in economic power, there has been a steady retreat from town planning and redevelopment. All the impulse and ideals of the 1940s to re-create, re-build and re-plan have now collapsed. At the level of central government planning, as Professor Matthew has said, 'all is silence'.[76] The drift south continues. Without planned redevelopment 'on a really heroic scale in the next few years, obsolescence and traffic volume alone between them will kill the quality of urban living upon which we, above all people, depend'.[77] This is retreat from government; a retreat into irresponsibility.

VII

Underlying the notions of continued economic growth is the assumption of a dwindling role for government. The public services are increasingly seen, as Galbraith says, as an incubus; an unnecessary, doctrinaire burden on private enterprise.[78] The act of affirmation, the positive political decision about equality and its correlate freedom, becomes harder to make as the majority of voters (and not just the top 10 per cent) grow richer. Negatively, they assume – in so far as they are helped to think about these matters at all – that the unseen mechanisms of a more prosperous market will automatically solve the problems of the poverty of dependency, the slums of obsolescence, the growth of irresponsible power and all the contradictions that flow from undirected or misdirected social policies.

As society grows in scale and complexity, new social needs are created; they overlap with and often accentuate the more classical forms of dependent needs. Many of these new needs are born of the disservices of technological and scientific change which, in turn, give rise to new concentrations of self-interested professional and economic power. These needs call for services and social amenities; things which, in Galbraith's analysis, do not easily lend themselves to private production, purchase and sale.[79] If inequalities; individual and territorial, are not to grow and if public meanness is not to become public squalor, these things should be provided for everyone if they are provided for anyone.

The growth of a 'Pressure Group State', generated by more massive concentrations of interlocking economic, managerial and self-regarding professional power, points in the other direction; towards more inequality; towards the restriction of social rights and liberties and the muffling of social protest among a large section of the population. The growing conservatism of professionalism, of the imposed inequalities resulting from the decisions of congeries of social power, were remarked, with extraordinary foresight, by Graham Wallas in his chapter on 'Professionalism' in *Our Social Heritage* in 1921.[80] He was concerned as I have been (though in a much more limited context) with the fundamental problem of re-interpreting social equality and personal liberty in the conditions of a new age and a changed society.

Accelerating Inequality

Those aspects of economically determined power with which I have been chiefly concerned function, if not socially controlled, as accelerators of inequality; inequalities in the distribution of income and wealth, educational opportunity, vocational choice, pension expectations, and in the right to change one's job, to work in old age, and in other spheres of individual and family need. Some part of this process is expressed through the multiplication and division of occupational and fiscal benefits. Some part is traceable to the separation of 'ownership' from the rights of stockholding, and the organized concentration of control over the 'economic surplus' which represents a primary source of power in our society. The answers lie in many fields and forms of public ownership, public responsibility, and public accountability. The expansion and re-shaping of social policy is but one.

To grow in affluence then does not mean that we should abandon the quest for equality. In some senses at least the quest becomes harder to undertake as the cruder injustices of yesterday are reduced and blurred. But new forms and manifestations of social injustice take their place. To substitute the professional protest for the social protest and the arbitrary power of the City for the accountable power of the Commons is no answer. No answer for ourselves; no prescription for a participating democracy; no example for Africa and the poverty stricken peoples of the world. It is simply the mark of an irresponsible society.

Notes

A revised and expanded version of a lecture given before a Fabian audience in London in November 1959. Printed as Fabian Tract 323.

1 Tawney, R. H., 'The choice before the Labour Party', published in 1934 and reprinted in 1953 in *The Attack*. Most of it might have been written in 1960, so apposite is the discussion of principles.

2 Crossman, R. H. S., *Socialism and the New Despotism*, Fabian Tract 298 (1955).

3 At 1958 prices, local authorities spent £20½m. on these services in 1949. In 1958 they spent £24m.

4 Insurance and other interests providing private medical care benefits (now developing with some rapidity in the United Kingdom) generally exclude 'non-white nationalities', the elderly and other specified classes from certain group schemes. This is but one example from a long catalogue of discriminatory private policies exercised by insurance companies, building societies, property owners, hire purchase firms, banks and other commercial institutions against those with 'handicaps' — legal, physical, psychological, racial and so forth.

5　Gellner, E., *Words and Things* (1959).

6　Mr Marples, Minister of Transport, in the House of Common, 10 December 1959, *Hansard*, vol. 615, cols 769–84.

7　Rostow, W. W., *Stages of Economic Growth* (1960).

8　15–18: *Report of the Central Advisory Council for Education: England*, Newsom Report, vol. 1 (1959), p. 114.

9　Hutchins, R. M., 'Is democracy possible?', *Bulletin of the Fund for the Republic* (February 1959), p. 4.

10　Hailsham, Lord, *The Conservative Case* (Penguin edition, 1959).

11　*The Times*, 27 October 1959. In one of the highest polls for some years (48 per cent) Lord Hailsham received 1,428 votes, Mr B. Butlin 1,182 and the Rev. Michael Scott 493.

12　*Daily Sketch*, 'Odd-job Gestapo – if you don't vote right', 8 October 1959, pp. 1, 12, 13.

13　Townsend, Peter, 'A society for people' in N. Mackenzie (ed.), *Conviction* (1958), pp. 103–4.

14　*Hearings before the Sub-committee on the Aged and Aging*, US Senate, 86 Congress, June 1959, Report 43350, p. 167.

15　The proportion of retired couples with no income other than OASI benefit or less than $75 was nearly one-fifth in 1957 as it had been in 1951 (*Report on Hospitalisation Insurance for OASDI Beneficiaries by the Secretary of Health, Education and Welfare*, US Government Printing Office, 1959, p. 12).

16　*Hearings before the Sub-committee on the Aged and Aging, op. cit.*, p. 166. Less than $1,000 a year. Translated into sterling at $5 to the £, using purchasing power parity rather than the official rate of exchange.

17　Surveys of the resources of beneficiaries were carried out by the Bureau of Old Age and Survivors Insurance in 1949, 1951 and 1957 (see *Social Security Bulletin*, US Dept. of Health, Education and Welfare, vol. 21, no. 8, 1958).

18　See Table on p. 18 of *National Superannuation* (The Labour Party, 1958).

19　In answer to a plea for more generous National Assistance disregards the Minister of Pensions and National Insurance said: 'I do not think we want to encourage more people to rely on Assistance' (*Hansard*, vol. 532, HC, 1 November 1954, col. 15).

20　The following are some examples. The limit to capital assets (other than an owner-occupied house or 'war savings') above which assistance is not granted is now £600. In 1932, for purposes of outdoor relief, the limit was £300 (Transitional Payments (Determination of Needs) Act, 1932). Equivalent value at July 1959 prices would be £887 (LCES Retail Price Index). Under the Pensions and Determination of Needs Act, 1943, the limit was raised to £400 (equivalent value July 1959 £766). The limit to 'war savings' was £375 in 1941 (Determination of Needs Act). It is still £375. The maximum disregard today for certain forms of income, such as sick pay from trade unions and clubs, occupational pensions, voluntary allowances from relatives, friends and charities, is 15s. Under the Pensions and Determination of Needs Act, 1943, the occupational pension disregard was 10s 6d (equivalent value July 1959 20s 1d). Under the Outdoor Relief (Friendly Societies) Act, 1904, the sick pay disregard was 5s (equivalent value July 1959 22s 11d).

21　*The Economist*, 20 January 1951, p. 118.

22 White Paper on *National Assistance*, Cmnd 782 (1959).

23 Rev. Eric James reported in *The Times*, 30 November 1959.

24 *The Economist*, 6 June 1959, p. 925.

25 *The Economist*, 6 September 1958, p. 724.

26 Though not a very informative source in other respects, see the account by the City editor of the *Evening Standard*, 'This fantastic year in the City', 22 December 1959.

27 *The Economist*, 21 November 1959, p. 704.

28 Durham, W., *The LSD of Welfare in Industry*, Industrial Welfare Society (1958), table 9.

29 Tax free lump sums of £60,000 to £100,000 as compensation for loss of office (following take-over bids which may or may not have been 'arranged') are not uncommon today. One typical case reported in *The Times* on 22 June 1959, was for £60,000 plus a pension of approximately £4,000 a year. No comprehensive information on these benefits can be obtained from the Board of Inland Revenue or any government source.

30 See booklets published by the Permanent Sickness Insurance Co. Ltd, the British United Provident Association and other insurance companies. At the end of 1958, BUPA reported, for example, 2,900 group or 'staff' schemes covering 350,000 people. Sickness benefits up to £50 per week are not taxed unless they extend for more than a year. Contributions are allowed as a business expense. Consultant and hospital charges are largely 'policed' or controlled by the National Health Service. The Service therefore functions to keep down some of the costs of private medical care for higher paid executives.

31 Levitt, T., *Harvard Business Review*, September–October 1958.

32 This argument was put forward, for example, in an article 'Company pensions and the state scheme', in *The Times*, 15 January 1960.

33 Pound, Roscoe, *Kentucky Law Journal*, vol. 19, no. 1 (1930), p. 14.

34 *The Times*, 14 October 1959.

35 Harrod, R., *Observer*, 20 September 1959.

36 Selvin, H. C., and Hagstrom, W. C., 'Determinants of support for civil liberties' (subsequently published in *British Journal of Sociology*, vol. 11, no 1, March 1960).

37 It is not known how many senior academics in the social, medical and natural sciences now hold paid directorships on the boards of commercial concerns (including insurance companies). One doctor, writing to the *Lancet* in 1949 (*i*, 584) said, 'Very few in our profession and practically none of the general public realize that some holders of professorial chairs and other important positions in the medical world also act as expert advisers to industrial concerns. This may not affect their judgment, but they may reasonably be asked to "declare their interest".'

38 See discussion on the influence of drug firms on university departments and doctors, 'Symposium on clinical trials', *British Medical Journal*, 1958, *ii*, 1056; a letter from Dr E. Cronin on fees for drug trials in the *British Medical Journal*, 1959, *ii*, 954; and a commentary on the methods employed by private enterprise to introduce a new penicillin (*British Medical Journal*, 1959, *ii*, 940). 'Medicine', according to Professor Means, 'is showing an alarming

tendency to slip from the place of a profession into the behaviour pattern of the market place' (Means, J. H., *New England Journal of Medicine*, 15 October 1959).

39 Hutchins, R. M., 'Is democracy possible?', p. 7.

40 Excluding companies in the banking, insurance & finance sector, *Report of Committee on The Working of the Monetary System*, Cmnd 827, p. 90.

41 *The Times*, 18 October, 1958.

42 *The Times*, 13 November 1958.

43 *The Times*, 27 October 1958, and 30 November 1959.

44 The relative percentages are 12.3 and 5.7. For sources see the *Radcliffe Report*, Cmnd 827, tables 15, 16 and 36; *The Times* (*Annual Financial and Commercial Review*), 19 October 1959, p. xiii; Tilove, R., *Pension Funds and Economic Freedom*, A Report to the Fund for the Republic (1959), pp. 29–39 and table 8.

45 Tilove, R., *Pension Funds*, p. 39, and US Senate, Committee on Banking and Currency, 84th Congress, 1st Session, Report 376, (1955).

46 Tilove, R., *Pension Funds*, p. 39.

47 Cmnd 827, p. 290.

48 The companies involved in the 1959 amalgamations were Alliance Assurance and Sun Insurance; Scottish and Norwich Unions; Commercial Union and North British and Mercantile; Royal Exchange and Atlas; Eagle Star and Midland Employers' Mutual.

49 Pitt, Miss E., joint parliamentary secretary to the Ministry of Pensions and National Insurance, *The Policy-Holder*, vol. 77, no. 18 (1959), p. 536.

50 Tilove, R., *Pension Funds*, pp. 85–6.

51 Cmnd 827, p. 285.

52 *The Economist*, Supplement on British Insurance, 19 September 1959, p. 4.

53 The primitive nature of the estimates made since 1945 are illustrated in Clarke, W. M., *The City's Invisible Earnings*, The Institute of Economic Affairs (1958), pp. 56–64.

54 'No comprehensive statistics are published of total business in force on a single date according to types of policy, nor is any breakdown available of endowment assurances into those connected with staff schemes, "top hat" and other, and those which are "individual".' (*The Economist*, Supplement on British Insurance, 16 July 1955). In addition, it should be noted that no statistics have ever been published showing breakdowns by age, sex, occupation, type of contribution, distribution of back-service, lump sum and pension benefits and vesting provisions.

55 For some discussion of the problems of accepting or rejecting 'bad risks' – especially suspected cases of coronary thrombosis – see pp. 164–8 of vol. 4 of the *Transactions of XVth International Congress of Actuaries* (1957). Most offices appear to refuse the right to any re-assessment. No light is thrown on the consequences of rejection and sub-standard rating irrespective of the validity of the diagnosis or examination.

56 The Noble Lowndes Pension Service. It is reported that the total sums assured under Noble Lowndes schemes now exceed £350m. (*The Times*, 13 January 1960).

57 According to the President of the Guild of Insurance Officials, the insurance

industry is 'semi-feudal' in its approach to staff matters. In his 1959 address he said that the whole trend of insurance employment was towards immobility as a result of non-transferable pension schemes, 'gentlemen's agreements' between members of the British Insurance Association to prevent changes of jobs and so forth (*The Times*, 29 May 1959). If this is the situation in the insurance industry it is hardly likely that the pension schemes they sell allow or encourage labour mobility.

58 The most recent evidence about vesting provisions comes from a report published in *The Professional Engineer*, vol. 6, no. 4 (1959). This relates to a joint survey conducted by the Engineers Guild with the Social Survey Division of the Central Office of Information. It covered some 6,000 engineers in 1956. As regards the preservation of pension rights by these professional engineers in schemes wholly or partly financed by employers, the 'results show that no less than 88 per cent of those who replied (5,945 out of 6,137) are in such schemes, but despite the slowly increasing tendency to look on pension benefits as a form of deferred pay, less than one in ten of these are entitled to retain the benefit of the employer's contribution without restriction, and nearly half are not entitled to this benefit at all'.

59 Whittaker, E. B., *Transactions of XVth International Congress of Actuaries*, vol. 4 (1957), p. 155.

60 Whittaker, E. B., *Transactions of XVth International Congress*, p. 155.

61 Tilove, R., *Pension Funds*, pp. 42–8. For example: 'Life assurance companies domiciled in New York are limited to acquiring no more than 2 per cent of any issuer's common stock, and they may not invest more than 0.2 per cent of their assets in the stock of any company' (p. 76).

62 Hansson, K., 'Life assurance in Sweden', *The Policy-Holder Journal* (20 November, 1958), p. 7.

63 A future historian, interested in the relationships between professional power and financial power, will have to take note of the several thousand statements made since 1945 attacking 'the immense and corrupting burden' of the 'Welfare State' by insurance companies, banks, investment and hire purchase firms, the *British Medical Journal*, the Institute of Chartered Accountants, the British Employers' Confederation, the Association of British Chambers of Commerce, the Institute of Directors, actuaries, judges, doctors and other professional men. Even as late as January 1960, the chairman of Barclays Bank could say that the 'Welfare State' had 'removed financial anxiety about illness and old age and had diminished in the ordinary man the sense of personal responsibility for his own future and that of his family' (Address by the chairman to the Stockholders, January 1960).

64 *Transactions*, vol. 4, (1957) pp. 136 and 140.

65 *Some Principles of Conservatism*, Conservative Political Centre (1956), p. 14.

66 Gerth, H. H., and Mills, C. W., *From Max Weber* (1947), pp. 233–5.

67 See the Radcliffe Report. This claim was accepted by the Radcliffe Committee without apparently gaining access to the necessary facts (Cmnd 827, pp. 87, 285 and 290). According to the investment manager of the Legal and General Assurance Society the Investment Protection Committee of the British Insurance Association does 'endeavour to speak with a single voice' in such matters as capital reconstruction, company amalgamations and other

investment matters (Ginsburg, L., *The Policy-Holder Journal*, Supplement on Investment Policies, 30 April 1959, p. 11).

68 There is no reference in the Radcliffe Report to the role played by the Prudential Assurance Co. Ltd in the affairs of the Birmingham Small Arms Co. Ltd, in 1956. The Prudential, 'one of the largest shareholders' (holding approximately 5 per cent of the equity), took certain action to have the affairs of the company investigated; the Prudential was apparently also asked by some of the directors to negotiate with the chairman and managing director who, finally, was removed from office. See reports in *The Times*, 2 June, 5 July, 21 July and 2 August 1956, and the comments by the chairman of the Prudential at its Annual General Meeting in 1959 (*The Times*, 15 May 1959).

69 See letter from the Chairman of the Investment Protection Committee of the British Insurance Association in *The Times*, 9 November 1959.

70 I am indebted to Mr T. A. Lynes for assembling and analysing this information, which it is hoped to publish in more detail later. It is, however, impossible to trace all these connections; the chain of sub-infeudations, subsidiary companies, affiliated companies and holding companies has come to be as intricate as that of mesne tenancies before *Quia Emptores*.

71 Abel-Smith, Brian, 'Whose welfare state?', in N. Mackenzie (ed.), *Conviction*, (1958).

72 Radcliffe Report, Cmnd 827, p. 87.

73 *The Times*, 24 November 1959.

74 See reports in *The Times* 11 August 1959, and *Observer*, 20 December 1959.

75 Opinion seems to differ as to whether the proposed new building in the Circus is 'crude and banal', 'a sign of England's greatness', 'the world's biggest aspidistra' or just a 'monster'. The Legal and General Assurance Co. are principally concerned (see reports of the public inquiry into this development proposal in *The Times* and *Observer*, December 1959).

76 Matthew, R., *Listener*, 6 August 1959, p. 204.

77 *Ibid.*

78 Galbraith, J. K., *The Affluent Society* (1958), pp. 104–5.

79 *Ibid.*, pp. 105–6.

80 Graham Wallas was also one of the first to see the importance of the transferability of pension rights as an element in personal freedom (*Our Social Heritage*, 1921, pp. 150–1).

CHAPTER

— 4 —

The Position of Women
Some Vital Statistics

In a period when the possibilities of social progress and the practicability of applied social science are being questioned it is a source of satisfaction to recall some of the achievements of the Women's Suffrage Movement in Britain. The development of the personal, legal and political liberties of half the population of the country within the span of less than eighty years stands as one of the supreme examples of consciously directed social change.

There have been numerous historical and biographical studies of this movement and of Millicent Fawcett and its other leaders.[1] Many of these studies have analysed the political, legal and vocational consequences, though largely within a middle-class ethos. Few have been concerned with the working-class woman, and particularly with the conditions of life of the working-class mother.[2] Yet, during the present century, far-reaching changes, social, economic and technological, have affected her status and role as a wife and mother, as a home-maker, as a contributor to the economy of the family, and in a variety of situations in the cycle of married life. Social historians and sociologists have been curiously neglectful of such studies and have allowed the subject of the position of women in modern society to be dominated by the psychologist, the psychiatrist and the sexologist.[3]

The purpose of this essay is twofold. First, to draw together some of the vital statistics of birth, marriage and death for the light they shed on the changes that have taken place since the beginning of the century in the social position of women. Secondly, to suggest that the accumulated effect of these changes now presents the makers of social policy with some new and fundamental problems.

The fall in the birth rate in Western societies is one of the dominating biological facts of the twentieth century. Commenting on the British statistics, the 1949 Report of the Royal Commission on Population noted the rapidity of the decline in family size after 1900.[4] Viewed within the context of the long period of industrial change since the seventeenth century, it is the rapidity of this fall which is as remarkable as the extent of the fall over the past fifty years. By and large, these trends have been shaped by changes in the family building habits of the working classes during the present century. The first phase of declining family size among non-manual workers, and particularly middle and upper-middle class groups, took place earlier. The absolute difference in the average size of completed families of non-manual and manual workers which was 1.15 for 1900–9 marriages fell by one third to .76 for 1925–9 marriages. From a mid-Victorian family size of six or more the average size of completed working-class families of marriages contracted in 1925–9 had fallen to just under 2½. For all classes, the proportion of couples having seven or more children during the second half of the nineteenth century was 43 per cent; for marriages contracted in 1925 this proportion had fallen to 2 per cent.[5] It would probably be true to say that at the end of the century about half of all working-class women over the age of 40 had borne between seven and fifteen children.

To speak of a revolutionary change in working-class attitudes to childbearing would hardly be an exaggeration in any attempt to interpret figures of this magnitude. Since the lowest levels in rates of fertility registered before the Second World War there have been minor fluctuations; a short-lived postwar rise and fall; and some indication that family building habits have settled at a little below replacement level. But, as Mr Carrier has observed, this 'apparent stability' provides 'no indication that the future prospects represent full replacement'.[6] The great gains in declining mortality during this century have, so to speak, held population replacement at substantially higher levels than would otherwise have been the case. Little help can be looked for in the future from this source. Moreover, over the past decade or so the indices of replacement have been temporarily inflated by earlier marriages (and earlier births) and true replacement may thus turn out to be appreciably below unity when we are in a position to judge the family building habits of postwar generations.

However, it is not my purpose to speculate about the future. I mention these more recent data simply to point the contrast between now and fifty years ago. This contrast, remarkable as it is in average family size, is even more so in terms of the number of pregnancies – that is, when allowance is made for the losses from stillbirths, miscarriages and deaths in infancy experienced at the beginning of the century.

When this is done it would seem that the typical working-class mother of the 1890s, married in her teens or early twenties and experiencing ten pregnancies, spent about fifteen years in a state of pregnancy and in nursing a child for the first year of its life. She was tied, for this period of time, to the wheel of childbearing. Today, for the typical mother, the time spent would be about four years.[7] A reduction of such magnitude in only two generations in the time devoted to childbearing represents nothing less than a revolutionary enlargement of freedom for women brought about by the power to control their own fertility. This private power, what Bernard Shaw once described as the ultimate freedom, can hardly have been exercised without the consent – if not the approval – of the husband. The amount and rapidity of the change together support such a proposition. We are thus led to interpret this development as a desired change within the working-class family rather than as a revolt by women against the authority of men on the analogy of the campaign for political emancipation.

What do these changes signify in terms of 'the forward view' – the vision that mothers now have and have had about their functions in the family and in the wider society? At the beginning of this century, the expectation of life of a woman aged 20 was forty-six years.[8] Approximately one-third of this life expectancy was to be devoted to the physiological and emotional experiences of childbearing and maternal care in infancy. Today, the expectation of life of a woman aged 20 is fifty-five years.[9] Of this longer expectation only about 7 per cent of the years to be lived will be concerned with childbearing and maternal care in infancy.

That the children of the large working-class families of fifty years ago helped to bring each other up must have been true; no single-handed mother of seven could have hoped to give to each child the standard of care, the quantity of time, the diffusion and concentration of thought that most children receive today. In this context, it is difficult to understand what is meant by those who generalize about the 'lost' functions of parents in the rearing of children. Certainly the children themselves, and especially girls, have lost some of these functions. But despite the help that the mother had from older children she could not expect to finish with the affairs of child care until she was in the middle 50s. Only then would the youngest child have left school. By that time too her practical help and advice would be increasingly in demand as she presided over, as the embodiment of maternal wisdom, a growing number of grandchildren. In other words, by the time the full cycle of child care had run its course the mother had only a few more years to live – an analogous situation to the biological sequence for many species in the animal world. The typical working-class mother in the industrial towns in 1900 could expect, if she survived to 55, to live not much more than another twelve years by the time she reached the comparative ease, the reproductive grazing field, of the middle 50s.[10]

The situation today is remarkably different. Even though we have extended the number of years that a child spends at school and added to the psychological and social responsibilities of motherhood by raising the cultural norms of child upbringing, most mothers have largely concluded their maternal role by the age of 40. At this age, a woman can now expect to live thirty-six years.[11] And if we accept the verdict of Parsons and Bales, Margaret Mead and others, she has also been largely divested of her role as a grandmother by the professional experts in child care.[12]

What these changes mean is that by the time the typical mother of today has virtually completed the cycle of motherhood she still has practically half her total life expectancy to live. Should she have only had boys, instead of girls, or children of both sexes, the necessary adjustments in outlook may seem more obvious, the diminution in role sharper. For the generality of women in most societies of which we have any reliable records this is a new situation. It presents an industrialized society, based on an extensive division of labour, on the early acquisition of occupational skills, on the personal achievement of status through educational and other channels which steadily narrow after the first ten years of adult life, with a host of new social problems. They are problems in the sense that these can be situations in which uncertainty and conflict develop over the individual's future role. What is socially approved behaviour is to recognize the need of the young adolescent for a growing measure of independence. Yet to relinquish the reins of motherhood today is no longer – as it was fifty years ago – a seemingly natural process of life closing in; of adjusting to the disabilities and tiredness of a long cycle of childbearing. Many mothers of today are not worn out by their forties. Nor may it be supposed that they are any more psychologically prepared to become more dependent on their husbands. For that is what the adjustment could spell to some wives as they consciously relinquish the independence-giving and emotionally expressive maternal role. What was in the past an almost unconscious process is now becoming a conscious one. This is to be expected as a natural corollary to the development of self-consciousness, as part of the intellectualization of child rearing, in the parental role.[13]

These questions are being formed by the conjunction and combination of many forces. Changes in family building habits is one; changes in rates of dying since the nineteenth century is another.

It is common knowledge that there have been great reductions in mortality over the past fifty years, particularly in infancy and childhood where rates of dying have fallen by approximately 75 per cent. What is less well known is that death rates among women have been declining faster than among men. A comparison of the standardized mortality rates (which allow for differences in the age structure of the male and female populations) shows that the rate among men today exceeds that for women by about 50 per cent.[14] This excess has accumulated steadily throughout the century. If rates of mortality are any guide to the general level of health of a population then these trends suggest that, since 1900, the health of women has improved, and is still improving, at a considerably faster rate than that of men.

The relative gains, as measured by death rates, of women over men apply to all age groups, but the really striking changes have taken place over the age of 45. This is shown by the percentage male excess at 10-year age groups for two periods:[15]

	25–34	35–44	45–54	55–64	65–74	75–84	85+
	%	%	%	%	%	%	%
1896–1900	15	22	29	24	17	13	9
1951–1955	28	28	62	91	65	37	20

Easily the greatest gains have been registered by women aged 45 to 74. There is no justification here for a lower pensionable age for women. Their expectation of life at 60 now exceeds that for men by nearly four years, which means that they are covered for national retirement pensions for about nine years longer than are men. Thus, with a pension running for nineteen years from 60,[16] and if a family allowance and an income tax child allowance runs to age 18, there are, in all, a total of thirty-seven years of 'dependency' recognized by the state in social policy.

A large part of these gains in mortality by women has been achieved since 1931. To quote the government actuary in reporting on mortality changes between the census of 1931 and 1951:

> At ages over forty, hoiwever, the experience of the two sexes has diverged. For women, there has been a continued substantial lightening of mortality, extending to age eighty and beyond. For men, on the other hand, the improvement has been much less; at age sixty the 1951 rate is almost the same as that of twenty years earlier. At that age the women's rate of mortality in 1950–2 was about 45 per cent less than that forty years before, while the men's rate was only 22 per cent less.[17]

These conclusions are more pronounced in the case of married women (and to a somewhat less extent for widows) for all ages up to 70 in contrast with the experience of single women. Not only do married women show much lower rates, but the gains they have made since 1930–2 are more substantial. But even single women show much lower rates than married men after the middle 40s.

Working-class women still show, however, substantially higher rates of mortality than the national average for all women. The expectation of life at age 45 for Glasgow women was four years lower than that for London women of the same age in 1950–2.[18] But, even so, all the declines registered by women in recent decades (in contrast with the trends for men) can only be summed up, to use the words of the Registrar-General for Scotland, 'as sensational'.[19]

This phenomenon is not peculiar to Britain. The relative gains by women over men since 1900 appear to be even more sensational in the United States, a fact that has been explained by one medical commentator in these words: 'In this patriarchal American culture males preserve their masculinity complex. Striving to live up to the expectations of maleness, men blow out their coronaries and cerebral arteries, making wealthy widows out of their wives. Men die five years before women in this country, and women possess 83 per cent of the wealth.'[20]

Whatever the reasons may be for the relative – if not the absolute – worsening in mortality rates for men[21] such comments do not explain the dramatic improvements shown by the rates for women. So far as Britain is concerned, a reasonable hypothesis would be that these improvements are in large part attributable to the decline in the size of the family since 1900. This receives support from the remarkable change, after 1930–2, in the relationship between the mortality of single women and that of married women. In Scotland, for instance, while the rates of single women in youth and early middle age fell by something like 25 per cent between 1930–2 (when they were lower than those for married women) and 1950–2, the rates for married women in the same range fell by about 60 per cent by 1950–2. This fall puts the rates for single women about 60 per cent in excess up to the age of 42.[22]

Among married women, not only have the hazards of childbirth and the frequency of confinements been greatly diminished, but the number and proportion of mothers worn out by excessive childbearing and dying prematurely from such diseases as tuberculosis, pneumonia and so forth are but a fraction of what they were fifty years ago. Above all, the decline in the size of the family has meant, in terms of family economics, a rise in the standard of living of women which has probably been of more importance, by itself, than any change since 1900 in real earnings by manual workers. Nor would it be hard to argue that this factor was far more influential up to the Second World War than any additional benefits derived from the expansion of the social services and improvements in medical care.

Yet when one turns to the history of the women's movement in

Britain it is odd to find that little attention was given to the problem of continuous childbearing with all its attendant evils of chronic ill-health and premature ageing. The social freedom of working-class women to control their own fertility was not an issue of any importance. Nevertheless, the Victorian myth about the biological inferiority of women was still powerful. For example, the manifesto of 1889, signed by Beatrice Webb, Mrs Humphrey Ward and others, protesting against Women's Suffrage, observed: 'We believe that the emancipating process has now reached the limits fixed by the physical constitution of women.'[23] Such an argument could hardly be brought forward today by those who oppose the principle of equal pay for women.

Before I turn to my last heading of marriage I would make one general point about the long term consequences of these trends in mortality and fertility. At the beginning of this century, when the total population of England and Wales was 32,500,000, there were 661,000 men aged over 65 and 1,337,000 women aged over 60 – a total of 1,998,000 or 6 per cent of the population. Today (1956), we have 2,045,000 men aged over 65 and 4,395,000 women aged over 60 – a total of 6,440,000 people of pensionable ages – or 14 per cent of the population. According to the Registrar-General's projections we are likely to have, by 1975, approximately 750,000 more men aged over 65 but 1,250,000 more women aged over 60.[24] About 18 per cent of the population will then be of pensionable age. While this proportion is not abnormally high for a more or less stable population, it does contain a preponderance of women. The problem of social policies for old age today and tomorrow is thus mainly a problem of elderly women – a fact that is generally overlooked by those who consider that private occupational schemes for men will answer all the questions of income maintenance in old age.

When the women's movement was in full flood, early this century, most thoughtful observers believed that to release women from the domination of men, exercised through what John Stuart Mill called 'the foul means of marriage',[26] would lead to fewer marriages in the future. No student of society would have had the temerity at that time to forecast the remarkable changes which the institution of marriage has undergone since those days. On the subjective plane, it can be said with some degree of truth that the mutual relationships of husband and wife are very different today from the picture of married life which emerges from the literature and social investigations of Edwardian times. The extent to which fertility has come under control by married couples is evidence of this. New patterns in the psychological management of married life have been slowly evolving; the idea of companionship in marriage is being substituted for the more sharply defined roles and codes of behaviour set by the Victorian patriarchal system with (to quote Virginia Woolf) 'its nullity, its immorality, its hypocrisy, its servility'.[27]

It seems that we are at some as yet undefinable stage in the process of 'democratizing' marriage. It follows, therefore, that as the size of the family has declined we have gradually come to expect more and more of our marriages.

> We are more inclined now than we used to be to demand a capacity for response between the partners, to look for intellectual and temperamental compatibility, as well as purely material welfare, in addition to the ordinary social and parental satisfactions. The more we demand in these respects, the more frequently, perhaps, we shall have to count our failures, but also the higher may be our level of achievement.[28]

Perhaps that is why the Royal Commission on Marriage and Divorce saw that its primary task was to seek out 'ways and means of strengthening the resolution of hubsand and wife to realize the ideal of a partnership for life'.[29]

No doubt the political and legal emancipation of women has contributed to these changes in what is expected from marriage. A more socially equal relationship was foreseen by the leaders of the Women's Movement but what they could hardly have envisaged is the rise in the popularity of marriage since about 1911. Here we turn from the debatable field of value judgments about the quality of married life to the statistics of marriage, distinguishing, as we must, between the amount of marriage taking place in a given population and the age at marriage.

As to the first, it is clear that for about forty years before 1911 marriage rates among women were declining. But somewhere around this time a change occurred; the amount of marriage began to increase. It has been increasing ever since, and in a striking fashion since the mid-1930s. An increase of nearly one-third between 1911 and 1954 in the proportion of women aged

20 to 40 married represents, as the Registrar-General has said, 'a truly remarkable rise'.[30] Never before, in the history of English vital statistics, has there been such a high proportion of married women in the female population, under the age of 40 and, even more so, under the age of 30. Since 1911 the proportion at age 15 to 19 has risen nearly fourfold; at age 20 to 24 it has more than doubled. Such figures as these hardly support the conclusion of the Royal Commission on Marriage and Divorce that 'matrimony is not so secure as it was fifty years ago'.[31]

More marriage has been accompanied by a great increase in the years of married life experienced by married couples. Declining death rates have not only lengthened marriage (and with earlier childbearing very substantially lengthened the years of married life during which there are no children to be cared for), but they have brought about a striking fall in the proportion of marriages broken by widowhood and widowerhood under the age of 60. It is highly probable that the proportion of broken marriages under the age of 60, marriages broken by death, desertion and divorce, is, in total, smaller today than at any time this century. It is also relevant to point out that the greater the amount of marriage becomes the greater will be the chances that men and women, with impaired health and handicaps, physical and psychological, and unstable personalities will be exposed to the hazards of married life and child-rearing. In other words, a wider range of personality and character variation may now be drawn into the ambit of marriage and parenthood. Formerly, this segment of the population (some part of which could be distinguishable by the incidence of acquired and inherited physical handicaps) might not have entered matrimony.[32] No interpretation of recent divorce statistics or of the facts about 'broken homes' can be satisfactory unless account is taken of this factor; and of the strikingly high rates of remarriage of divorced men and women in recent years. By 1955 this was in the region of three-quarters.[33]

Married life has been lengthened not only by declining mortality but by earlier marriage. It is a fact of the greatest social significance that for the past forty years a trend towards more youthful marriage has been in progress. In 1911, 24 per cent of all girls aged 20 to 24 were married; by 1954 this proportion had risen to 52 per cent.[34] As a result of this trend and rising marriage rates the proportion of women still single at the age of 35 has fallen to only about 13 per cent.[35] There are now fewer unmarried women aged 15 to 35 in the country than at any time since 1881, when the total population was only 60 per cent of its present size. Yet 'the last generation in this country to reproduce itself completely was born as long ago as 1876 or thereabouts'.[36]

What broadly emerges from this incursion into the statistics of marriage is, first, a remarkable increase in the amount of marriage in the community, secondly, more and more youthful marriage – especially among women, thirdly, a concentration of family building habits in the earlier years of married life and, fourthly, a substantial extension in the years of exposure to the strains and stresses of married life. All these changes have taken place during a period of increasing emancipation for women. Paradoxically, therefore, fewer social and legal restraints and more equality and freedom for women have been accompanied by an increase in the popularity of the marriage institution.

To survey the changed position of women in English society from the standpoint of the vital statistics of birth, marriage and death raises a great many questions. While it has not been the purpose of this essay to analyse the causes of these changes, or to examine the modern family in sociological terms, it is nevertheless possible to discern from the bare facts the outlines of new social problems which, as yet, we have hardly begun to contemplate, while other problems, long recognized, have now to be seen in a different frame of reference. The problem, for instance, of the dual roles of women in modern society; of the apparent conflict between motherhood and wage-earning which now has to be viewed in relation to the earlier and much more compressed span of life during which the responsibilities of motherhood are more intense. With an expectation of another thirty-five to forty years of life at the age of 40, with the responsibilities of child-upbringing nearly fulfilled, with so many more alternative ways of spending money, with new opportunities and outlets in the field of leisure, the question of the rights of women to an emotionally satisfying and independent life appears in a new guise.

Yet, at present, practically all forms of educational and vocational training, along with entry to many pensionable occupations, are shut to the woman who has reached the age of 40. Motherhood and date of birth disqualify her, while the unthinking and unknowing may condemn her in moralizing terms for seeking work outside the home. Few subjects are more surrounded with prejudice and moral platitude than this; an approach which perhaps deepens the conflict for the women themselves about their roles as mothers, wives and wage-earners.

Already, it seems, more and more middle-aged mothers are seeking to find some solution to the social, economic and psychological problems which face them, or may do so in the future. Dimly they may be perceiving the outline of these problems in the years ahead when the days of child upbringing are over.

Between 1946 and May 1955 the number of married women in gainful employment rose by 2¼ million to 3¾ million or 48 per cent of all women at work.[37] The biggest source of recruitment in recent years has been married women over 30 years of age.[38] Today, the most important group, relatively and absolutely, are those aged 40 to 50. There are now over one million married women of these ages at work, or one in three of all married women in this group.[39] Of all married women under the age of 50 at work in 1951 at least one-fifth had children of school age.[40] The proportion is probably substantially higher now.

Making allowance for seasonal and other work changes, it is probable that the lives of about 4 million families in Britain are now affected by the paid employment of the wife or mother outside the home.[41] This development has no doubt contributed substantially to the standard of living of a large proportion of working-class families – as it has to that of the nation as a whole. Mothers and wives are likely to be affected first by any rise in unemployment.

In the field of employment opportunities, as in so many other fields, new issues for social policy are taking shape as a consequence of these changes in the position of women in society. The problems for state policy which the women's movement of fifty years ago brought to the fore were largely political; those raised by the women's movements of today are largely social.

Notes

The substance of the Millicent Fawcett Lecture given at Bedford College, London, on 19 February 1952. Some additional material of a factual nature has been inserted for publication. Other statistics have been brought up to date and references added.

1 Since this lecture was given Mr O. R. McGregor has published his valuable bibliography on 'The social position of women in England, 1850–1914' (*British Journal of Sociology*, vo. 6, no. 1, March 1955). Every student of the subject will be grateful to him, as the present writer is, for this extensive, witty and penetrating commentary on the literature.

2 Even in the field of women's employment nothing has been published for the period since 1850 to rank with Dr Ivy Pinchbeck's scholarly work, *Women Workers and the Industrial Revolution, 1750–1850*.

3 Particularly in the United States. The main index of the New York Central Library, for instance, lists 10,600 separate published volumes under *Woman* and *Women*. By contrast, *Child* and *Children* scores 7,800; *Man* (which includes *Mankind*) 2,200, and *Men* only 446.

4 *Report of the Royal Commission on Population*, 1949, Cmd 7695, p. 25.

5 See *Report of the Royal Commission*, pp. 24–30; Glass, D. V., and Grebenik, E., *The Trend and Pattern of Fertility in Great Britain: a Report on the Family Census of 1946* (1954), and Registrar-General, *Census of England and Wales, 1911*, vol. 13, pts 1 and 2.

6 Carrier, N. H., 'An examination of generation fertility in England and Wales', *Population Studies*, vol. IX, no. 1 (July 1955), p. 19. The average family size at nine completed years of marriage of those marrying in 1945 at ages under 25 was lower than that for a corresponding group married in 1930 (*Registrar-General's Statistical Review*, England and Wales, 1954, pt 3, p. 22).

7 Actual number of years, not consecutive years. If estimated in terms of the distribution of pregnancies over the childbearing period the contrast would probably be greater.

8 English Life Table, no. 7 for 1901–10, *Supplement to the 75th Annual Report of the Registrar-General*, 1914, pt 1. It was precisely the same for males in Glasgow in 1950–2 (Glasgow Life Tables, *Supplement to the 99th Annual Report of the Registrar-General for Scotland*, 1954).

9 England and Wales, 1953–5, *Registrar-General's Quarterly Return*, September 1956, App. B.

10 Estimated from the Registrar-General's Occupational Mortality and Life Table Reports, 1891–1900, *Supplement to the 75th Annual Report*, pts 1 and 2, Cd 2618/9.

11 England and Wales, 1953–5. *Registrar-General's Quarterly Return*, September 1956, App. B.

12 This may be true of middle-class white populations in the United States, but there are no systematic studies in Britain to support such a conclusion. On the contrary, Young and Willmott have shown that in Bethnal Green, London, for instance, the mother, whatever her age, rarely ceases to play an important part in the lives of her children and grandchildren (Young, M., and Willmott, P., *Family and Kinship in East London*, 1957).

13 See Parsons, Talcott & Bales, R. F., *Family, Socialization and Interaction Process* (1956), especially chs 2 and 3 in which the authors discuss marriage as an 'achieved' status.

14 1954–5, table 3, *Registrar-General's Statistical Review, England and Wales*, 1955, pt 1.

15 Calculated from table 4, *Registrar-General's Statistical Review, England and Wales*, 1955, pt 1.
16 Expectation of life at 60 in 1952–4, *Registrar-General's Statistical Review, England and Wales*, 1954, pt 3, table 30).
17 *Registrar-General's Decennial Supplement*, England and Wales, 1951, Life Tables, p. 11.
18 *Registrar-General's Decennial Supplement*, England and Wales, 1951, Life tables, table V4, and *Registrar-General for Scotland*, Life Tables, 1950–2, App. 2, table 3.
19 Life Tables, 1950–2, p. 12.
20 Moloney, J. C., in *Symposium on the Healthy Personality*, ed. by M. J. E. Senn (New York, 1950), p. 51.
21 Some fascinating material on the medical causes of these trends is analysed by J. N. Morrris in *Uses of Epidemiology* (1957).
22 *Registrar-General for Scotland*, Life Tables, 1950–2, p. 12.
23 Strachey, R., *The Cause* (1928), p. 285.
24 *Registrar-General's Quarterly Return for England and Wales*, December 1955, App. B.
25 On the basis of mortality in 1953–5, 22 per cent of males and 40 per cent of females born would reach the age of 80.
26 Mill, J. S., *The Subjection of Women* (1869), p. 81.
27 Woolf, V., *Three Guineas* (1943), p. 135.
28 Slater, E., and Woodside, M., *Patterns of Marriage* (1951), p. 126.
29 Report of the Royal Commission on Marriage and Divorce, 1951–5, Cmd 9678, p. 7.
30 *Registrar-General's Statistical Review*, England and Wales, 1940–5, Civil Text, vol. 2. For other recent material on marriage trends see the *Reviews* for 1946–50 (Civil Text), 1951 (Text), 1954 (pt 3), and 1955 (pt 3); and Hajnal, J., *Population Studies*, vol. 1, no. 1, June 1947, and vol. 7, no. 2, November 1953.
31 Report 1951–5, Cmd 9678, p. 24.
32 Support for this thesis comes from the trend of mortality rates for married and single women since the 1930s. 'It is to be supposed', wrote the government actuary, 'that those persons who marry are likely, on average, to be in better health than the unmarried; it was, therefore, to be anticipated that, as the number of spinsters became progressively smaller, a higher proportion of them would be of inferior vitality and that their mortality, relative to that of married women, would become heavier.' This expectation is borne out in a striking manner by the comparative mortality rates discussed in these paragraphs (*Registrar-General's Decennial Supplement*, England and Wales, Life Tables, 1951, pp. 14–15).
33 The 1954 level of incidence of decrees, when related to the number of antecedent marriages from which they arise, indicates that about 7 per cent of marriages are terminated by divorce (*Registrar-General's Statistical Review*, England and Wales, 1955, pt 3, pp. 2–3). The statistics of divorce petitions and maintenance orders are critically examined by Mr O. R. McGregor in his book *Divorce in England* (1957), esp. ch. 11.
34 According to a survey of 'Britain's six or seven leading marriage bureaux',

conducted by *The Economist* in 1955, those who remain single and approach these agencies 'always want to marry a professional man, as do the heroines of women's magazine stories'. But 'it is the civil servants who really go like hot cakes, because of the pension' (*The Economist*, 27 August 1955, pp. 678–9).

35 The rise in the proportion of all marriages which are of minors is another illustration of the trend towards earlier marriage. In 1938 this proportion for females was 16.4 per cent; in 1955 it was 30.3 per cent. For males it rose from 3.4 per cent to 7.8 per cent respectively (*Registrar-General's Statistical Review*, England and Wales, 1955, pt 3, p. 48).

36 *Registrar-General's Statistical Review*, England and Wales, 1946–50, Civil Text, p. 83.

37 *Report by the Government Actuary on the Provisions of the National Insurance Bill*, 1946, Cmd 6750, and *The Economist*, 14 July 1956, p. 131. These figures include full time and part time.

38 *Ministry of Labour Gazette*, June 1954.

39 *Ministry of Labour Gazette*, August 1952.

40 *Ministry of Labour Gazette*, May 1951.

41 Some aspects of these changes among families in East London were being studied by Miss Pearl Jephcott and her colleagues in a project undertaken by the Social Science Department of the London School of Economics (subsequently published as Jephcott, A. P. *et al.*, *Married Women Working* (London: Allen & Unwin, 1962).

CHAPTER

— 5 —

War and Social Policy

Professor Gibbs, in reappraising the contribution made by Clausewitz to military studies,[1] has politely but firmly criticized past historians for bringing their histories to a stop when the guns started firing, and in opening a new chapter only with the return of peace – of normal diplomatic and institutional relationships between sovereign states. Following Clausewitz – a much misunderstood thinker – Professor Gibbs deplored this historical interregnum. He was faced with a lack of balance in the material available to him in reflecting upon the nature of war and society. He could hardly complain, however, about the *quantity* of historical studies at his disposal. Military and naval documents, regimental histories, the lives of captains and kings, political, diplomatic and even philosophical works jostle each other for a place in the crowded 'war' index and bear witness to the energy and interests of past students of war, and to the endemic character of war in the history of man.

By contrast, I am doubly handicapped in discussing the relationship of war and social policy. So far as the story of modern war before 1939 is concerned, little has been recorded in any systematic way about the social and economic effects of war on the population as a whole. Only long and patient research in out of the way documentary places can reveal something of the characteristics and flavour of social life during the experience of wars in the past. And these records are often undisciplined and unreliable. There are, for example, somewhat highly coloured accounts of popular reactions on the south coasts of England to the threat of invasion when Napoleon Bonaparte was master of all Western Europe; of the effects of the Crimean and Boer Wars on poor law policy in those days; of a remarkable decline in criminal behaviour among civilians in Britain during the First World War and an equally remarkable outbreak of panic among the civilians of London when the first Zeppelins arrived with their primitive bombs, most of which failed to explode.[2] But even such accounts, unreliable as they may be, are hard to come by. And, strangely enough, one often turns away from the novelists in disappointment; it is difficult to believe, for instance, that some of Jane Austen's novels were written during one of the great wars in history; a war which signified for this country, if the late Professor Greenwood got his sums right, a proportionately greater loss of life among soldiers and sailors than during the First World War and, consequently, more widespread effects among the families of those who served in the Armed Forces.[3]

These are some of the reflections which I have recalled – though in a more tranquil mood – from the days when I was engaged on the social policy history of the Second World War. In studying the effects of the evacuation of civilians from London and other cities, I was led to wonder whether there were any recorded accounts of the movement of civilian populations in past wars as a calculated element in war strategy. I had to go back to the Greeks – to the great Hellenic wars – before I was rewarded. Here is Plutarch's description of the evacuation of the civilian population of Athens as a military necessity during the Persian invasion in 480 BC. The Peloponnesian city of Troezen, on the far side of the Saronic Gulf, became (what we now call) a 'reception area'. According to Plutarch,

> The most part of them [the Athenians] did convey their aged fathers and mothers, their wives and little children, into the city of Troezen, where the Troezenians received them very lovingly and gently. For they gave order that they should be entertained of the common charge, allowing them apiece, two oboloes of their money a day, and suffered the young children to gather fruit wheresoever they found it, and furthermore, did hire schoolmasters at the charge of the common-wealth, to bring them up at school.[4]

From this account it would seem that conscious thought was given by the responsible authorities to the social and psychological needs of the evacuated population. There was, in fact, a plan; a concerted social policy, a deliberate public attempt to foresee events, to estimate behaviour, to minimize hardships and to control a social situation in the interests of a community at war.

It was this fragment of history, illuminating the way in which war and social policy influence each other, that helped to shape the ideas for this essay. In discussing social policy, I mean those acts of government deliberately designed and taken to improve the welfare of the civil population in time of war. I am not, therefore, simply concerned with the social and biological consequences of war; my main interest, then, is with the organized attempts of governments to control these consequences. Much of what I have to say will be confined to the experiences of this country since the middle of the nineteenth century. For a definition of 'social', I take, for convenience, the scope of the two published volumes on social policy during the Second World War. There is, however, a difficulty here which cannot be so lightly resolved. In essence, it is the problem of distinguishing between policies related to peace-time needs and policies concerned only with the immediate wartime situation. It is bound up with the assumption that war is an abnormal situation; that peace is – or ought to be – the normal lot of mankind.

In considering, however, the results of deliberate attempts to organize a society for war – either in the military, economic or social spheres – we are confronted with one of the major characteristics of large scale, modern war; the fact that modern war casts its shadow long before it happens and that its social effects are felt for longer and longer periods after armed conflict has ceased. In the time scale of these effects, modern war stretches over a greater span of men's lives, unlike the wars of religion and those wars which Toynbee called in his studies of *War and Civilization*, 'The sport of Kings'.[5] Many of them started abruptly, without planning; without any preparatory action to provide for the needs of the civilian population; without any consideration of how war might affect the social and economic life of the country. They were, in fact, organized military wars; otherwise, and apart from the particular territories over which battles were fought, normal life proceeded – and was assumed to proceed – normally. By contrast, however, as the plans and policies of twentieth-century governments for war and peace have become more inter-related it is, in consequence, increasingly difficult to detach the 'abnormal' from the 'normal', and to attribute precisely the acts of government to one or other of these situations.

I turn now to consider how developments in modern war have affected social policy. It is a commonplace among students of the subject that in our recent Western history war has been following war in an ascending order of intensity. In scale, in depth and in time, war has been waged more intensively and ferociously. This crescendo in the organization of war has enveloped a larger proportion of the total population and, as I said earlier, has left its marks on them for a longer period of time. These developments during the past hundred years have affected social policy in a variety of ways. Among these, perhaps the dominating one has been the increasing concern of the state in time of war with the biological characteristics of its people. The growing scale and intensity of war has stimulated a growing concern about the quantity and quality of the population.

We may mark certain well-defined stages in this progression of biological interests. The first stage of organized interest was with quantity; with the number of men available for battle. This, of course, developed as the scale upon which war was fought increased, and it was no longer safe for the authorities to assume that there were abundant supplies of men available. This growing concern with quantity at different periods and in different societies has been one of the forces which has stimulated the interest of governments in population trends and in the taking of national censuses. As we know from our own history of vital statistics, opposition was raised in the nineteenth century to census operations because of a fear that they were being carried out for military reasons.

The second stage in this progression is marked by the increasing adoption of qualitative standards applied to military and naval recruits. No doubt a connection can be traced between secular changes in these standards as to what constitutes 'fitness for service' and the increasing mechanization and division of labour in the armed forces. The standards demanded have risen enormously in this country since the day, just over one hundred years ago, when Florence Nightingale discovered that the British Army Medical Service was staffed by a few clerks and an odd messenger boy or two. We now have the most complex system of standards comprising a variety of physical, functional, psychological and social attributes. According to the editor of the *International Journal of Psycho-Analysis*, 'It was not love but war-time necessity which made American psychiatry turn towards Freud'.[6] He suggests that one of the principal reasons why psychiatry occupies such a commanding position in the American social scene today is because of what he calls the 'unforgettable role' that psychiatrists played in the organization of the war effort.

All this has two important implications for social policy; first, that increasingly higher demands are made upon society for those who are physically and psychologically fit, intellectually bright, and socially acceptable on grounds of personal character; second, that, as a result, the proportion of men rejected and invalided from the Armed Forces tends to rise rather than fall. Many then become the clients of the social services. This is one example which shows that what is done in the name of 'defence' determines, in substantial measure, some of the roles and functions of the social services. The social costs of the Boer War and the First World War, as measured by expenditure on pensions, widows' benefits, medical care, rehabilitation, sickness claims, rent subsidies, and national assistance, represent a substantial proportion of the social service budget today.

The third stage of interest is reached when public concern about the standard of fitness of men of military age moves out, in a widening circle of policy, to embrace concern about the health and well-being of the whole population and, in particular, of children – the next generation of recruits. This stage was reached in Britain at the beginning of the century, and it is worth enquiring a little more closely into events at that time because of their importance for the subsequent development of public health policies.

It was the South African War, not one of the notable wars in human history to change the affairs of men, that touched off the personal health movement which led eventually to the National Health Service in 1948. Public concern was roused at the end of the war by the facts that were published about sickness and mortality among the troops, and by a report from the inspector-general of recruiting which spoke of 'the gradual deterioration of the physique of the working classes from whom the bulk of the recruits must always be drawn'.[7] At a time when many leaders of opinion still held to the nineteenth-century doctrine of the inevitability of social progress, this report from the inspector-general came as a shock. Could it be, at the end of a century of unprecedented material progress, that the health and fitness of the bulk of the population was deteriorating? There followed, in rapid succession, one commission of inquiry after another into these questions of physical deterioration, systems of medical inspection, the causes of high infant mortality and many other matters affecting the well-being of the population.

As a consequence of this ferment of inquiry we may trace the establishment in 1906 of the school medical service, the school feeding of children in elementary schools, a campaign to reduce infant mortality and many other social measures.

All these elements of social policy stemmed directly from the Boer War and show how, in modern times, our concern for communal fitness has followed closely upon the course of our military fortunes. The story repeats itself in the First World War. In 1917, for example, we may note the introduction of the first instalment of a free National Health Service when facilities were offered, to civilians and soldiers alike, for the treatment and prevention of venereal disease. At the close of the war a new phrase 'a C3 nation' crept into contemporary journalism after the report of the Ministry of National Service had told the country that only one man in three of nearly 2½ million examined was completely fit for military service.[8] Most of these men are now in their sixties and account, in substantial measure, for the high proportion who are retiring from work today on grounds of ill-health – a matter to which a recent report from the Ministry of Pensions and National Insurance has drawn attention.[9] It is possible that, among many other reasons, the age of retirement for men in the National Insurance Scheme has not been raised because of the long range effects of the First World War.

The ancient Greeks, in attaching some moral significance to the idea of keeping fit, almost as though they had convinced themselves that vigour of body was an absolute good, had, we may now remember, sound reasons for keeping fit. Their civilization involved them in continuous wars; and so, we must admit, has our civilization of the twentieth century.

When we consider the effects of the Second World War, a war in Britain which depended not on the efforts of a fraction of the population but on the efforts of virtually all citizens, we reach a fourth stage in our ascending scale of interest. Not only was it necessary for the state to take positive steps in all spheres of the national economy to safeguard the physical health of the people; it was also an imperative for war strategy for the authorities to concern themselves with that elusive concept 'civilian morale'; with what Professor Cyril Falls called, in his Lees Knowles lectures in 1941, 'demostrategy'.[10] By this he meant, in military terms, that the war could not be won unless millions of ordinary people, in Britain and overseas, were convinced that we had something better to offer than had our enemies – not only during but after the war. This requirement of war strategy was stated, more explicitly, in a memorable leader in *The Times*[11] soon after the last British troops had left the Dunkirk beaches. It was a call for social justice; for the abolition of privilege, for a more equitable distribution of income and wealth; for drastic changes in the economic and social life of the country.

The effect on social policy of these ideas about war strategy was profound. It was increasingly sharpened as the war went on, for not until three years had passed, and victory was at last a rational – rather than an emotional – conception, could the enemy claim that he had killed as many British soldiers as women and children.

Much of the story of the war effort in terms of applied social policies is told in the series of volumes in the Official War History by myself and my colleagues. I shall not attempt to recount the story here, except to draw out of it one or two general conclusions.

The social measures that were developed during the war centred round the primary needs of the whole population irrespective of class, creed or military category. The distinctions and privileges, accorded to those in uniform in previous wars, were greatly diminished. Comprehensive systems of medical care and rehabilitation, for example, had to be organized by the state for those who were injured and disabled. They could not be exclusively reserved for soldiers and sailors, as in the past, but had to be extended to include civilians as well – to those injured in the factories as well as the victims of bombing. The organization and structure of the Emergency Medical Service, initially designed to cater for a special section of the population, became in the end the prototype of a medical service for the whole population.

In the sphere of food policy, it was no longer thought

appropriate for members of the Armed Forces to receive better diets than the civilian population. The scales of rationing – as in many other spheres of need as well – had to be kept in balance between civilian and non-civilian.

This wartime trend towards universalizing public provision for certain basic needs did not come about as a result of the traffic of ideas in one direction only. It also worked the other way; from civilians to non-civilians. Educational facilities in the form of music, drama and the arts, open to civilians in time of war, could not be withheld from men and women in the Forces. No longer could it be said that soldiers 'would get above themselves' if, instead of drinking, they read books and papers, and that army discipline would thereby be endangered – as was said in May 1855 by the War Office to Florence Nightingale when she opened a reading room for injured soldiers in Scutari.[12] By the 1940s the military authorities in Britain had taken to heart – no doubt unwittingly – Aristotle's epitaph on the 'Lycurgean' system of Spartan training for war. This was the way he summed it up:

> Peoples ought not to train themselves in the art of war with an eye to subjugating neighbours who do not deserve to be subjugated . . . The paramount aim of any social system should be to frame military institutions, like all its other institutions, with an eye to the circumstances of peace-time, when the soldier is off duty; and this proposition is borne out by the facts of experience. For militaristic states are apt to survive only so long as they remain at war, while they go to ruin as soon as they have finished making their conquests. Peace causes their metal to lose its temper; and the fault lies with a social system which does not teach its soldiers what to make of their lives when they are off duty.

To apply this Aristotelian precept to the modern world means, in effect, that a social system must be so organized as to enable all citizens (and not only soldiers) to learn what to make of their lives in peacetime. In this context, the Education Act of 1944 becomes intelligible; so does the Beveridge Report of 1942 and the National Insurance, Family Allowances and National Health Service Acts. All these measures of social policy were in part an expression of the needs of wartime strategy to fuse and unify the conditions of life of civilians and non-civilians alike. In practice, as we have seen, this involved the whole community in accepting an enlargement of obligations – an extension of social discipline – to attend to the primary needs of all citizens.

In no particular sphere of need is the imprint of war on social policy more vividly illustrated than in respect to *dependant* needs – the needs of wives, children and other relatives for income-maintenance allowances when husbands and fathers are serving in the Forces. To trace in detail the system of Service pay and allowances from the Napoleonic Wars to the Second World War is to see how, as war has followed war in an ascending order of intensity, so have the dependant needs of wives and children been increasingly recognized. The more, in fact, that the waging of war has come to require a total effort by the nation the more have the dependant needs of the family been recognized and accepted as a social responsibility.

This trend in the wartime recognition of family dependencies has also profoundly affected social security policies in general. New systems of Service pay and allowances threw into sharper prominence the fact that in industrial society money rewards take no account of family responsibilities. Nor, until 1939, did many of the payments made under various social services. Thus, one immediate effect was that dependants' allowances were added to workmen's compensation and other schemes. Another was that in many respects war pensions and industrial injury pensions had to be brought into line. This was done – as so many other things were done – because it seemed inappropriate to make distinctions between war and peace, civilians and non-civilians.

Looking back over the various points I have made about the relationship between the war effort of a community and its social policies in peace as well as in war one general conclusion may, I think, be ventured. The waging of modern war presupposes and imposes a great increase in social discipline; moreover, this discipline is only tolerable if – and only if – social inequalities are not intolerable. The need for less inequality is expressed, for example, in the changes that take place in what is socially approved behaviour – marked differences in standards of living, in dress, in luxury entertainment and in indulgencies of many kinds are disapproved. They were not only disapproved in wartime Britain but, in fact, there is evidence to show that they were greatly reduced.

It follows that the acceptance of these social disciplines – of obligations as well as rights – made necessary by war, by preparations for war, and by the long-run consequences of war, must influence the aims and content of social policies not only during the war itself but in peacetime as well. 'The discipline of the army', wrote Max Weber, 'gives birth to all discipline.'[13] In some senses he was not far wrong, but it should be remembered that this thesis rested on an analysis of military organization from the days of Sparta down to the professional European armies at the beginning of the twentieth century. Britain's war effort in 1930 did not rest on a professional military base. Nevertheless, it is, I think, a tenable proposition that military wars demand a military discipline, and that this kind of discipline (or 'warrior communism' as Weber described it) demands certain kinds of perfected conduct from a small section of the population. We have some classic examples of this perfection of discipline in the infantry drill of Spartan soldiers and the exquisite movements of Lord Cardigan's cavalry in the Crimean War. Both inevitably required – and this was the point of Weber's analysis – an 'aristocratic' structure in military organization and in society as a whole. Both essays in war came to a bad end. The social disciplines demanded by the civilians' war in Britain of 1939 were very different; they derived their strength from internal sources rather than from external commands, and had to rest on a social system which sought to teach all its soldiers what to make of their lives when off duty.

The aims and content of social policy, both in peace and in war, are thus determined – at least to a substantial extent – by how far the co-operation of the masses is essential to the successful prosecution of war. If this co-operation is thought to be essential, then inequalities must be reduced, and the pyramid of social stratification must be flattened. This, in part, is the thesis advanced by Andrzejewski in a sweeping, untidy but brilliant study recently published under the title *Military Organization and Society*.[14] In analysing the character of war and its conduct from pastoral and pre-literate societies down to the advent of atomic war, he argues that what he calls the military participation ratio determines the social stratification of a society. Mass war, involving a high proportion of the total population, tends to a levelling in social class differences. On the other hand, professional wars, conducted by military leaders recruited from a social élite and depending on support from only a small proportion of the population, tend to heighten existing social inequalities. This study, in my view, effectively answers Herbert Spencer's theory that war conduces to greater social inequalities. It may have been true of some wars in some periods and cultures but not of all wars. However, we must fairly admit that Spencer was writing before the advent of the mass wars of the twentieth century.

The work of these sociologists does, in general, support the arguments I have advanced: that modern war has had – at least in Britain – a profound ⁻influence on social policy and that, reciprocally, the direction of social policy has influenced the way in which war is prosecuted. But this, I am confident – more perhaps by faith than by reason – is not the whole of the story in the evolution of social policy. Man does not live by war alone. To explain the social life of a community in terms of aggression and struggle is to explain only part of 'this sorry scheme of things entire'.

Notes

Delivered at King's College, London, on 3 March 1955, in a series of public lectures on 'War and society'. A shortened version was published in the *Listener*, 3 November 1955.

1 Printed in the *Listener*, 6 October 1955.
2 See Titmuss, R. M., *Problems of Social Policy* (1950); Trotter, W., *Instincts of the Herd in Peace and War* (1916); and *British Medical Journal* (1940), i, 270.
3 Greenwood, M., 'British loss of life in the wars of 1794–1815 and 1914–1918', *Journal of the Royal Statistical Society*, vol. 105, pt 1 (1942).
4 *Vita Themistoclis*, 10, 5 (North's translation).
5 Toynbee, A., *War and Civilization* (1951).
6 Hoffer, W., *Lancet* (1954), ii, 1234.
7 See *Report of the Inter-Departmental Committee on Physical Deterioration*, vol. 1, especially App. 1, p. 96, Cd 2175, 1904.
8 *Report of the Ministry of National Service 1917–1919*, vol. 1.
9 *Reasons for Retiring or Continuing at Work*, Ministry of Pensions and National Insurance, 1954.
10 Falls, C., *The Nature of Modern Warfare* (1941), p. 13.
11 1 July 1940.
12 Woodham-Smith, C., *Florence Nightingale* (1950), p. 239.
13 Gerth, H. H., and Wright Mills, C., *From Max Weber: Essays in Sociology* (1947), p. 261.
14 Andrzejewski, S., *Military Organization and Society* (1954).

CHAPTER

— 6 —

Social Welfare and the Art of Giving

I

The history of social welfare in Western countries as an organized system of 'giving' shows that over the past century it has played a variety of roles in the processes of change. One of the most important but least acknowledged in the historical literature has been its educational role. In Britain and other countries exposed to the early stages of industrialization, it was a major force in sustaining the social conscience. To give aid without regard to economic criteria and to differences in race, colour, religion, and class brought it into direct conflict with the values of the market place. To act as an agent of redistributive social justice meant opposing discrimination; the concept of economic man had to be confronted with non-economic criteria; the natural dignity and uniqueness of every man had continually to be publicly re-stated, fought for, and demonstrated.

While time and circumstances have changed for the mass of the people in the West, the fundamental need for social welfare as an instrument of social justice and community education remains. This is one of the underlying themes of this essay; a second and less explicit one is that only a society which is firmly dedicated to the principle of greater equality and the diffusion of humanistic values will have sufficient moral conviction to make available the resources necessary to help close the gap between the 'have' and the 'have-not' nations of the world. The ideas which move men and which they hold about their own societies must influence

113

them in their attitudes toward the need for change in other societies.

It is of course possible to preach reform for others but not for one's own social group. The history of colonialism and race relations in the East and the West is littered with sad examples of hypocrisy. But, considered in collective terms, such attitudes today require a high degree of calculated cynicism. In effect, they can mean that the rich nations advocate social reform for the poor nations in order to prevent the spread of communism or some other hostile ideology or to further the defence and economic interests of the rich. According to Professor Seymour Martin Lipset (writing of underdeveloped countries): 'only parties which promise to improve the situation of the masses through widespread reform . . . can hope to compete with the Communists'.[1] A philosophy of the status quo at home can cynically purvey the notion of social welfare as a reforming agent among the poorer nations of the world simply to protect an already established 'good' society in the West. Fortunately, the development of social welfare values and policies among the poorer nations does not wholly depend on the influence or attitudes of the rich nations.

Nevertheless, however determined and able the 'have-not' nations are to shape their own internal policies, there will still remain a major dilemma of 'giving' on an international scale. The income gap between the rich and poor nations is continually widening and, more serious still, there is evidence that this widening is now proceeding at an alarming rate. Professor Gunnar Myrdal has recently drawn the conclusion that 'without a radical change in policies in both groups of countries, the world is headed for an economic and political cataclysm'.[2] How societies give collectively and their motives for giving are questions as fundamental to the health of social welfare systems at home and abroad as the question of what they give.

II

We come then to the question of the present and future role of social welfare in the West – particularly in Britain and the United States. If there is any substance in the foregoing view, then this question is of more than national interest: how we conduct our own domestic affairs will influence the quality of our relationships with our poorer neighbours.

'Modern social welfare', it has been said in the United States, 'has really to be thought of as help given to the stranger, not to the person who by reason of personal bond commands it without asking.'[3] It has, therefore, to be formally organized, to be administered by strangers, and to be paid for collectively by strangers.

Social welfare or the social services, operating through agencies, institutions, and programmes outside the private market, are becoming more difficult to define in any society with precision. As societies become more complex and specialized, so do systems of social welfare. Functionally, they reflect, and respond to, the larger social structure and its division of labour. This process makes it much harder today to identify the causal agents of change – the microbes of social disorganization and the viruses of impoverishment – and to make them responsible for the costs of 'disservices'. Who should bear the social costs of the thalidomide babies, of urban blight, of smoke pollution, of the obsolescence of skills, of automation, of the impact of synthetic coffee – which will dispense with the need for coffee beans – on the peasants of Brazil? The private benefits are to some extent measurable and attributable, but the private losses are not. Neo-classical economics and the private market cannot make these allocations; they are not organized to estimate social disruption and are unable to provide adequately for the public needs created by social and economic change.

Our growing inability to identify and connect cause and effect in the world of social and technological change is thus one reason for the historical emergence of social welfare institutions in the West. Altruism by strangers for strangers was and is an attempt to fill a moral void created by applied science. The services and programmes developed in the West to give aid to the stranger victims of industrialism and change have inevitably and necessarily become more specialized and complex. In this paper we shall only be able to speak of them in general terms.

III

The social services, as they are named in Britain, are largely the product of the twentieth century – a delayed response to the industrialism of the nineteenth century. The term is generally and loosely interpreted today to cover such public (or publicly supported) services as medical care, education, housing, income maintenance in old age and during periods of unemployment, sickness, disability and so forth, child allowances, and a variety of specific services for particular groups of people with special needs, e.g. neglected children, unmarried mothers, the blind, mental defectives, young delinquents, discharged prisoners, and other categories. All these services came apologetically into existence to provide for certain basic needs which the individual, the family, and the private market in capitalist societies were unable or unwilling to meet. In the United States and other Western countries, the terms 'social welfare' or 'social policy programmes' are used as alternative generic labels to embrace a similar variety of collectively organized services which may differ widely in scope and structure, methods of administration and finance, and in the fundamental objectives underlying them.

The concept of the 'Welfare State', which entered the arena of political thought in the 1940s, is generally accepted as a wider definition of the role of the state in the field of social and economic policy, embracing more than the provision of social services. Most writers on the subject, whether on the right or left politically, take it to mean a more positive and purposeful commitment by government to concern itself with the general welfare of the whole community and with the social costs of change. In his book *Beyond the Welfare State*, Gunnar Myrdal concluded that

In the last half-century, the State, in all the rich countries in the Western world, has become a democratic 'Welfare State', with fairly explicit commitments to the broad goals of economic development, full employment, equality of opportunity for the young, social security, and protected minimum standards as regards not only income, but nutrition, housing, health and education, for people of all regions and social groups.[4]

116

In this view it can be argued that 'Welfare Statism', either as an established fact or as a political objective, is a common phenomenon of large scale, industrialized societies. The renaissance of private enterprise during the past two decades in North America and Europe, the Keynesian Revolution and the adoption of techniques of economic management, rising standards of living and the achievements of political parties and trade unions on behalf of the underprivileged – have led all these culturally different societies along the same road to 'Welfare Statism' – a road unforeseen by Marx. Whether they know it or not, and whether they like it or not, Democrats and Republicans, Conservatives, Socialists, and Liberals in North America and Europe have become 'welfare statists'. The Germans and the Swedes may have more 'advanced' pension systems, the British a more comprehensive health service, the French more extensive family allowances, and the Americans may spend more on public education but, when all these national differences are acknowledged, the generalized welfare commitment is nevertheless viewed as the dominant political fact of modern Western societies. Governments of the liberal right and the liberal left may come and go; the commitment to welfare, economic growth, and full employment will remain with minor rather than major changes in scope and objectives.

IV

In historical and comparative terms, these are sweeping conclusions and leave many questions of values and facts unexamined. To what extent are they based on the real facts of income and wealth distribution, property, power, and class? Has the 'Welfare State' abolished poverty, social deprivation, and exploitation? Has man a greater sense of social control and participation in the work and life of his community? What will be the human consequences of further social and technological changes? Will the future resemble the immediate past, or are these views a simple projection of a transient phase in the development of large scale and predominantly competitive societies?

In recent years a growing number of political commentators, economists, and sociologists on both sides of the Atlantic, in proclaiming the end of political ideology in the West, have either ignored such questions or have tended to imply that they are no longer of primary importance for our societies. Their reasons for doing so are explicit in their general thesis. Professor Lipset in his book *Political Man* (1960) spoke for many when he said (in summarizing the discussions of a world congress of intellectuals in 1955) that 'the ideological issues dividing left and right [have] been reduced to a little more or a little less government ownership and economic planning'; and there was general agreement that it really makes little difference 'which political party controls the domestic policies of individual nations'. With minor differences, parties of both the right and the left will attempt to alleviate those social injustices that still remain, and will continue to seek improvements in social welfare, education, medical care, and other sectors of the economy for the general well-being. All will share, rich and poor, in the benefits of growth. By a natural process of market levitation all classes and groups will stand expectantly on the political right as the escalator of growth moves them up. Automatism thus substitutes for the social protest.

To quote Lipset again (though writers in a similar vein in England, France, and Germany could equally be cited):

the fundamental political problems of the industrial revolution have been solved: the workers have achieved industrial and political citizenship, the conservatives have accepted the welfare state, and the democratic left has recognised that an increase in overall state power carries with it more dangers to freedom than solutions for economic problems. This very triumph of the democratic social revolution in the West ends domestic politics for those intellectuals who must have ideologies or utopias to motivate them to political action.[5]

As a generalization, it is conceivable that this statement may serve as a summing-up for the 1950s in the history books of the next century. But from the perspective of 1960 it is, to say the least, a dubious proposition. However, we would not wish this essay to take the form of a critique of any one particular writer. To do so would carry with it the obligation to discuss in detail an individual interpretation of recent trends and the many qualifications attached to them. We shall, therefore, treat these statements as an expression not of the views of Professor Lipset but of a collective *Weltanschauung*, and one that seems to be growing in influence in the West, to judge by the number of its adherents.

Though we make no attempt to examine the thesis at length, we shall speculate about some of its basic assumptions so far as they relate to the future role of a humanist social policy in Britain and the USA.

First, it is unhistorical. Implicit in the thesis is the assumption that the 'Industrial Revolution' was a once and for all affair. Thus, it ignores the evidence concerning the trend toward monopolistic concentrations of economic power, the role of the corporation as private government with taxing powers, the problems of social disorganization and cultural deprivation, and the growing impact of automation and new techniques of production and distribution in economically advanced societies. If the first phase of the so-called revolution was to force all men to work, the phase we are now entering may be to force many men not to work. Without a major shift in values, only an impoverishment in social living can result from this new wave of industrialism.

Secondly, it states that the workers have achieved 'industrial citizenship'. The only comment we feel able to make on this is to say that it is a misuse of language to imply that membership of a trade union is synonymous with 'industrial citizenship'. Conceptions of what constitutes 'citizenship' for the worker must be related to what we now know about man's potential and his basic social and psychological needs; they cannot be compared with conditions of industrial slavery in the nineteenth century.

Third, the thesis implies that the problem of the distribution of income and wealth has either been solved or is now of insignificant proportions in Western society. In any event, such disparities as do exist are justified on grounds of individual differences and the need for economic incentives, and are considered to present no threat to democratic values.

In the 1950s, 1 per cent of the British population owned 42 per cent of all personal net capital and 5 per cent owned 67.5 per cent.[6] Even these proportions are underestimates for the figures exclude pension funds and trusts (which have grown enormously in recent years), and they do not take account of the increasing tendency for large owners of property to distribute their wealth among their families, to spread it over time, to send it abroad, and to transform it in other ways.

119

This degree of concentration in the holding of wealth is nearly twice as great as it was in the United States in 1954, and far higher than in the halcyon days of ruthless American capitalism in the early 1920s. Since 1949, wealth inequality has been growing in the United States, the rate of increase being more than twice as fast as the rate of decline between 1922 and 1949. Measured in terms of the increase in the percentage of wealth held by the top 1 per cent, the growth of inequality during 1949–56 (the latest available data) was more striking than at any time during at least the past forty years. Not unexpectedly, the distribution of income also appears to be becoming more unequal in recent years, affecting in particular the one fifth to one quarter of the United States population living below the currently defined 'poverty line'.[7] These are not all Negroes; 80 per cent of the American poor are white, and only one-fifth receive welfare aid. Economic growth in the richest society in the world has not been accompanied by any automatic, built-in equalizer. Crime for the young unemployed acts as a substitute within the prevailing system of values – the modern form of acquisitive social mobility for the lower classes.

There is no evidence to suggest that Britain has not been following in the same path since the end of the 1940s. It is even possible that inequality in the ownership of wealth (particularly in terms of family holdings) has increased more rapidly in Britain than in the United States since 1949. The British system of taxation is almost unique in the Western world in its generous treatment of wealth-holders in respect of settlements, trusts, gifts and other arrangements for redistributing and rearranging income and wealth. This is reflected in the remarkable fact that, in the mid-1950s, it was in the young adult age group that the tendency for wealth to be concentrated in a few hands was most marked.

Such evidence as this is ignored by those who proclaim the end of political ideology. Similar trends are probably in operation in De Gaulle's France and Erhard's Germany.[8] Over a quarter of a century of political upheaval, global war, 'welfare statism', managed economies, and economic growth have made little impression on the holdings of great fortunes in at least two of the largest industrial nations: the United States and Britain. The institution of concentrated wealth appears to be as tenacious of life as Tawney's intelligent tadpoles. Wealth still bestows political and economic power, more power than income, though it is probably exercised differently and with more respect for public opinion than in the nineteenth century.

Changes in the distribution of incomes appear to be following a similar pattern in Britain as in the United States. Toward the end of the 1940s a wartime movement toward more equality (before and after tax) in both Britain and the United States was reversed. The poorest tenth of the British population were relatively worse off compared with the higher standards of the rest of the nation in 1963 than they were in 1948.[9]

How can these great disparities in the private ownership of wealth and in the exercise of economic power be viewed as consistent with the thesis that we have reached the end of the political dialogue? No political utopia since Plato has ever envisaged such degrees of economic inequality as permanent and desirable states for man. Socialists protest at such disparities not because they want to foster envy; they do so because, as Tawney argued, these disparities are fundamentally immoral. History suggests that human nature is not strong enough to maintain itself in true community where great disparities of income and wealth preside.

Fourth and finally, there is in this thesis an assumption that the establishment of social welfare necessarily and inevitably contributes to the spread of humanism and the resolution of social injustice. The reverse can be true. Welfare, as an institutional means, can serve different masters. A multitude of sins may be committed in its appealing name. Welfare can be used simply as an instrument of economic growth which, by benefiting a minority, indirectly promotes greater inequality. Education is an example. We may educate the young to compete more efficiently as economic men in the private market with one another, or we may educate them because we desire to make them more capable of freedom and more capable of fulfilling their personal differences irrespective of income, class, religion, and race.

Welfare may be used to serve military and racial ends – as in Hitler's Germany. More medical care was provided by state and voluntary agencies not because of a belief in every man's uniqueness, but because of a hatred of men.

Welfare may be used to narrow allegiances and not to diffuse them – as in employers' fringe benefit systems. Individual gain and political quietism, fostered by the new feudalism of the corporation, may substitute for the sense of common humanity nourished by systems of non-discriminatory mutual aid.

What matters then, what indeed is fundamental to the health of welfare, the objective toward which its face is set? To universalize humanistic ethics and the social rights of citizenship, or to divide, discriminate, and compete?

V

In reality, of course, the issues are never as clear cut as this. The historical evolution of social security measures in Britain since the end of the nineteenth century shows how complex and various were the forces at work. Fear of social revolution, the need for a law abiding labour force, the struggle for power between political parties and pressure groups, a demand to remove some of the social costs of change – for example, industrial accidents – from the back of the worker, and the social conscience of the rich, all played a part.

But the major impulse came from below – from the workingman's ethic of solidarity and mutual aid. It found expression and grew spontaneously from working-class traditions and institutions to counter the adversities of industrialism. By means of a great network of friendly societies, medical clubs, chapel societies, brotherhoods, co-operatives, trade unions, and savings clubs, schemes of mutual insurance were developed as a method of pre-payment for services the members could claim when they were in need – in sickness, disablement, unemployment, old age, widowhood, and death. The 'good' risks and the 'bad' risks, the young and the old, shared one another's lot. They constituted microscopic welfare states, each struggling to demonstrate that man could still exercise some control over the forces of technology. By the end of the century some 24,000 different friendly societies were in existence, with a total membership representing about half the adult male population of the country. Aptly and significantly named, during a century of unbridled competition, they were *the* humanistic institution for the artisan and his family, far outdistancing in active membership all trade unions, political parties and religious bodies.

122

We can now see this great movement as the amateur's compassionate answer to the challenge of the economic and psychological insecurities of industrialism and individualism. It expressed also the ordinary man's revulsion from a class conscious, discriminating charity and a ruthless, discriminating poor law. The poor law was hated because it spelled humiliation; it was an assault on the individual's sense of self-respect in an age when 'respectability' – the quality of meriting the respect of others – governed the mores of society.

The values and objectives which underlay in the past the search for security in an increasingly insecure world are still relevant to an understanding of the role of social welfare in Britain today. The ways in which they shaped its origins and early development still permeate the principles on which the systems of medical care and social security operate today – comprehensive in scope, universal in membership. That they have not yet solved the problems of poverty and neglect, and still provide little place for citizen participation, is another story, and one that remains as a formidable challenge for socialism. But we cannot retrace our footsteps to the intimate 'friendly societies' of yesterday; we must find imaginative ways and new institutional means of combining humanity in administration with redistributive social justice in the future development of welfare policies.

VI

These are two of the central unresolved issues for humanists: the problem of bigness and the problem of inequality. They affect every aspect of social policy: education from the primary school to the university and into adult life; social security in unemployment, sickness, and old age; the care of the physically and mentally ill; housing and urban planning, leisure and recreation.

The demand for these services will grow in the future as living standards rise among some sections of the population and fall, relatively or absolutely, among others. The consequences of automation and its technological cousins on the one hand, and more dependent needs in childhood and old age on the other, will call for a much greater investment in people and social service than in consumption goods. Science and technology are today beginning to accomplish as thorough a revolution in social and economic theory as they are in the theory of war and international relations. The conventional doctrine that machines make work is losing its validity; machines are now replacing workers. It is already clear from American experience that these victims of technological displacement are no longer 'resting between engagements' (which is the theory of unemployment insurance); they are *permanently* out of work; permanently liberated from work. By the end of 1962 nearly one third of all young Negroes between the ages of 16 and 21 who were out of school were also out of work. Relatively speaking, they were also more handicapped educationally than unemployed young Negroes twenty years earlier. Between 1939 and 1958 the disadvantage of not having a college diploma grew in the USA.[10]

In an age of abundance of things, the production of consumption goods will become a subsidiary question for the West. The primary question will be just distribution; in particular, the distribution of services according to needs in place of the principle of productivity and performance in a market economy which today powerfully influences access to education and other social services.

In the past we have distributed resources on the basis of success and failure in economic competition; in the future we must decide whether it is morally right to do so in an economy of abundance. To distribute services on the basis of needs will help us to discover equality in our neighbours. 'Awareness of equality', wrote Daniel Jenkins, 'always arises in personal relationships and nearly always confronts us as a challenge, for it means placing a greater value upon our neighbour than we have previously been disposed to do. We are all ready to love ourselves. The discovery of equality might be defined as the discovery that we have indeed to love our neighbours as ourselves.'[11]

And so we have to ask, 'What are we to do with our wealth?' This is a more relevant question to ask today than those that seek to find more effective ways of punishing criminals, enforcing the law against deviants, preventing abuse of public assistance, forcing men to search for work, compelling them to save for old age when they cannot feed their children adequately, shifting them out of subsidized housing, inventing cheap technological substitutes for education, and charging them more for access to medical care.

Yet these aims reflect the values which are often applied today

124

in the administration of social services. According to one writer, Professor Mencher, 'The present United States welfare [public assistance] program is in keeping with the philosophy of 1830' – the philosophy of less eligible citizens enshrined in the English Poor Law Act of 1834.[12] Social workers, teachers, doctors, and social administrators find their functions imprisoned by the 'virtues' of hard work and profit; virtues that are rooted in the economics of scarcity. Their role is to police these virtues as, in a more ruthless context, medical certification of fitness for work became one of the central directives under the Stalinist regime. They have no relevance to the economics of abundance.

And, as Gerard Piel has emphasized, any

> hard work that a machine can do is better done today by a machine; 'hard' these days means mostly boring and repetitive work, whether in the factory or the office. But the instinct for workmanship, the need to feel needed, the will to achieve, are deeply felt in every human heart. They are not universally fulfilled by the kind of employment most people find. Full employment in the kind of employment that is commonly available, whether blue-collar or white-collar, has been plainly outmoded by technology. The liberation of people from tasks unworthy of human capacity should free that capacity for a host of activities now neglected in our civilisation: teaching and learning, fundamental scientific investigation, the performing arts and the graphic arts, letters, the crafts, politics, and social service. Characteristically these activities involve the interaction of people with people rather than with things. They are admittedly not productive activities; nor are they profitable in the strict sense.[13]

Science and technology in alliance with other structural and demographical changes under way in our societies will call for a major shift in values; for new incentives and new forms of reward unrelated to the productivity principle; for new criteria applied to the distribution of resources which are not tied to individual 'success' as a measure; for new forms of socially approved 'dependencies'. They will make the conventional criteria of capitalism largely irrelevant.

Many years ago Keynes foresaw that the time would come when these changes would be needed:

> we shall be able to rid ourselves of many of the pseudo-moral principles which have hag-ridden us for 200 years, by which we have

exalted some of the most distasteful of human qualities into the position of the highest virtues . . . All kinds of social customs and economic practices affecting the distribution of wealth and of economic rewards and penalties, which we now maintain at all costs, we shall then be freed to discard.

We shall need different rules domestically to live by; more examples of altruism to look up to. Indeed, our societies in Britain and the United States are already in need of them. In no other way in the long run will it be possible for us to prevent the deprived and the unable from becoming more deprived and unable; more cast down in a pool of apathy, frustration, crime, rootlessness, and tawdry poverty.

In all this, what we call the social services will have a central role to play. If this role is defined at all it will have to be defined by socialists in the language of equality. Here it is that ethics will have to be reunited to politics. The answers will not come and, indeed, logically cannot come from those who now proclaim 'the end of political ideology'; those who would elevate the principle of pecuniary gain and extend it to social service by equating education and medical care with refrigerators and mink coats; and those who advocate that more and more people should 'contract out' of universal social services and create for themselves new areas of privilege and discrimination. They, today, are the utilitarian doctrinaires; prisoners of the economics of scarcity; oblivious to the social consequences of the march of science and technology; and blind to the need for a sense of moral purpose in their own societies as the motive power in the art of giving to our international neighbours.

Notes

From Titmuss, R. M., 'Social welfare and the art of giving', in E. Fromm (ed.), *Socialist Humanism* (New York: Doubleday & Company, Inc., 1965).

1 Lipset, S. M., *Political Man: the Social Bases of Politics* (New York: Doubleday & Company, Inc., 1960), p. 416.
2 Myrdal, G., *The Urgent Need for Scientific Breakthroughs if Great Misery shall not be the Destiny of Underdeveloped Countries*, paper presented to the Conference on Global Impacts of Applied Microbiology, Stockholm, 2 August 1963.

3 Wilensky, H. L., and Lebeaux, C. N., *Industrial Society and Social Welfare* (New York: Russell Sage Foundation, 1958), p. 141.

4 Myrdal, G. (Yale University Press, 1960), p. 45.

5 Lipset, *Political Man*, pp. 404–6. For other references to this thesis see Lipset and also Daniel Bell, *The End of Ideology: on the Exhaustion of Political Ideas in the Fifties* (Glencoe, Ill.: Free Press, 1960).

6 See my Introduction to the third edition of R. H. Tawney's, *Equality*, reproduced as Chapter 1 in this volume.

7 Lampman, R. J., *The Share of the Top Wealth-Holders in National Wealth 1922–56* (1962); Harrington, M., *The Other America: Poverty in the United States* (1962); Conference on Economic Progress, *Poverty and Deprivation in the United States* (1961), known as the Keyserling Report.

8 According to Mr Christopher Johnson, 'The statistics which are available show what is evident to anyone living in France; that the rich are getting richer while the poor are barely maintaining their standard of living' (*New Society*, 21 February 1963, p. 15).

9 Lynes, T., 'Poverty in the Welfare State', *Aspect*, no. 7, August 1963.

10 Miller, H. P., 'Money value of an education', *Occupational Outlook Quarterly* (September 1961), p. 4.

11 Jenkins, D., *Equality and Excellence* (1961), p. 21.

12 Mencher, S., 'Perspectives on recent welfare legislation', *Social Work*, vol. 8, no. 3 (1963), p. 62.

13 Piel, G., *Consumers of Abundance*, Center for the Study of Democratic Institutions (1961), p. 9.

CHAPTER

7

Universal and Selective Social Services

I

The American 'War on Poverty', urgently launched in 1964 under the Economic Opportunity Act, is now seen to be failing; the early idealism is waning, cynicism grows. The reasons are many and complex. The strategy attempted was basically a technical short-cut; a series of programmes to by-pass the established structures of power, governmental, state and local; to reach the poor directly and concentrate resources on them without the support of an infrastructure of social welfare utilized and approved by the non-poor as well as the poor.

What was insufficiently recognized in 1964 was the extent to which many of these programmes would require the poor to define themselves; to stand up and declare themselves poor people, eligible for 'maximum feasible participation' in special poverty programmes. In the Act and, in particular, the regulations under the Act, there is a curious affinity with the New Poor Law Act of 1834 in England. Both endorsed and legitimated prevailing social values, both believed in redemption through work regardless of whether work was available; both were rooted in pathological explanations of poverty. But there was one fundamental difference.

The framers of the New Poor Law deliberately intended the system to operate as an assault on personal dignity and self-respect. Shame was needed to make the system work; many

128

techniques were to hand, the inquisition of the relieving officer being only one. The framers of the American Act vehemently rejected the instrument of shame; in any event, the civil rights movement, 'midnight searches' in the homes of poor people and other indignities of public assistance condemned its use as a servant of policy.

Nevertheless, the 'War on Poverty', despite its radicalism and its unorthodoxies of 'opting out' of the power structure, has not found the answers to the challenge of how to provide benefits in favour of the poor without stigma. What makes this problem of redistribution such a formidable challenge today – both in Britain and the USA – is that it is now inextricably mixed up with the challenge of social rights as well as civil rights for 'coloured' citizens. Two standards of service, in quality and methods of administration, one for the black and one for the white, are now seen to be more intolerable to the public conscience than two standards of service for the poor and the non-poor.

The American failure has been due to the belief that poverty was the problem, and that the advance of the poor Negro could be presented as a pro-Negro enterprise; it has not been seen as a universalist problem of inequality, social injustice, exclusion. The faults were not political and structural; technical know-how, project innovation, self-help and consumer aggression could eradicate the 'poverty disease' by 1970.

II

How to include poor people, and especially poor coloured people, in our societies, and at the same time to channel proportionately more resources in their favour without inducing shame or stigma, remains one of the great challenges for social policy in Britain and the USA. The answers will not be found by creating separate, apartheid-like structures and 'public burden' services for poor people; nor will they be found through short term 'gimmicks' and slogans or by expecting the computer to solve the problems which human beings have not yet adequately diagnosed.

Those in Britain who are now muddled about the current debate, headlined as 'universalism versus selectivity', should study American experience. They are muddled because of the mixture of ideas in the apparently simple cries 'let us concentrate help on those whose needs are greatest'; 'why provide benefits for those who do not really need them'.

Many people are muddled because there is a case for more selective services and benefits provided, as social rights, on the basis of the *needs* of certain categories, groups and territorial areas (e.g. Plowden's 'educational priority areas')[1] and not on the basis of individual *means*; there is a problem (as there always has been) of priorities in the allocation of scarce resources in the social policy field; there is a case for more redistribution through taxing the middle and upper-middle classes more heavily by making them pay higher contributions for, e.g. medical care and higher education; there is a problem of finding more money for social security, education, health, the welfare services, housing, roads and all sectors of all the public services.

'Selectivity' can mean many different things (which is rarely understood) but to most critics of 'Welfare Statism' it denotes an individual means-test; some inquiry into resources to identify poor people who should be provided with free services or cash benefits; be excused charges, or pay lower charges.

The Economist (to cite one school of thought) has been campaigning for more means-tests for years; in 1951 it said that the stigma of the test had gone; that national assistance was too lavish; that it was 'weakening the sense of individual pride and family unity' and discouraging thrift and incentives to work.[2] Now it is arguing that it is not lavish enough. Instead of raising retirement pensions and family allowances more should have been spent on supplementary benefits.[3] The Institute of Economic Affairs (another school) has similarly been campaigning for 'selectivity' since its foundation as a trust in 1957 in order to encourage the growth of private markets in education, medical care and social security. Its latest effort is to reprint an address (*Paying for the Social Services*) by Mr Douglas Houghton in which he advocates the use of a standard income tax means-test 'for a variety of social purposes'.[4] In particular, he suggests prescription charges and charges for hospital treatment. He envisages an extension of the coding system below the point of no tax liability which could be used to determine entitlement to supplementary cash benefit, graduated according to income assessment, and also for rent rebates, rate rebates, school meals, welfare services, health service charges and so on. 'Not only could the structure of PAYE and its ingenious and flexible coding system and tax tables be used to provide an automatic minimum income, it could be adapted to a scheme for payment for state services.' Inland Revenue computers would allocate to everyone a code number based on PAYE assessments. Armed with this number, all would pay according to ability.

III

Before examining the practicalities of the computer solution it is necessary to examine more thoroughly the case for more means-tested selective services. The nature, content, scope, characteristics and frequency of a means-test depend to a great extent on its functions and purposes. What are these? This question cannot be answered, however, without considering more specific policy objectives. Means-testing, *as a method*, may in theory be used (to cite a few of its many possible functions):

(*a*) to define for people outside the labour market (whose needs for income maintenance and whose resources are relatively ascertainable and predictable, e.g. old people) the level of income which is to be taken as the minimum for the purposes of income maintenance;

(*b*) to fix charges or rents for services and to decide who should and who should not pay charges;

(*c*) to determine those who should receive a 'free' public service or benefit – the rest of the population buying services or benefits in the private market or paying the full cost of the publicly provided service or benefit;

(*d*) to determine entitlement to the remission (or reduction) of a universal charge (e.g. rate rebates).

Broader social objectives lie behind these functions of determining minimum income levels, fixing charges, remissions, entitlements and so on. The aim may be to deter people from using or 'abusing' a service; to induce a sense of inferiority among those using a public service; to develop two standards of service; to raise more revenue; to help students of poor parents enter universities; to ration resources and so on.

At this point, I do not want to discuss the political values and choices involved except to say this. Socialist social policies are, in my view, totally different in their purposes, philosophy and attitudes to people from Conservative social policies. They are (or should be) pre-eminently about equality, freedom and social integration.

The limited and deliberate intention of this article is to dissect the computer solution; a solution which seems to have muddled quite a lot of well-meaning people. Hence, it is necessary to present a picture (though, admittedly, a small one) which shows something of the administrative, technical and real life complexities of the issues involved. There can be no return to the simplicity of the Poor Law (with its inevitable corollary of brutality) – American experience is sufficient warning of that. We have, therefore, painfully to understand that methods of allocating resources (like means-testing and charges) cannot be separately considered from (*a*) functions, specific purposes and general social objectives and (*b*) the infinite and infinitely changing circumstances of individuals and families. What follows, therefore, is not easy reading. Ideological reasoning there must be – but superficial administrative proposals cannot be countered with superficial political answers.

IV

Not only must means-tests differ in content, scope, characteristics and frequency according to their particular functions but, more complex still, they must differ in all these factors according to (*a*) the kind of service or benefit provided and, to some extent, the causes of the need; (*b*) the actualities of the need; immediate and temporary, weekly, monthly, yearly, etc.; (*c*) the characteristics of the consumer (age, sex, marital and household status, dependants, etc.) and (*d*) the extent to which a variety of economic, social and psychological incentives and disincentives have to be taken into account in the structure and operation of the test. A brief explanation must suffice of some of the reasons for differential treatment in respect of these four categories.

Services in kind and in cash may fulfil, singly or in combination, a large number of functions. They may represent not a benefit at all but a compensation for disservices caused by society and especially those disservices (or social costs) where the causal agent, or agents, cannot be identified, legally held responsible, and charged with the costs. When one examines in detail the social consequences in modern society of technological, industrial, economic and other processes of change it is evident that the problem of compensation is an immense one, and immensely complex. Unless the social costs of these disservices are to lie where they fall (as they did in nineteenth-century Britain and as they do to a large extent in the USA today) then we have to find ways and means of compensating people without stigma.

I have discussed this particular function of the social services elsewhere; here I can only give an example.

Consider the serious and growing problem of industrial accidents and diseases. The computer selectivity proposal linked to a charge for medical care (inpatient and outpatient and general practitioner) would involve $1\frac{1}{4}$ million individuals (new injury claimants each year plus existing disablement pensioners) and their dependants;[5] means-tests to select those who cannot pay, and, later in life, more means-tested selective benefits in respect of income maintenance for the earnings-affected victims of industrial accidents and their wives (widows) and other dependants. Should all these victims of industrial accidents and their families now be charged (as they were in the nineteenth century) with part of the costs, and be means-tested to decide whether the charge should be remitted, and whether and to what extent they should receive additional selective cash benefits? Is this what Mr Gunter wants?

If industrial accidents and diseases are to be excluded (though there is an appallingly difficult medical problem of diagnosis, attribution and checking in distinguishing these medical needs from other medical needs) what about road accidents, medical error, cross-infection in hospitals, and many other categories of accidents and disease? How would one justify and administer charges and means-tests for a variety of services for some groups (e.g. on criteria of *occupational causation*) and not for others?

But the list of claimants for exclusion from charges does not end there. What about the war disabled, war widows and industrial widows, the blind, the mentally retarded, the mentally ill (occupying nearly one-half of all hospital beds), the large number of over-70s in hospital, those who die in hospital, those with infectious diseases, the tubercular, the chronic bronchitic victims of the coal mines and other industries, the unemployed and their families, unmarried mothers, deprived children, fatherless families, and so on and so on? Where in the end does one draw the line among over 5 million inpatient cases and over 35 million outpatient attendances annually and how often? It is possible to make a strong case (most politicians would say a cast iron case) for exemption from charges for medical care and other services (starting with the war disabled, industrial accidents and the mentally ill) for over forty distinguishable categories or classes in the population. Then, if one is practical, it is necessary in considering inpatient care to take account of length of stay (for all acute cases down to an average of 12.3 days in 1966);[6] the position of other members of the family in all these classes; and the administrative costs of the whole operation of charges, reimbursements, means-tests and the massive burden on employers of supplying and verifying essential data.

This is but one example of how the *cause* of the need giving rise to demands for different services and benefits must be taken into account in considering how and to what extent charges, remissions and means-tests should, in actual practice, differ in content, scope, characteristics and frequency.

But social services fulfil many other different functions apart from compensation and, in each case, different sets of factors have to be considered. For instance, they may represent a form of protection for society; an investment for a future personal or collective gain (e.g. higher education); an immediate and/or deferred increment to personal welfare (e.g. pensions).

If equity is to be served – one of the touchstones of a civilized society – then the content, scope, characteristics and frequency of means-tests and charges must differ according to the type of service to be provided. Different rules must apply to different groups in different circumstances for different types of services. There is no standardized answer.

V

Secondly, the time-scale of need introduces another set of differentiating factors. Means-tests and charges cannot be determined in cases of immediate need (evicted families with unemployed fathers, unmarried mothers, deserted wives, individuals with recurrent spells of sickness and unemployment, and many other categories of emergency needs in changed circumstances) in, say, January 1968, on the basis of the reported earnings (PAYE form P 60) of one earner only in the tax year April 1966–April 1967. But this is what Mr Douglas Houghton, *The Economist*, the Bow Group (*Policies for Poverty*), the Conservative Political Centre,[7] the Confederation of British Industries,[8] and other theoreticians are, in fact, proposing though their intentions are different.

Thirdly, it should not be necessary to remind these theoreticians that there are no standard families with standard or uniform requirements and resources; not only does family (or houshold or 'needs unit') composition, its requirements and resources vary greatly in modern society but the majority are in a constant state of flux and change. How would a computerized code number relating to circumstances $1\frac{1}{2}$ to $2\frac{1}{2}$ years ago deal with changes in requirements and resources brought about by birth, children leaving school, marriage and re-marriage, divorce, separation, desertion, death, adoption, illness, disablement, retirement, fires and disasters, institutional care (hospitals, homes for old people, children's institutions and many other forms of institutional care), unemployment, new jobs, new housing and rents, boarders, inheritance, capital appreciation, windfalls and a multitude of change factors altering the composition, responsibilities, requirements and resources of individuals and families?

Let us suppose the impossible: that the PAYE system could be adapted as proposed and computerized by the year 1980. All employers would then have to give to the Inland Revenue at weekly or monthly intervals what they now give once a year (often months after the end of the tax year), a statement of earnings and tax paid by the individual employee, which would have to be married with information on incomes from other sources. It would likewise follow that where the system showed no tax liability for the employee but a title to receive benefits of any kind the employer would be the natural instrument of payment. If he were not, then there would have to be very rapid communication week by week from the employer about each and all employees' earnings to the local office of the Inland Revenue, and thence, if no tax were due, to the paying authority for issue of the benefit. For British industry, this could represent an administrative cost nightmare. Why have the CBI not thought of this one?

Fourthly, there are fundamental issues of moral values and equity which, in the wider interests of society, must be taken into account in the scope, content, characteristics and frequency of means-tests and charges for services and benefits, and which introduce further reasons for different treatment in different circumstances. Again, in abbreviated fashion, some of these issues may be expressed in the form of questions:

(i) Should men and women who are cohabiting have a financial advantage over husbands and wives?

(ii) Should men who do not work be better off than men who do (the wage-stop problem)?

(iii) Should those with unearned incomes have an advantage over those with earned incomes?

(iv) Should those who give away their capital assets to kin receive more favourable treatment compared with those who do not or who have no such assets?

(v) Should those who save be penalized as compared with those who do not?

(vi) Should wives be encouraged or discouraged, penalized or not for going out to work?

(vii) Should families be encouraged or discouraged from maintaining at home elderly relations, mentally retarded children and other disabled kin?

(viii) Should income tests and charges disregard capital assets, house property, discretionary trusts, education covenants, insurance policies, reversionary interests, fringe benefits, tax free lump sums, share options, occupational benefits in kind and such like?

(ix) Should those who are on strike, or refuse employment, or who are in prison be treated differently from those who are not in these situations?

VI

Computers cannot answer these questions. Virtually all types of means-tests designed for individual selective benefits and all schemes for charges with a related right to remission, *involving the population of working ages*, run into these problems of moral values, incentives, and equity. If father gets a wage increase (due perhaps to rising prices), works overtime, moves to a cheaper house, or experiences many other changes in responsibilities and circumstances, at what point does he lose part or all of a family allowance or have to pay a series of charges for various services? Where does the 'cut-off' come and what would 'tapering' involve? Similar problems arise if mother goes to work and incomes are aggregated – as, in equity, they would have to be – but a data marriage of this kind must involve employers and the Inland Revenue in another administrative cost nightmare.

To consider each of these nine questions in all their diverse ramifications would be tedious. In any event, it should now be clear that the computer code number proposal is not, and never can be, the answer to child poverty or to any of the other issues raised by the protagonists of selective services, means-tests and charges. Moreover, computermania appears to have blinded many people to the simple fact that the critical form (P 2) on which the present computer case rests is *not* a means-test. It is simply a guide to the employer (for those who have employers) about certain allowances to be set against an individual's earnings for tax deduction purposes. It does not, therefore, relate to wives' earnings nor to a whole host of circumstances, resources and requirements only some of which have been discussed here.

Even more nonsensical are the proposals put forward in a recent Conservative Political Centre booklet *The New Social Contract*[9] for a reorganization of the income tax and social security system by servicing them through the proposed new Post Office Giro. They do not even begin to understand the administrative, technical, social and psychological issues so briefly surveyed in this article.

VII

What I find so frightening is the extraordinary administrative naivety of those who argue in such terms for 'selectivity'. The superficiality of much of the recent outpourings from the City, the Conservative Political Centre and elsewhere suggests that the writers have made no attempt to understand the complexities involved. If this is indicative of the current level of managerial thinking, cost consciousness and export marketing then it throws some light on Britain's productivity performance in recent years.

There are alternative ways of finding more money for the social services; reducing subsidies and 'indiscriminate' benefits for the higher income groups, and redistributing more resources in favour of poor areas and particular groups on criteria of need without involving individual means-tests.

Is it not time the NHS contribution became a graduated contribution? Why not re-introduce Schedule A tax on owner-occupiers – its disappearance has left us with an indiscriminate social service subsidy if there ever was one. It was abolished by the 'selectivists' in 1963; it has not been mentioned by them since. Charging tax on replacement values, and allowing for depreciation, the removal of this subsidy would bring in over £300 million a year today. Why not raise fees for all university students; stiffen the parental means-test (which at present subsidizes other children at public schools) and abolish other and substantial public school subsidies? The revision and reduction of tax allowances for children and old people is by far the simplest, most equitable and least costly administrative device for preventing 'excessive benefits being paid to those who do not really need them'. Moreover, these and other changes in the structure of taxation would help to diminish the highly regressive incidence of direct and indirect taxation on poorer families. For example, married couples with two children struggling to live on £13 a week pay about one-fifth of their income in total taxation, rates and insurance contributions. Housing allowances on criteria of need as an integrated part of (and not an alternative to) other policies to relieve poverty could also produce savings. And how much longer are we to be burdened with the heavy and wasteful administrative costs (to say nothing of the misuse of computer time) of the chaos of something like 60,000 private pensions schemes?

The purpose of this article was not, however, to discuss the financing of the social services or the reform of taxation. I have tried to be severely practical and to examine some of the hard, inescapable facts and moral dilemmas which must face any government concerned to find the best possible balance between equity, adequacy and administrative efficiency. The fundamental ideological issues of socialist social policies and the private market are not, therefore, discussed here. Had this been my purpose I would have elaborated on my general conclusion. It is this. The challenge that faces us is not the choice between universalist and selective services. The real challenge resides in the question: what particular infrastructure of universalist services is needed in order to provide a framework of values and opportunity bases within and around which can be developed acceptable selective services provided, as social rights, on criteria of the *needs* of specific categories, groups and territorial areas and not dependent on *individual tests of means*? It is in such practical ways which do not involve an assault on human dignity, which are not socially divisive and which do not lead to the development of two standards of services for two nations that more redistribution can be effected through the social services in favour of those whose needs are greatest.

There can, therefore, be no answer in Britain to the problems of poverty, ethnic integration, and social and educational inequalities without an infrastructure of universalist services. These are the essential foundations. We have to build on them and around them; face the hard, detailed challenge of how precisely to do so and not run away in search of false gods or worn out doctrines. Some of the answers have been hammered out and are known in Whitehall; what is now required is the courage to implement them.

Notes

Published in the *New Statesman*, 15 September 1967.

1 *Children and their Primary Schools* (Plowden Report), Vol. 1, (London, HMSO, 1967).
2 *The Economist*, 20 January 1951, pp. 118–19.
3 *The Economist*, 8 April (pp. 109–11), 24 June (pp. 1326–31) and 29 July 1967 (pp. 388–9).
4 Occasional Paper 16, The Institute of Economic Affairs, 1967.
5 *Annual Report of the Ministry of Social Security for 1966*, Cmnd 3338 (London, HMSO, 1967). See also *Annual Reports of HM Chief Inspector of Factories for 1966*, Cmnd 3358–9 (London, HMSO, 1967).
6 *Annual Report of the Ministry of Health for 1966*, Cmnd 3326 (1967).
7 Sewill, H., *Auntie*, Conservative Political Centre (1967).
8 Report of CBI Economic Committee summarized in *The Times*, 4 August 1967.
9 Rhys Williams, B., Conservative Political Centre (1967).

CHAPTER

8

Welfare State and Welfare Society

Introduction

I did not choose this title. It was chosen for me. Despite this assistance, I must say I am no more enamoured today of the indefinable abstraction the 'Welfare State' than I was some twenty years ago when, with the advent of the National Health, National Insurance and other legislative promissories, the term acquired an international as well as a national popularity.

The consequences have not all been intellectually stimulating. Generalized slogans rarely induce concentration of thought; more often they prevent us from asking significant questions about reality. Morally satisfied and intellectually dulled, we sink back into our presumptive cosy British world of welfare. Meanwhile, outside these islands (as well as inside) there are critics – economic and political critics – who are misled into confusing ends and means, and who are discouraged from undertaking the painful exercise of distinguishing between philosophical tomorrows and the current truths of reality in a complex British power structure of rationed resources, and great inequalities in incomes and wealth, opportunities and freedom of choice.

From what little is known about the reading habits of international bankers and economists, I think it is reasonable to say that they do not include much in the way of studies on welfare and the condition of the poor. How then are their views shaped about the British 'Welfare State'? This we do not know, but at least we can say that if we mislead ourselves, we shall mislead them. But the matter does not end there. Models of public welfare can assume different forms and contain different assumptions about means and ends. Concepts of welfare can imply very different things to different people – as we can see from the Study Group Reports to this Conference.

One particular model is the *Public Burden Model of Welfare*. In general terms, this sees public welfare expenditure – and particularly expenditure which is redistributive in intent – as a burden; an impediment to growth and economic development. Given this model of the British patient, the diagnosis seems simple. We are spending too much on the 'Welfare State'. Such explanations are, moreover, encouraged by the concept of private economic man embedded in the techniques of national income accounting. An increase in public retirement pensions is seen (as it was seen internationally during the balance of payments crisis in 1964) as an economic burden.[1] A similar increase in spending power among occupational (publicly subsidized private) pensioners is not so seen. Yet both involve additions to consumption demand.

Or take another example: medical care, public and private. It is being argued today that by encouraging the growth of private medical care through a voucher system and by allowing people to contract out of taxation, the 'burden' of the Health Service would be reduced. The objective it seems is to reduce the assumed 'burden'; thus, those who contract out diminish the burden. Logically, we should extend to them our gratitude and moral respect for contracting out of public commitments. But, if Mr Enoch Powell may be accepted as an authority (and I quote from his recent book *Medicine and Politics*[2]) this 'voucher scheme resolves itself merely into a method of increasing state expenditure upon medical care'. In other words, it is a proposal for redistributing more medical resources in favour of private patients. The case for contracting out must, therefore, be justified on grounds other than the 'welfare burden' argument.

International Aspects of Welfare

If we insist, come what may, on the continued use or misuse and misapplication of the term the 'Welfare State' then we must accept the consequences of international misunderstanding. We cannot assume that observers abroad share, or will share, the social or moral criteria we may apply to welfare; to many of our creditors and currency colleagues in Western Germany, France and the United States, the 'Welfare State' is equated with national irresponsibility and decadence; an easy way of living off foreign loans. To the political scientist as well as the economist these opinions are relevant facts in the same way as (according to some sociologists) social class is what men think it is. These opinions do not, moreover, differ markedly from those expressed in the published statements on welfare during the past fifteen years by bankers, insurance directors, financiers and others in the City of London.[3]

Many of these monetary experts abroad appear to place a different valuation on countries which depend heavily on 'borrowing' human capital as distinct from those which borrow financial capital. For such transactions, no payment is made to the lending country; there are no interest charges, and there is no intention of repaying the loan.

Since 1949 the United States has absorbed (and to some extent deliberately recruited) the import of a hundred thousand doctors, scientists and engineers from developed and developing countries. In about 18 years the United States will have saved some $4,000 million by not having to educate and train, or train fully, this vast quantity of human capital.[4] It has spent more on consumption goods; less on public services. It has taxed itself more lightly while imposing heavier taxation on poorer countries. Estimates have been made that foreign aid to America is as great or greater than the total of American aid to countries abroad since 1949. Moreover, such estimates leave out of account the social and economic effects in Britain (and more significantly in the poor countries of the world) of having to train more doctors, scientists and engineers, and of having to pay heavily inflated rewards to prevent American recruitment with all their harmful repercussions on incomes, prices and levels of taxation.

In medicine alone, foreign doctors now account for nearly 20 per cent of the annual additions to the American medical profession.[5] The world now provides as much or more medical aid to the United States in terms of dollars as the total cost of all American medical aid, private and public, to foreign countries.[6] A study I have made recently of the columns of the *British Medical Journal* and the *Lancet* from 1951 to 1966 shows that advertisements for British doctors (often accompanied by recruiting campaigns and sometimes actively encouraged by senior British doctors[7]) rose from a yearly average of 134 in 1951 to over 4,000 in 1966.[8] The total number of newly qualified doctors in Britain in 1966 was around 1,700; each of them cost about £10,000 to train, excluding expenditure on student maintenance.[9]

The United States is not alone in attempting to develop its welfare systems (and Medicare) at the expense of poorer countries through the discovery that, today, it is much cheaper and less of a public burden to import doctors, scientists and other qualified workers than to educate and train them. Britain is also relying heavily on the skills of doctors from poorer countries – due in part to the belief less than five to ten years ago among ministers and leaders of the medical profession that we were in danger of training too many doctors.[10] And, we may add, the belief among liberal economists and sections of the medical profession that Britain was spending too much on the Health Service which was in danger of bankrupting the nation. Even as late as 1962, there were influential voices in the British Medical Association who were speaking of the profession's recent experience of a 'glut of doctors' and the need to avoid medical unemployment in the late 1960s.[11] Guilty as we have been in our treatment of doctors from overseas, and in our failure in the past to train enough health workers for our own national needs, at least it cannot be said that we are deliberately organizing recruitment campaigns in economically poorer countries.

These introductory reflections on some of the international aspects of welfare point, I believe, to three general conclusions. First, they underline the dangers in the use of the term the 'Welfare State'. Secondly, they remind us that we can no longer consider welfare systems solely within the limited framework of the nation-state; what we do or fail to do in changing systems of welfare affects other countries besides ourselves. Thirdly, to suggest one criterion for the definition of a 'Welfare Society'; namely, a society which openly accepts a policy responsibility for educating and training its own nationals to meet its own needs for doctors, nurses, social workers, scientists, engineers and others. Just as we have recognized the injustices and the waste in the unrestricted free international movement of goods, material and capital, so we must now recognize the need for the richer countries of the world to take action to protect the poorer countries of the world from being denuded of skilled manpower.

To this end, a number of measures could be taken, some unilaterally, some by international agreement. Among the most important would be for the rich countries to decide to spend less on personal consumption goods and more on training young people for the social service professions; to decide to devote more of their resources for genuine international aid to the poorer countries; to decide to ban the deliberate recruitment overseas of skilled manpower; to decide to revise and broaden their immigration policies so that movement between countries is not restricted to the highly educated and trained; and to take other measures too complex to discuss in this paper.

For the rich countries of the world to take action in such ways would represent a few modest steps towards the notion of a 'Welfare World'. Those countries assuming leadership with policies of this nature might then with some justification regard themselves as 'Welfare Societies'.

This principle of community responsibility for the provision of adequate resources to implement the objectives of national legislation is particularly relevant to the whole field of welfare. The quantity, territorial distribution and quality of any country's social services – education, medical care, mental health, welfare, children's and other personal community services – depends enormously on the quantity and quality of staff, professional, technical, auxiliary and administrative. To enact legislation designed to create or develop services yet not to invest adequately in the training of doctors, nurses, social workers, teachers and many other categories of skilled manpower and womanpower is a denial of this principle of community responsibility. To rely on the private market and autonomous professional bodies to fulfil these training needs is nothing less than a ridiculous illusion. The private national market has failed lamentably in this country and in the United States to produce enough doctors, teachers, social workers and nurses. To resort to the international market to remedy the deficiency of national social policies can only have tragic consequences for the poorer countries of the world.

In considering the international aspects of these welfare

manpower issues there is one further observation I wish to make before turning to other Conference themes. It seems to me the height of collective immorality for the rich countries of the world to preach to the poorer countries about the economic benefits of family planning while, at the same time, making it more difficult for these countries to develop family planning programmes by drawing away the skilled manpower they need for the infrastructure of services required in which to provide birth control as well as death control services.

Having delivered myself of these thoughts under the conveniently broad umbrella theme of this Conference, I want now to consider certain other questions of principle in systems of welfare.

Universalist and Selective Social Services

In any discussion today of the future of (what is called) the 'Welfare State' much of the argument revolves round the principles and objectives of universalist social services and selective social services. Prominence was given to this issue in Chapters 2 and 4 of the *Guide to Studies* prepared two years ago for this Conference. Time does not seem to have eroded the importance of this issue.

I think it is unnecessary, therefore, to remind you in detail of the many complex questions of principles, goals, methods and assumptions involved in this debate. In regard to some of them – and particularly the question of freedom of choice – I have set out my views in a recently published lecture *Choice and 'The Welfare State'*.[12]

Briefly, then, I will restate certain of the more general points emphasized in this *Guide*. Consider, first, the nature of the broad principles which helped to shape substantial sections of British welfare legislation in the past, and particularly the principle of universalism embodied in such postwar enactments as the National Health Service Act, the Education Act of 1944, the National Insurance Act and the Family Allowances Act.

One fundamental historical reason for the adoption of this principle was the aim of making services available and accessible to the whole population in such ways as would not involve users in any humiliating loss of status, dignity or self-respect. There should be no sense of inferiority, pauperism, shame or stigma in the use of a publicly provided service; no attribution that one was being or becoming a 'public burden'. Hence the emphasis on the social rights of all citizens to use or not to use as responsible people the services made available by the community in respect of certain needs which the private market and the family were unable or unwilling to provide universally. If these services were not provided for everybody by everybody they would either not be available at all, or only for those who could afford them, and for others on such terms as would involve the infliction of a sense of inferiority and stigma.

Avoidance of stigma was not, of course, the only reason for the development of the twin concepts of social rights and universalism. Many other forces, social, political and psychological, during a century and more of turmoil, revolution, war and change, contributed to the clarification and acceptance of these notions. The novel idea of prevention – novel, at least, to many in the nineteenth century – was, for example, another powerful engine, driven by the Webbs and many other advocates of change, which reinforced the concepts of social rights and universalism. The idea of prevention – the prevention and breaking of the vicious descending spiral of poverty, disease, neglect, illiteracy and destitution – spelt to the protagonists (and still does so) the critical importance of early and easy access to and use of preventive, remedial and rehabilitative services. Slowly and painfully the lesson was learnt that if such services were to be utilized in time and were to be effective in action in a highly differentiated, unequal and class saturated society, they had to be delivered through socially approved channels; that is to say, without loss of self-respect by the users and their families.

Prevention was not simply a child of biological and psychological theorists; at least one of the grandparents was a powerful economist with a strongly developed streak of nationalism. As Professor Bentley Gilbert has shown in his recent book, *The Evolution of National Insurance: the Origins of the Welfare State*, national efficiency and welfare were seen as complementary;[13] The sin unforgivable was the waste of human resources; thus, welfare was summoned to prevent waste. Hence the beginnings of four of our present day universalist social services: retirement pensions, the Health Service, unemployment insurance and the school meals service.

The insistent drumming of the national efficiency movement in those far off days before the First World War is now largely forgotten. Let me then remind you that the whole welfare debate was a curious mixture of humanitarianism, egalitarianism, productivity (as we would call it today) and old-fashioned imperialism. The strident note of the latter is now, we may thank our stars, silenced. The Goddess of Growth has replaced the God of National Fitness. But can we say that the quest for the other objectives is no longer necessary?

Before discussing such a rhetorical question, we need to examine further the principle of universalism. The principle itself may sound simple but the practice – and by that I mean the present operational pattern of welfare in Britain today – is immensely complex. We can see something of this complexity if we analyse welfare (defined here as all publicly provided and subsidized services, statutory, occupational and fiscal) from a number of different standpoints.

An Analytical Framework

Whatever the nature of the service, activity or function, and whether it be a service in kind, a collective amenity, or a transfer payment in cash or by accountancy, we need to consider (and here I itemize in question form for the sake of brevity) three central issues:

(*a*) What is the nature of entitlement to use? Is it legal, contractual or contributory, financial, discretionary or professionally determined entitlement?

(*b*) Who is entitled and on what conditions? Is account taken of individual characteristics, family characteristics, group characteristics, territorial characteristics or social-biological characteristics? What, in fact, are the rules of entitlement? Are they specific and contractual – like a right based on age – or are they variable, arbitrary or discretionary?

(*c*) What methods, financial and administrative, are employed in the determination of access, utilization, allocation and payment?

Next we have to reflect on the nature of the service or benefit. What functions do benefits, in cash, amenity or in kind, aim to fulfil? They may, for example, fulfil any of the following sets of functions, singly or in combination:

(1) As partial compensation for identified disservices caused by society (for example, unemployment, some categories of industrial injuries benefits, war pensions, etc.). And, we may add, the disservices caused by international society as exemplified recently by the oil pollution resulting from the Torrey Canyon disaster costing at least £2 million.[14]

(2) As partial compensation for unidentifiable disservices caused by society (for example, 'benefits' related to programmes of slum clearance, urban blight, smoke pollution control, hospital cross-infection and many other socially created disservices).

(3) As partial compensation for unmerited handicap (for example, language classes for immigrant children, services for the deprived child, children handicapped from birth, etc.).

(4) As a form of protection for society (for example, the probation service, some parts of the mental health services, services for the control of infectious diseases, and so on).

(5) As an investment for a future personal or collective gain (education – professional, technical and industrial – is an obvious example here; so also are certain categories of tax deductibles for self-improvement and certain types of subsidized occupational benefits).

(6) As an immediate and/or deferred increment to personal welfare or, in other words, benefits (utilities) which add to personal command over resources either immediately and/or in the future (for example, subsidies to owner-occupiers and council tenants, tax deductibles for interest charges, pensions, supplementary benefits, curative medical care, and so on).

(7) As an element in an integrative objective which is an essential characteristic distinguishing social policy from economic policy. As Kenneth Boulding has said, 'social policy is that

which is centred in those institutions that create integration and discourage alienation'.[15] It is thus profoundly concerned with questions of personal identity whereas economic policy centres round exchange or bilateral transfer.

This represents little more than an elementary and partial structural map which can assist in the understanding of the welfare complex today. Needless to say, a more sophisticated (inch to the mile) guide is essential for anything approaching a thorough analysis of the actual functioning of welfare benefit systems. I do not, however, propose to refine further this frame of study now, nor can I analyse by these classifications the several hundred distinctive and functionally separate services and benefits actually in operation in Britain today.

Further study would also have to take account of the pattern and operation of means-tested services. It has been estimated by Mr M. J. Reddin, my research assistant, that in England and Wales today local authorities are responsible for administering at least 3,000 means-tests, of which about 1,500 are different from each other.[16] This estimate applies only to services falling within the responsibilities of education, child care, health, housing and welfare departments. It follows that in these fields alone there exist some 1,500 different definitions of poverty or financial hardship, ability to pay and rules for charges which affect the individual and the family. There must be substantial numbers of poor families with multiple needs and multiple handicaps whose perception today of the realities of welfare is to see only a means-testing world. Who helps them, I wonder, to fill up all those forms?

I mention these social facts, by way of illustration, because they do form part of the operational complex of welfare in 1967. My main purpose, however, in presenting this analytical framework was twofold. First, to underline the difficulties of conceptualizing and categorizing needs, causes, entitlement or gatekeeper functions, utilization patterns, benefits and compensations. Second, to suggest that those students of welfare who are seeing the main problem today in terms of universalism versus selective services are presenting a naive and oversimplified picture of policy choices.

Some of the reasons for this simple and superficial view are, I think, due to the fact that the approach is dominated by the concept or model of welfare as a 'burden'; as a waste of resources in the provision of benefits for those who, it is said, do not need them. The general solution is thus deceptively simple and romantically appealing; abolish all this welfare complexity and concentrate help on those whose needs are greatest.

Quite apart from the theoretical and practical immaturity of this solution, which would restrict the public services to a minority in the population leaving the majority to buy their own education, social security, medical care and other services in a supposedly free market, certain other important questions need to be considered.

As all selective services for this minority would have to apply some test of need – eligibility, on what bases would tests be applied and, even more crucial, where would the lines be drawn for benefits which function as compensation for identified disservices, compensation for unidentifiable disservices, compensation for unmerited handicap, as a form of social protection, as an investment, or as an increment to personal welfare? Can rules of entitlement and access be drawn on purely 'ability to pay' criteria without distinction of cause? And if the causal agents of need cannot be identified or are so diffuse as to defy the wit of law – as they so often are today – then is not the answer 'no compensation and no redress'? In other words, the case for concentrated selective services resolves itself into an argument for allowing the social costs or diswelfares of the economic system to lie where they fall.

The emphasis today on 'welfare' and the 'benefits of welfare' often tends to obscure the fundamental fact that for many consumers the services used are not essentially benefits or increments to welfare at all; they represent partial compensations for disservices, for social costs and social insecurities which are the product of a rapidly changing industrial urban society. They are part of the price we pay to some people for bearing part of the costs of other people's progress; the obsolescence of skills, redundancies, premature retirements, accidents, many categories of disease and handicap, urban blight and slum clearance, smoke pollution, and a hundred and one other socially generated disservices. They are the socially caused diswelfares; the losses involved in aggregate welfare gains.

What is also of major importance today is that modern society is finding it increasingly difficult to identify the causal agent or agencies, and thus to allocate the costs of disservices and charge those who are responsible. It is not just a question of benefit allocation – of whose 'Welfare State' – but also of loss allocation – whose 'Diswelfare State'.

If identification of the agents of diswelfare were possible – if we could legally name and blame the culprits – then, in theory at least, redress could be obtained through the courts by the method of monetary compensation for damages. But multiple causality and the diffusion of disservices – the modern choleras of change – make this solution impossible. We have, therefore, as societies to make other choices; either to provide social services, or to allow the social costs of the system to lie where they fall. The nineteenth century chose the latter – the *laissez faire* solution – because it had neither a germ theory of disease nor a social theory of causality; an answer which can hardly be entertained today by a richer society equipped with more knowledge about the dynamics of change. But knowledge in this context must not, of course, be equated with wisdom.

If this argument can be sustained, we are thus compelled to return to our analytical framework of the functional concepts of benefit and, within this context, to consider the role of universalist and selective social services. Non-discriminating universalist services are in part the consequence of unidentifiable causality. If disservices are wasteful (to use the economists' concept of 'waste') so welfare has to be 'wasteful'.

The next question that presents itself is this: can we and should we, in providing benefits and compensation (which in practice can rarely be differentially provided), distinguish between 'faults' in the individual (moral, psychological or social) and the 'faults of society'? If all services are provided – irrespective of whether they represent benefits, amenity, social protection or compensation – on a discriminatory, means-test basis, do we not foster both the sense of personal failure and the stigma of a public burden? The fundamental objective of all such tests of eligibility is to keep people out; not to let them in. They must, therefore, be treated as applicants or supplicants; not beneficiaries or consumers.

It is a regrettable but human fact that money (and the lack of it) is linked to personal and family self-respect. This is one element in what has been called the 'stigma of the means test'. Another element is the historical evidence we have that separate discriminatory services for poor people have always tended to be poor quality services; read the history of the panel system under National Health Insurance; read Beveridge on workmen's compensation; Newsom on secondary modern schools; Plowden on standards of primary schools in slum areas; Townsend on Part III accommodations in *The Last Refuge*,[17] and so on.[18]

In the past, poor quality services for poor people were the product of a society which saw 'welfare' as a residual; as a public burden. The primary purpose of the system and the method of discrimination was, therefore, deterrence (it was also an effective rationing device). To this end, the most effective instrument was to induce among recipients (children as well as adults) a sense of personal fault, of personal failure, even if the benefit was wholly or partially a compensation for disservices inflicted by society.

The Real Challenge in Welfare

Today, with this heritage, we face the positive challenge of providing selective, high quality services for poor people over a large and complex range of welfare; of positively discriminating on a territorial, group or 'rights' basis in favour of the poor, the handicapped, the deprived, the coloured, the homeless, and the social casualties of our society. Universalism is not, by itself alone, enough: in medical care, in wage-related social security, and in education. This much we have learnt in the past two decades from the facts about inequalities in the distribution of incomes and wealth, and in our failure to close many gaps in differential access to and effective utilization of particular branches of our social services.[19]

If I am right, I think that Britain is beginning to identify the dimensions of this challenge of positive, selective discrimination – in income maintenance, in education, in housing, in medical care and mental health, in child welfare, and in the tolerant integration of immigrants and citizens from overseas; of preventing especially the second generation from becoming (and of seeing themselves as) second class citizens. We are seeking ways and means, values, methods and techniques, of positive discrimination without the infliction, actual or imagined, of a sense of personal failure and individual fault.

At this point, considering the nature of the search in all its ramifying complexities, I must now state my general conclusion. It is this. The challenge that faces us is not the choice between universalist and selective social services. The real challenge resides in the question: what particular infrastructure of universalist services is needed in order to provide a framework of values and opportunity bases within and around which can be developed socially acceptable selective services aiming to discriminate positively, with the minimum risk of stigma, in favour of those whose needs are greatest?[20]

This, to me, is the fundamental challenge. In different ways and in particular areas it confronts the Supplementary Benefits Commission, the Seebohm Committee, the National Health Service, the Ministry of Housing and Local Government, the National Committee for Commonwealth Immigrants, the policy-making readers of the Newsom Report and the Plowden Report on educational priority areas, the Scottish Report, *Social Work and the Community*, and thousands of social workers and administrators all over the country wrestling with the problems of needs and priorities. In all the main spheres of need, some structure of universalism is an essential prerequisite to selective positive discrimination; it provides a general system of values and a sense of community; socially approved agencies for clients, patients and consumers, and also for the recruitment, training and deployment of staff at all levels; it sees welfare, not as a burden, but as complementary and as an instrument of change and, finally, it allows positive discriminatory services to be provided as rights for categories of people and for classes of need in terms of priority social areas and other impersonal classifications.

Without this infrastructure of welfare resources and framework of values we should not, I conclude, be able to identify and discuss the next steps in progress towards a 'Welfare Society'.

Notes

Lecture delivered at the British National Conference on Social Welfare, London, April 1967, and published in the *Proceedings of the Conference*.

1 See, for example, *The Times*, 28 July 1965, and 6 August 1965; article by Heymann, H., 'Gnomes of Zurich with a London address', in *The Times*, 18 January 1966, and *The Times*, 4 April 1967 (report by P. Jay, Economics Correspondent), and *The Economist*, editorial 'Into the Wasteland', 23 July 1966, and editorial note on 'Poverty', 22 April 1967.

2 Powell, J. Enoch, *Medicine and Politics*, (London: Pittman, 1966), p. 72.

3 See Titmuss, R. M., *Income Distribution and Social Change* (London: Allen & Unwin, 1962).

4 Henderson, G., Institute for Training and Research, *New York Times*, 6 November 1966, p. E 11. See also Perkins, J. A., President of Cornell University and chairman of the President's Advisory Committee on Foreign Assistance Programmes, *Foreign Affairs*, July 1966; Brinley, T., in 'The new immigration', *The Annals of the American Academy of Political and Social Science* (September 1966); Sutherland, G., *Political Quarterly*, vol. 38, no. 1 (January–March 1967); Lord Bowden, House of Lords, *Hansard*, 20 December 1966, cols 1971–80; and Grubel, H. G., and Scott, A. D., *Journal of Political Economy*, University of Chicago, vol. 14, no. 4 (1966), p. 231.

5 West, K. M., 'Foreign interns and residents in the United States', *Journal of Medical Education*, vol. 40, December 1965, pp. 1110–29.

6 'The dollar value per year of this "foreign aid" to the United States approximately equals the total cost of all our medical aid, private and public, to foreign nations' (West, K. M., *ibid.*, p. 1127). About three-fourths of all foreign medical trainees in the USA are from developing countries.

7 Gibson, T. C., 'British physicians on medical school faculties in North America', *British Medical Journal*, 1967, i, 692.

8 Israel, as well as many other countries, is affected by the shortage of doctors in the USA. Of the 265 doctors graduating from Israeli medical schools in 1963–5, nearly 40 per cent left for the USA (statement by Minister of Health quoted in *Haaretz*, 21 March 1967).

9 Hill, K. R., 'Cost of undergraduate medical education in Britain', *British Medical Journal*, 1964, i, 300–2.

10 Ministry of Health and Department of Health for Scotland, *Report of the Committee to Consider the Future Numbers of Medical Practitioners and the Appropriate Intake of Medical Students* (London: HMSO, 1957). Seven of this eleven-man Committee were eminent members of the medical profession and the chairman was an ex-Minister of Health, Sir Henry Willink.

11 In May 1962 a special committee set up by the British Medical Association to consider recruitment to the medical profession concluded in its report that in spite of certain obvious indications of a shortage of doctors it was not prepared to commit itself on the need for more medical students (*The Times*, 11 May 1962). Dr R. G. Gibson, chairman of this committee (and now chairman of the Council), said two months later that the profession had recently experienced a 'glut of doctors. At present there seemed to be a shortage but care must be taken not to create unemployment in the profession a few years from now' (*British Medical Journal*, Supp., ii, 26, 28 July 1962).

12 See Chapter 9 in this volume.

13 Gilbert, B. B. (London: Michael Joseph, 1966).

14 *The Torrey Canyon*, Cmnd 3246 (London: HMSO, 1967).

15   Boulding, K. E., 'The boundaries of social policy', *Social Work*, vol. 12, no. 1 (January 1967), p. 7.

16   Reddin, M., 'Local authority means tested benefits', in P. Townsend (ed.), *Social Services for All?* (London: Fabian Society, 1968).

17   Townsend, P., *The Last Refuge* (London: Routledge, 1964).

18   See also Titmuss, R. M., *Problems of Social Policy* (London: HMSO, 1950).

19   See Townsend, P., *Poverty, Socialism and Labour in Power*, Fabian tract, 371 (1967), and Nicholson, R. J., 'The distribution of personal income', *Lloyds Bank Review* (January 1967), p. 11.

20   For a more specific formulation see Chapter X, of Titmuss, R. M., *Commitment to Welfare* (London: Allen & Unwin, 1968).

CHAPTER

9

Choice and 'The Welfare State'

For those of us who are still socialists the development of socialist social policies in the next few years will represent one of the cardinal tests on which the Labour Government will be judged – and sternly judged – in the early 1970s. Economic growth, productivity and change are essential; about this there can be no dispute. But as we – as a society – become richer shall we become more equal in social, educational and material terms? What does the rise of 'affluence' spell to the values embodied in the notion of social welfare?

For the purposes of this lecture I have, in asking these questions, to take a long view and disregard our immediate economic and social problems. One assumption I have to make is that over the next ten years (and thereafter) British society will be substantially richer; that, on average, the population of Britain will be living at a higher standard than today. In his pamphlet *Labour's Social Plans*[1] Professor Abel-Smith dealt with what he called the 'ugly imbalance between private affluence and public squalor' and went on to direct a searching attack on the social policy content of the government's *National Plan*.[2]

He assumed (as I do) that over the period of the National Plan we may expect to be (in company with other highly industrialized countries of the West) a richer society in the 1970s. Now that the government has begun to lay a sounder basis for a higher rate of growth in the future after inheriting a decade or more of incompetence and dereliction it is, I think, more rather than less likely that our economic targets will be broadly attained.

But, at the present time, economic and industrial policies are involving much hardship for a minority of workers; whether this was or was not inevitable is a matter on which a great deal more could be said, and no doubt will be said. The acid test will come, however, in the next few years; there will be many who will want to know by the time the life of this government comes to its natural end whether those who are making sacrifices now in the general interest will be more than justly compensated.

This question of who should bear the social and economic costs of change is relevant to the larger issue of the future role of the social services in a more affluent society. First, however, let us remember the general thesis about 'freedom of choice' now being forcefully presented by various schools of 'liberal' economists in Britain, Western Germany and the United States – notably in the writings of Professor Friedman of Chicago and his friends and followers in London and elsewhere.[3] Broadly, their argument is that as large scale industrialized societies get richer the vast majority of their populations will have incomes and assets large enough to satisfy their own social welfare needs in the private market without help from the state. They should have the right and the freedom to decide their own individual resource preferences and priorities and to buy from the private market their own preferred quantities of medical care, education, social security, housing and other services.

Unlike their distinguished predecessors in the nineteenth century, these economic analysts and politicians do not now condemn such instruments of social policy (in the form of social services) as politically irrelevant or mistaken in the past. They were needed then as temporary, *ad hoc* political mechanisms to ameliorate and reduce social conflict; to protect the rights of property, and to avoid resort to violence by the dispossessed and the deprived. This contemporary redefinition of the past role of social policy thus represents it as a form of social control; as a temporary short term process of state intervention to buttress and legitimate industrial capitalism during its early, faltering but formative years of growth. We are now told that those who in the past were critical of state intervention in the guise of free social services were misguided and short-sighted. The Bourbons of today disavow the Bourbons of yesterday. The times, the concepts, the working classes, and the market have all changed. They have been

158

changed by affluence, by technology, and by the development of more sophisticated, anonymous and flexible mechanisms of the market to meet social needs, to enlarge the freedom of consumer choice, and to provide not only more but better quality medical care, education, social security and housing.

In abbreviated form, these are some of the theories of private social policy and consumer choice now being advanced in Britain[4] and other countries. Like other conceptions of social policy presented in large and all-embracing terms, these theories make a number of basic assumptions about the working of the market, about the nature of social needs, and about the future social and economic characteristics of our societies. These assumptions require examination: the task alloted to me by the Fabian Society in preparing this lecture.

I cannot, however, discuss them all in as much detail as I would like. I propose, therefore, to make more explicit four important assumptions and, in respect of each, to raise some questions and add some comments.

Assumption No. 1: That economic growth without the intervention of comprehensive and deliberately redistributive social policies can, by itself alone, solve the problem of poverty.

None of the evidence for Britain and the United States over the past twenty years during which the average standard of living in real terms rose by 50 per cent or more supports this assumption. The most recent evidence for Britain has been examined by Professors Abel-Smith and Townsend in their study *The Poor and the Poorest*.[5] Had private markets in education, medical care and social security been substituted for public policies during the past twenty years of economic growth their conclusions, in both absolute and relative terms, as to the extent of poverty in Britain today would, I suggest, have been even more striking.

For the United States the evidence is no less conclusive and can be found in the recent studies of Orshansky, Brady, S. M. Miller and Rein, Moynihan, Schorr, Herman Miller and Richard Elman, whose book, *The Poorhouse State: the American Way of Life on Public Assistance*,[6] provides a grim picture of degradation in the richest country the world has ever known.

Yet, in 1951, the first chairman of the Council of Economic Advisors under the Eisenhower administration said, before his appointment to the Council, 'the transformation in the distribution of our national income . . . may already be counted as one of the great social revolutions in history'.[7]

Economic growth spelt progress; an evolutionary and inevitable faith that social growth would accompany economic growth. Automatically, therefore, poverty would gracefully succumb to the diffusion of the choices of private market abundance. All this heralded, as Daniel Bell and others were later to argue, the end of ideological conflict.[8]

One is led to wonder what liberal economists would have said fifteen to twenty years ago had they had foreknowledge of the growth in American wealth and had they then been asked to comment on the following facts for the year 1966: that one American child in four would be regarded as living in poverty and that three elderly persons in ten would also be living in poverty;[9] that the United States would be moving towards a more unequal distribution of income, wealth and command over resources;[10] that many grey areas would have become ghettos;[11] that a nationwide civil rights' challenge of explosive magnitude would have to be faced – a challenge for freedom of choice, for the right to work, for a non-rat infested home,[12] for medical care and against stigma;[13] that, as a nation, the United States would be seriously short of doctors, scientists, teachers, social workers, nurses, welfare aids and professional workers in almost all categories of personal service; and that American agencies would be deliberately recruiting and organizing the import of doctors, nurses and other categories of human capital from less affluent nations of the world.

Britain, we should remember, is also relying heavily on the skills of doctors from poorer countries – due in part to the belief less than five to ten years ago among Conservative ministers and leaders of the medical profession that we were in danger of training too many doctors.[14] And, we should add, the belief among liberal economists and sections of the medical profession that Britain was spending too much on the Health Service which was in danger of bankrupting the nation.

Guilty as we have been and are in our treatment of doctors from overseas, at least it cannot be said that we are deliberately organizing recruitment campaigns in India, Pakistan and other developing countries.

Assumption No. 2: That private markets in welfare can solve the problem of discrimination and stigma.

This assumption takes us to the centre of all speculations about choice in welfare and the conflict between universalist social services and selective means-tested systems for the poor. It is basically the problem of stigma or 'spoiled identity' in Goffman's phrase;[15] of felt and experienced discrimination and disapproval on grounds of poverty, ethnic group, class, mental fitness and other criteria of 'bad risks' in all the complex processes of selection–rejection in our societies.

How does the private market in education, social security, industrial injuries insurance, rehabilitation, mental health services and medical care, operating on the basis of ability to pay and profitability, treat poor minority groups? All the evidence, particularly from the United States and Canada, suggests that they are categorized as 'bad risks', treated as second class consumers, and excluded from the middle-class world of welfare. If they are excluded because they cannot pay or are likely to have above average needs – and are offered second class standards in a refurbished public assistance or panel system – who can blame them if they come to think that they have been discriminated against on grounds of colour and other criteria of rejection? Civil rights legislation in Britain to police the commercial insurance companies, the British United Provident Association, and the BMA's Independent Medical Services Ltd would be a poor and ineffective substitute for the National Health Service.

Already there is evidence from recently established independent fee paying medical practices that the 'bad risks' are being excluded, and that the chronic sick are being advised to stay (if they can) with the National Health Service.[16] They are not offered the choice though they may be able to pay. In point of fact, their ability to choose a local doctor under the Health Service is being narrowed. This is a consequence, I suppose, of what Mr Arthur Seldon of the Institute of Economic Affairs in his most recent essay on 'Choice in welfare' describes as 'a new stirring in medical insurance and a new class of doctors with a grain of entrepreneurial determination to supplement or abandon the NHS and to find salvation in the market'.[17]

The essential issue here of discrimination is not the problem of choice in private welfare markets for the upper and middle classes but how to channel proportionately more economic and social resources to aid the poor, the handicapped, the educationally deprived and other minority groups, and to compensate them for bearing part of the costs of other people's progress. We cannot now, just because we are getting richer, disengage ourselves from the fundamental challenge of distributing social rights without stigma; too many unfulfilled expectations have been created, and we can no longer fall back on the *rationale* that our economies are too poor to avoid hurting people. Nor can we solve the problems of discrimination and stigma by re-creating poor law or panel systems of welfare in the belief that we should thereby be able to concentrate state help on those whose needs are greatest. Separate state systems for the poor, operating in the context of powerful private welfare markets, tend to become poor standard systems. In so far as they are able to recruit at all for education, medical care and other services, they tend to recruit the worst rather than the best teachers, doctors, nurses, administrators and other categories of staff upon whom the quality of service so much depends. And if the quality of personal service is low, there will be less freedom of choice and more felt discrimination.

Assumption No. 3: That private markets in welfare would offer consumers more choice.

As I have said, the growth of private markets in medical care, education and other welfare services, based on ability to pay and not on criteria of need, has the effects of limiting and narrowing choice for those who depend on or who prefer to use the public services.

But let us be more specific, remembering that the essential question is: *whose* freedom of choice. Let us consider this question of choice in the one field – private pension schemes – where the insurance market already operates to a substantial extent and where the philosophy of 'free pensions for free men' holds sway.[18] It is, for example, maintained by the insurance industry that private schemes 'are arrangements made voluntarily by individual employers with their own workers';[19] that they are tailor made and shaped to meet individual (consumer) requirements. This is, *par excellence*, the model of consumer choice in the private welfare market.

What are the facts? For the vast majority of workers covered by such private schemes there is no choice. Private schemes are compulsory. Workers are not offered the choice of deferred pay or higher wages; funded schemes or pay as you go schemes. They are not asked to choose between contributory or non-contributory schemes; between flat rate systems or earnings related systems. Despite consumer evidence of a widespread wish for the provision of widows' benefits, employees are not asked to choose. There is virtually no consultation with employees or their representatives. They have no control whatsoever over the investment of funds in the hands of private insurance companies which now total some £2,500 million.[20] And, most important of all, they are rarely offered on redundancy or if they freely wish to change their jobs the choice of full preservation of pension rights.[21]

These issues of transferability and the full preservation of pension rights underline strongly the urgency and importance of the government's current review of social security. We have now been talking for over ten years about the need for freedom of industrial movement, full transferability, and adequate, value-protected pensions as 'of right' in old age; it is time the government's proposals were made known. But they cannot now help with the immediate problem of the redundant workers in the Midlands and other parts of the country. Have these workers forfeited their full occupational pension expectations? What choices have been concretely offered to them by the private pension market? I have seen no statements or surveys or reports from the insurance industry or from the Institute of Economic Affairs. Surely, here was a situation in which one might have expected the protagonists of private welfare markets to have assembled the facts, and to have demonstrated the superiority of practice as well as theory in the matter of consumer choice. But it looks as though they failed in 1966 as they failed in 1956 when the British Motor Corporation announced on 27 June that 6,000 employees would be sacked on 29 June.[22] They were not offered the choice of full preservation of accrued pension rights.[23]

Assumption No. 4: That social services in kind, particularly medical care, have no characteristics which differentiate them from goods in the private market.

I propose to consider this last assumption in relation to medical care, and to pursue a little more intensively some of the central issues which I raised in 'Ethics and economics of medical care'.[24] This was written in response to the thesis advanced by certain 'liberal' economists in Britain and the United States who, after applying neo-classical economic theory to Western type systems of medical care, concluded that 'medical care would appear to have no characteristics which differentiate it sharply from other goods in the market'.[25] It should, therefore, be treated as a personal consumption good indistinguishable in principle from other goods. Consequently, and in terms of political action, private markets in medical care should be substituted for public markets. In support of this conclusion it is argued that the 'delicate, anonymous, continuous and pervasive' mechanism of the private market[26] not only makes more consumer choice possible but provides better services for a more discriminating public. Choice stimulates discrimination which, in turn, enlarges choice.

This thesis is usually presented as applying universally and in terms of the past as well as the present. It is presumed to apply to contemporary India and Tanzania as well as nineteenth-century Britain. It is, therefore, as a theoretical construct 'culture free'. It is also said to be value free. Medical care is a utility and all utilities are good things. But as we cannot measure the satisfactions of utilities – or compare individual satisfactions derived from different utilities – we should rely on 'revealed preferences'. Observable market behaviour will show what an individual chooses. Preference is what individuals prefer; no collective value judgment is consequently said to be involved.

In applying this body of doctrine to medical care we have to consider a large number of characteristics (or factors) which may or may not be said to differentiate medical care from personal consumption goods in the market. I want to concentrate discussion on two of these factors, chiefly because I believe that one of them is central to the whole debate about medical care, and because both of them tend to be either ignored or treated superficially by most writers on the subject. Broadly, they centre around the problems of uncertainty and unpredictability in medical care and, secondly, the difficulty, in theory as well as in practice, of treating medical care as a conceptual entity.

Consider first the problems of uncertainty which confront the consumer of medical care. Then contrast them with the problems of the consumer of, say, cars; there is clearly a risk to life in both situations if wrong choices are made. It is argued, for example, by Professor Lees and others that the market for consumer durables is affected both by unpredictability of personal demand and consumer ignorance about needs.[27] The more significant differentiating characters in the area of medical care would appear to be (though this is by no means an exhaustive list):

(1) Many consumers do not desire medical care.

(2) Many consumers do not know they need medical care.

(3) Consumers who want medical care do not know in advance how much medical care they need and what it will cost.

(4) Consumers do not know and can rarely estimate in advance what particular categories of medical care they are purchasing (such as surgical procedures, diagnostic tests, drugs, and so on).

(5) Consumers can seldom learn from experience of previous episodes of medical care consumption (not only do illnesses, or 'needs', vary greatly but utility variability in medical care is generally far greater than is the case with consumer durables).

(6) Most consumers cannot assess the value of medical care (before, during or after consumption) as an independent variable. They cannot be sure, therefore, whether they have received 'good' or 'bad' medical care. Moreover, the time-scale needed for assessment may be the total life duration.

(7) Most consumers of medical care enter the doctor–patient relationship on an unequal basis; they believe that the doctor or surgeon knows best. Unlike market relationships in the case of consumer durables, they know that this special inequality in knowledge and techniques cannot for all practical purposes be reversed.

(8) Medical care can seldom be returned to the seller,

exchanged for durable goods or discarded. For many people the consequences of consuming medical care are irreversible.

(9) Medical care knowledge is not at present a marketable advertised commodity. Nor can consumers exchange comparable valid information about the consumption of 'good' or 'bad' medical care.

(10) Consumers of medical care experience greater difficulties in changing their minds in the course of consuming care than do consumers of durable goods.

(11) Consumers of medical care may, knowingly or unknowingly, take part in or be the subject of research, teaching and controlled experiments which may affect the outcome.

(12) The concept of 'normal' or 'average' economic behaviour on the part of adult consumers, built into private enterprise medical care models, cannot be applied automatically to the mentally ill, the mentally retarded, the seriously disabled and other categories of consumer-patients.

(13) Similarly, this concept of 'normal' behaviour cannot be applied automatically to immigrant populations or peoples with non-Western cultures and different beliefs and value systems.

These thirteen characteristics are indicative of the many subtle aspects of uncertainty and unpredictability which pervade modern medical care systems. 'I hold', wrote Professor K. J. Arrow, in an article entitled 'Uncertainty and the welfare economics of medical care', in the *American Economic Review*,[28] 'that virtually all the special features of this (medical care) industry, in fact, stem from the prevalence of uncertainty.'

To grasp fully the significance of these differentiating characteristics, each one of them should be contrasted with the situation of the consumer of cars or other consumption goods; an exercise which I cheerfully leave to the reader.

I turn now to my second set of questions. Many economists who attempt to apply theories and construct models in this particular area conduct their analyses on the assumption that 'medical care' is (or can be treated as) an entity. Historically, perhaps this may once have been marginally valid when it consisted almost wholly of the personal doctor–patient relationship. Medical care, we would now say, was more a matter fifty years ago of spontaneous biological response or random chance.

Science, technology and economic growth have now, however, transformed medical care into a group process; a matter of the organized application of an immense range of specialized skills, techniques, resources and systems. If, therefore, we now wish to examine medical care from the standpoint of economic theory we need to break down this vague and generalized concept 'medical care' into precise and distinctive components.

To illustrate the importance of doing so let us consider one example; probably one of the more critical components in curative medicine today, namely, the procurement, processing, matching, distribution, financing and transfusion of whole human blood. Is human blood a consumption good?

Notes

London Fabian Lecture, November 1966, and published in Fabian Tract 370 (1967).

1 Fabian Tract 369.
2 Cmnd 2764 (London: HMSO, September 1965).
3 Friedman, M., *Capitalism and Freedom* (University of Chicago Press, 1962).
4 See, for example, Lees, D. S., 'Health through choice', in R. Harris, *Freedom or Free-for-all?*, Hobart Papers, vol. 3 (London: The Institute of Economic Affairs, 1965), and West, E. G., *Education and the State* (London: The Institute of Economic Affairs, 1965).
5 Occasional papers on Social Administration, no. 17 (London: Bell and Sons, 1965).
6 New York: Pantheon Books, 1966.
7 Quoted in Miller, H. T., 'Is the income gap closed? "No" ', *New York Times Magazine*, 11 November 1962.
8 Bell, D., *The End of Ideology: on the Exhaustion of Political Ideas in the Fifties* (New York: Collier Books, 1961).
9 Orshansky, M., in *Social Security Bulletin*, July 1963, January 1965 and July 1965, Social Security Administration, US Department of Health, Education and Welfare.
10 Brady, D. S., *Age and the Income Distribution*, Research Report no. 8, Social Security Administration, US Department of Health, Education and Welfare, 1965. For other evidence of recent trends see Miller, S. M., and Rein, M. 'Poverty, inequality and policy', in H. S. Becker (ed.), *Social Problems* (New York: John Wiley, 1967).

11 See Hunter, D. R., *The Slums: Challenge and Response* (New York: Glencoe Free Press, 1964); Gans, H., *The Urban Villagers* (New York: Glencoe Free Press, 1962); Taeuber, K. E., *Scientific American*, vol. 213, no. 2, 1965, and Taeuber, K. E., and Taeuber, F. Alma, *Negroes in Cities: Residential Segregation and Neighbourhood Change* (Chicago: Aldine, 1965).

12 'Welfare recipients in New York who live in rat-infested buildings can receive a so-called "rat allowance" to cover the cost of keeping their lights burning all night long' (Cloward, R. A., and Elman, R. M., 'Poverty, injustice and the Welfare State', *Nation*, 28 February 1966).

13 Office of Policy Planning and Research, US Department of Labor, *The Negro Family: the Case for National Action* (Washington, DC, 1965).

14 Seven of the eleven-man committee which drew up the Ministry of Health and Department of Health for Scotland's *Report of the Committee to Consider the Future Numbers of Medical Practitioners and the Appropriate Intake of Medical Students* (London: HMSO, 1957) were eminent members of the medical profession and the chairman was an ex-Minister of Health, Sir Henry Willink. In May 1962 a special committee set up by the British Medical Association to consider recruitment to the medical profession included in its report that in spite of certain obvious indications of a shortage of doctors it was not prepared to commit itself on the need for more medical students (*The Times*, 11 May 1962). Dr R. G. Gibson, chairman of this committee (and now chairman of the Council), said two months later that the profession had recently experience a 'glut of doctors. At present there seemed to be a shortage, but care must be taken not to create unemployment in the profession a few years from now' (*British Medical Journal*, Supp. ii, 26, 28 July 1962).

15 Goffman, E., *Stigma: Notes on the Management of Spoiled Identity* (Englewood Cliffs, NJ: Prentice-Hall, 1963).

16 Mencher, S., *Private Practice and the National Health Service*, Occasional Papers on Social Administration, No. 24 (London: Bell, 1967).

17 'Which way to welfare', *Lloyds Bank Review* (October 1966).

18 Seldon, A., *Pensions in a Free Society*, Institute of Economic Affairs (1957).

19 Life Offices' Association, *The Pension Problem: a Statement of Principle and a Review of the Labour Party's Proposals* (1957), p. 3.

20 Nursaw, W. G., *Principles of Pension Fund Investment* (1966), p. 19.

21 See Report of a Committee of the National Joint Advisory Council, *Preservation of Pension Rights*, Ministry of Labour (London: HMSO, 1966); the Government Actuary, *Occupational Pension Schemes: a New Survey* (London: HMSO, 1966), and two forthcoming studies by Lynes, T. A., *Pensions and Democracy*, and *French Pensions*, Occasional Papers on Social Administration.

22 Kahn, H. R., *Repercussions of Redundancy* (London: Allen & Unwin, 1965).

23 For a discussion of the concept of 'full preservation' see Ministry of Labour, *Preservation of Pension Rights*, and other references in Chapter XV of Titmuss, R. M., *Commitment to Welfare* (Allen & Unwin, 1968).

24 See ibid., Chapter XXI and also criticisms of this study by Professor Lees, Professor Jewkes and others in *Medical Care*, vol. 1, no. 4 (1963), pp. 234–55, and Lees, D. S., 'Health through choice'.

25 Lees, D. S., 'Health through choice', pp. 37–9 and 86–7.

26 ibid., p. 64.
27 ibid., p. 87.
28 vol. 53, no. 5 (December 1963).

CHAPTER

— 10 —

The Gift of Blood

There is a bond that links all men and women in the world so closely and so intimately that every difference of colour, religious belief and cultural heritage is insignificant beside it. Never varying in temperature more than five or six degrees, composed of 55 per cent water, the life stream of blood that runs in the veins of every member of the human race proves that the family of man is a reality.

The 'blood is the life', says Deuteronomy (12:23). 'For this is my blood of the New Testament which is shed for you' (Matthew 26:28). Ancient Egyptians were said to bathe in blood to refresh their powers, and to anoint heads with oil and blood to treat greying and baldness. Ovid describes how Aeson recovered his youthfulness after drinking the blood of his son Jason. The Romans were said to have drunk the blood of dying gladiators to imbue them with courage. Blood brother ceremonies in various countries of the world still fulfil functions of reconciliation and other social purposes, while blood feuds – blood being repaid with blood – represented a powerful institution in medieval Europe and form part of the conventions of some societies today.

Symbolically and functionally, blood is deeply embedded in religious doctrine, in the psychology of human relationships, and in theories and concepts of race, kinship, ancestor worship and the family. From time immemorial it has symbolized qualities of fortitude, vigour, nobility, purity and fertility. Men have been terrified by the sight of blood; they have killed each other for it, believed it could work miracles and have preferred death rather than receive it from a member of a different ethnic group.

In more recent times, the growth of scientific knowledge about blood has provided us with a more rational framework. But it is only in the last thirty years or so that scientific advances have made the transfer of blood from one human being to another an increasingly indispensable part of modern medicine.

Blood transfusion represents one of the greatest therapeutic instruments in the hands of contemporary physicians. It has made possible the saving of life on a scale undreamt of several decades ago, and for conditions that were long considered hopeless. Moreover, the demand for blood increases yearly in every Western country as physicians adopt more radical surgical techniques entailing the loss of massive amounts of blood, and as new uses are found for blood, both in the saving of life and in the prevention of disease and disability.

All these scientific and technical developments in the field of blood transfusion have not only produced new and as yet unsolved problems for the biological and medical sciences, they have also set in train social, economic and ethical consequences that present society with issues of profound importance. It is part of the purpose of this essay to explore these consequences.

Blood Banking in America

It is difficult to assemble information about the total activities of all blood banking systems in the United States. It has been estimated that there were in 1966–8 some 9,000 central, regional and local blood banks in the United States concerned with the collection of blood from donors. Some (for example, hospital blood banks) will also be concerned with processing, cross-matching and transfusion; some have the function of producing and preparing blood components; some operate solely as collectors, distributors and suppliers of whole blood; and some provide a comprehensive community service.

This diversity of single and multi-purpose agencies may be classified in terms of five distinct types of blood banks:

☐ Fifty-five independent but co-operating American Red Cross Regional Blood Centres based on 1,700 participating local chapters and accounting, according to rough estimates in 1967, for about 40 per cent of total blood supplies in the United States.

☐ Some 6,000 individual hospital blood banks, which perform a great variety of services and are estimated to be responsible for about 20 to 30 per cent of total blood supplies.

☐ About 100 non-profit organizations known as community blood banks, which generally aim to ensure an adequate blood supply for the communities in which they are situated. These agencies also perform various services, some simply acting as collectors and distributors to hospitals, others having a wide range of functions. The community banks were thought in 1966 to account for about 15 to 20 per cent of total blood supplies.

☐ An unknown number of independent profit-making commercial blood banks, which generally obtain their blood supplies from paid donors, process it and sell it to hospitals at a profit. These banks were believed in the early 1960s to account for some 10 to 15 per cent of total blood supplies. As we shall see, however, more recent estimates arrive at substantially higher figures. Indeed, there seems to be no doubt that in recent years the percentage of blood supplied by these commercial agencies has been increasing, partly at the expense of voluntary programmes.

☐ An unknown number of commercial blood banks directly operated by pharmaceutical firms which rely heavily on a newly developed method of drawing blood, plasmapheresis. In non-technical terms, this means that after the donor has given a pint of blood, the red cells are separated from the plasma (the liquid part of blood as distinguished from the suspended elements) and injected back into the donor. For the donor, the process takes less than an hour. Provided that the strictest medical standards are observed, and that the donor is in excellent health and eats a nutritious high-protein diet, it is claimed by some authorities that one individual can make several donations a week. Other authorities believe, however, that it is too soon to be certain that plasmapheresis may not involve serious long term hazards for the donors.

Plasmapheresis of donors is used by these blood banks to obtain plasma, plasma protein components and platelets, for all of which there has been an immensely increasing demand. Various estimates in 1968 suggested that pharmaceutical firms were paying for 1 to 1.5 million donations a year yielding, with 'double bleed' sessions, approximately 2 million units. A number of firms operate their own plasmapheresis centres; others obtain their supplies from 'independent blood contractors'. Some regular donors are, in effect, 'semi-salaried' and paid $150 to $200 a month for a specified number of donations; some are long term prisoners.

National estimates of the quantities of blood collected by these different types of blood banks generally exclude the commercial plasmapheresis centres because no comprehensive figures exist as to the scale of their operations. Excluding such supplies, however, national estimates of collections in the early 1960s range from 5 to 6 million units a year. Of this total, it has been suggested that anywhere from 17 to 20 per cent, and more, is provided by donors who are paid in cash for their blood. One might assume, therefore, that the remainder of the total annual collection was provided by voluntary donors. Much depends, however, on the definition of 'voluntary donor'.

The Gift Relationship

To 'donate' is to give implying an altruistic motive. Strictly and perhaps more neutrally speaking, 'suppliers' should replace 'donors' in the vocabulary of this study, as we shall see presently. We will, however, conform to the common usage, even though it is somewhat misleading.

To obtain sufficient quantities of blood in the required blood group proportions, at the required times and in the required places are not processes that can be determined and controlled by the medical profession alone, despite its power to decide who may and who may not give and the destination of the gifts. To give or not to give, to lend, repay or even to buy and sell blood – these are the questions that lead us beyond any one profession into the fundamentals of social and economic life.

The forms and functions of giving embody moral, social, psychological, religious, legal and aesthetic ideas. They may reflect, sustain, strengthen or lessen the cultural bonds of the group, large or small. They may inspire the worst excesses of war and tribal nationalism or the tolerances of the community. They may contribute to integrative processes in a society (binding together different ethnic, religious and generational groups), or they may spread, through separatist and segregationist acts, the sense and reality of alienation – as in South Africa and the southern states of the United States.

Customs and practices of non-economic giving – unilateral and multilateral social transfers – thus may tell us much (as Marcel Mauss so sensitively demonstrated in his book *The Gift*) about the texture of personal and group relationships in different cultures, past and present. But the gift of blood has about it certain unique attributes that distinguish it from other forms of giving. We enumerate some of these now; all derive from the assumption that the gift is a voluntary, altruistic act:

- The gift of blood takes place in impersonal situations, sometimes with physically hurtful consequences to the donor.
- The recipient is in almost all cases not personally known to the donor; there can, therefore, be no personal expressions of gratitude or of other sentiments.
- Only certain groups in the populations are allowed to give; the selection of those who can is determined on rational and not cultural rules by external arbiters.
- There are no personal, predictable penalties for not giving, no socially enforced sanctions of remorse, shame or guilt.
- For the giver there is no certainty of a corresponding gift in return, present or future.
- No givers require or wish for corresponding gifts in return; they do not expect and would not wish to have a blood transfusion.
- In most systems, there is no obligation imposed on the recipient himself to make a corresponding gift in return.
- Whether the gift itself is beneficial or harmful to an unknown recipient will depend to some extent on the truthfulness and honesty of the giver. Moreover, the intermediaries – those who collect and process the gift – may determine in certain systems whether it is potentially beneficial or harmful.
- Both givers and recipients might, if they were known to each other, refuse to participate in the process on religious, ethnic, political or other grounds.
- Blood as a gift is highly perishable (its value rapidly diminishes), but neither the giver nor the recipient wields any power in determining whether it is used or wasted.
- To the giver, the gift is quickly replaced by the body. There is no permanent loss. To the recipient, the gift may be everything: life itself.

174

The Source of Blood

There are many myths in all societies, and America is no exception. One of the most deeply held myths in this country today is that the voluntary donor is the norm, that most blood donations are contributed by volunteers.

In weighing the truth of this myth, one should bear in mind the many inadequacies, gaps and errors in the statistical data. At various points in the breakdown of types of donors that follows, we have been forced to employ what one can only call 'informed guesswork' based on months of work tabulating, checking and comparing statistics in all the survey reports since 1956. In general, we believe we have erred on the conservative side in our estimates of the proportions of paid blood supplies. However, with these cautions in mind, we now sum up these approximate figures:

Table 1 *Estimates of source of blood (including plasmapheresis programmes) collected by type, United States, 1965–7*

The paid donor The professional donor	47%
The paid-induced voluntary donor	3
The responsibility fee donor The family credit donor	39
The captive voluntary donor	4
The fringe benefit voluntary donor	0
The voluntary community donor	7
Total	100

This table shows that about one-third of all donations were bought and sold (types A, B and C). Approximately 52 per cent (types D and E) were 'tied' by contracts of various kinds; that is, these donations represented the contracted repayment in blood of blood debts, encouraged or enforced by monetary penalties. Some of these donors will have benefited financially, and some will have paid other donors to provide the blood. About 5 per cent were captive voluntary donors – members of the Armed Forces and prisoners. About 9 per cent approximated the concept of the voluntary community donor who sees his donation as a free gift to strangers in society.

But this picture is incomplete. We have already noted the recent growth of plasmapheresis programmes operated by commercial banks and pharmaceutical firms. Their annual harvest of 2 million units has had the effect of making the contribution of the voluntary donor an even less significant one in the United States, for almost all of these units were bought: some from registered, quasi-salaried donors, some from 'walk-in', irregular and occasional donors. In all, perhaps 400,000 or so different individuals are paid for this yield of 2 million units a year.

We now have to add these estimates to the totals in Table 1. The effect is to raise the annual national collection total to 8 million units and the combined figure for types A and B ('paid' and 'professional' donors) to 3,737,800 units. The adjusted percentages are:

Table 2   *Estimates of source of blood collected by type, United States, each year, 1965–7*

Type	Number of units	
The paid donor The professional donor	1,737,800	29%
The paid-induced voluntary donor	211,600	4
The responsibility fee donor The family credit donor	3,188,000	52
The captive voluntary donor	324,800	5
The fringe benefit voluntary donor	26,500	1
The voluntary community donor	561,300	9
Total	6,000,000	100

On the basis of 8 million units a year, then, approximately one half are bought and sold. The contribution of the voluntary community donor is only 7 per cent.

Apart from the great increase in paid plasma donations, all the evidence we have brought together suggests that the proportion of paid donations in the country as a whole has increased in recent years. Thirteen years ago the Joint Blood Council survey estimated the proportion of paid donations for the country as a whole at about 14 to 17 per cent. It would seem, therefore, from Table 1 that the proportion has doubled and, if the 2 million plasma donations are included, trebled.

The only other trend figures that have been published relate to New York City. The proportions of paid donations were: 1952, 14 per cent; 1956, 42 per cent; 1966, 55 per cent. The proportion of voluntary community donations fell from 20 per cent in 1956 to about 1 per cent in 1966.

As the blood transfusion services of the United States become increasingly dependent on the paid or professional donor, it is important that we have some sense of the social characteristics of those who sell their blood. A survey we conducted in 1968 was in part designed to produce some evidence on this matter. In all, I received statistics from a large number of commercial banks (some operated by pharmaceutical firms) accounting for some 366,000 units of blood. While very few appear to maintain detailed records on their sources of supply with respect to age, sex, marital status and other characteristics, many provided summary accounts. It would seem that most paid donors (apart from those in prisons, in the Armed Forces, or university students) fall into three categories:

- Professional donors – registered donors who contribute regularly and who are paid on a fee basis or are semi-salaried (this category figures largely in the plasmapheresis programmes).
- 'Call-in' donors – individuals (perhaps with less common blood groups) who are on a register of some kind and who respond to a call for blood on payments of a fee of $5 to $15 or more.
- 'Walk-in' donors, who may be attracted by advertisements, who are paid $5 or more a pint depending on local circumstances, such as the extent of the shortage of blood and other market considerations.

Many commercial blood banks, often open (at least in New York) from 7.30 in the morning to midnight, are better placed to attract walk-in donors because their 'store fronts' are located in Negro and ghetto areas. In 1966, according to one journalistic report, voluntary and private hospitals bought 100,000 pints of 'Skid Row blood from New York City's 31 pay-for-blood stores'. The hospitals paid $35 a pint or more for the blood. A typical journalistic account which appeared in 1963 described the scene at one of these blood banks:

> A bleary-eyed, vacant-faced man shuffles up to a building in an industrial part of town, checks the address with a scrap of paper in his shaking hand, and walks inside. In a bleak third-floor office, he joins a number of other men, many derelicts like himself. One by one they are summoned to a desk where an attendant asks a few quick questions and directs them to an inner room.
>
> This is not a flophouse. It is not an employment agency or a social service bureau for weary, homeless men. This is a blood donor center.

Similar accounts have appeared since 1963 of conditions in commercial blood banks in Chicago, Seattle, Georgia, Cleveland, Boston, Miami, Detroit, Cincinnati, Los Angeles, San Francisco, Washington, Baltimore, Philadelphia, New Jersey, Kansas City and many other places in addition to New York.

Most of these accounts, however, are not the products of keen-eyed journalists but of physicians concerned about the problem of serum hepatitis. We will discuss this problem in a moment. Meanwhile, we conclude that, despite all the statistical inadequacies in the data on blood transfusion services in America, the trend appears to be markedly in the direction of the increasing commercialization of blood and donor relationships. Concomitantly, we find that proportionately more blood is being supplied by the poor, the unskilled, the unemployed, Negroes and other low income groups and, with the rise of plasmapheresis, a new class is emerging of an exploited human population of high blood yielders. Redistribution in terms of 'the gift of blood and blood products' from the poor to the rich appears to be one of the dominant effects of the American blood banking systems.

Truth, Trust and Hepatitis

To the recipient the use of human blood for medical purposes can be more lethal than many drugs. The transfusion and use of whole blood and certain blood products carries with it the risk of transmitting disease, particularly serum hepatitis, malaria, syphilis and brucellosis. Not only are there risks in infected blood and plasma but there are also risks in the use of contaminated needles and apparatus in the collection and transfusion processes.

In the United States and other modern societies the most dangerous of these hazards is serum hepatitis. It is becoming a major public health problem throughout the world. No scientific means have yet been found to detect in the laboratory the causative agents of hepatitis in the blood before it is used for a transfusion or for conversion into various blood products. The quantity of infected blood that can transmit hepatitis may be as little as one-millionth of a millilitre. The absence of a scientific check on quality and safety means that the subsequent biological condition of those who receive blood constitutes the ultimate test of whether the virus was present in the donation; in effect, therefore, the patient is the laboratory for testing the quality of the gift of blood.

But few – if any – patients know that their bodies perform this role. They do not ask and in most cases are in no condition to ask: Will this blood cause hepatitis? Who supplied it? In what circumstances? What safeguards were employed to ensure as far as humanly possible that this blood is not going to harm or kill me? Even if such questions were asked, it has to be recognized that they could not be satisfactorily answered by those administering transfusions or blood products.

In these situations of consumer ignorance and uncertainty, as in many others in the field of medical care, the patient has to trust the medical profession and the organized system of medical care. He has no alternative but to trust. If, subsequently, he develops hepatitis and it is clinically diagnosed as such (which in many instances it is difficult to do), it is still virtually impossible in most cases to establish a causal relationship and to connect the infection or the ill health to the blood transfusion or the blood product. Many complex factors are involved in these difficulties of diagnosing, identifying and naming the causal agent(s), one being the long incubation period in serum hepatitis – possibly up to six months.

Not only, therefore, has the patient no alternative to trust when receiving blood but, subsequently, and apart from a very small proportion of obvious cases of infection where causal attribution can be established, he can have no redress. He is not only unknowingly the laboratory test of 'goodness', he and his family must bear the biological, social and economic costs of infected blood and misplaced trust in terms of physical incapacity, loss of earnings and career prospects, the effects on family life and other unquantifiable factors. These costs may be mitigated, but they may never be entirely eliminated. In many cases, the costs are irreversible.

For these and many other reasons those responsible for blood transfusion services have stressed the great importance of maintaining the most rigorous standards in the selection of donors. The state of health, the health history and the social habits of the donor become crucial because the laboratory cannot identify the virus. Again, however, there are definite limits to the clinical assessment of 'health'; no single test or battery of liver function tests has yet been devised which will reliably distinguish carriers of the virus from 'normal' subjects.

A great deal depends, therefore, on the truthfulness of the donor in the processes of medical examination, history taking and selection. Just as the recipient of blood has to trust the doctor, so the doctor has, within limits, to trust the giver. Those responsible for making medical decisions and administering blood have to act in certain circumstances on the assumption that donors have been truthful. In situations of total ignorance and total helplessness this is one social right the patient has – the right to truthfulness. Essentially, this is because he can exercise no preferences, and because one man's untruthfulness can reduce another man's welfare.

In different blood donation systems, therefore, we are led to ask: What particular set of conditions and arrangements permits and encourages maximum truthfulness on the part of donors? To what extent can honesty be maximized? Can this objective be pursued regardless of the donor's motives for giving blood? What principles should the medical profession, in the interests of patients and of the profession, consider as fundamental in the organization and operation of blood donor programmes?

Is the Gift a Good One?

Martin L. Gross has summarized the evidence on the risks of hepatitis:

Hepatitis is the most widespread transfusion danger for the hospital patient, the result of contaminated blood. Its exact toll is elusive, but the *Journal of the American Medical Association* has editorially indicated that the hepatitis transfusion problem is significant and considerably more prevalent than previously thought. 'It has been reliably shown', (ran the editorial), 'that an essential therapeutic measure, blood transfusion, causes death in approximately one of every 150 transfusions in persons over 40 years of age as a result of serum hepatitis. Since this is the age group to which most blood transfusions are given, and since many hundreds are given daily, such a high fatality rate becomes a problem.

Key area studies — in Chicago, New Jersey, Philadelphia, Los Angeles and Baltimore — which have carefully followed up transfused patients are discouraging. The hepatitis scourge, they show, strikes about one in 25 to 50 patients, with sizeable death rates of up to 20 per cent of those stricken. 'It appears that the incidence of hepatitis after blood transfusion is greater than prior estimates have indicated', states Dr John R. Senior, a Philadelphia researcher. Dr Garrott Allen of Chicago has reported hepatitis danger so extensive that it surprised the most inured of the profession: 3.6 per cent of all transfused hospital patients later contracted the disease (the risk rises with the number of units transfused). Judging from these samples, there may be 75,000 cases of hepatitis yearly, with almost 10,000 deaths.

More optimistic statistics have been garnered in Boston by Tufts University School of Medicine researchers with a hopeful transfusion rationale for the future. A twelve-year study of the nine Boston teaching hospitals has produced only 171 patients rehospitalized for post-tranfusion hepatitis, 12 per cent of whom died. Since their total study represents about 5 per cent of the nation's one-year blood use, we might thus expect 3,500 cases annually. The actual toll of blood transfusion hepatitis is possibly between the extremes of the Boston and Chicago studies.

Oneof the main keys to preventing hepatitis after transfusion, the Boston physicians found, was in the careful checking of the source of the blood. The epidemic-like hepatitis in other cities, they believe, is a direct result of prebottled blood supplied by commercial sources: 40 per cent of the blood in the Chicago sample was bought; and more than 75 per cent of the blood in the Baltimore group was commercial. In the teaching hospitals of

Boston, conversely, none of the blood was purchased from commercial blood firms.

'No matter what method of case finding was used, the lowest incidence of post-transfusion hepatitis was seen when commercially supplied blood was avoided', state the Tufts University researchers.

Dr Allen, one of the foremost authorities in the United States, has shown in a series of studies that the risk of serum hepatitis from transfusions derived from prison and skid row populations is at least ten times that from the use of voluntary donors.

> This greater risk rate is attributed to the fact that the paid donor is often a cloistered resident of Skid Row where he and his colleagues are alleged to enjoy frequently the practice of the communal use of unsterile needles and syringes for the self-administration of drugs. These rates increase with the number of transfusions, but they do not continue as a linear relationship after the first 5 or 6 units are given. There are also other unsanitary practices that prevail among this kind of population which favor repeated exposures to infectious hepatitis as well. Still another contributing factor, allegedly higher in this group than in the general population, is that of alcoholism, which appears to make such individuals more susceptible to an initial attack of either infectious or serum hepatitis.

A later study (in New Jersey) showed that the risk of hepatitis 'developing in recipients of blood known to have been donated by convicted or suspected narcotics addicts was 70 times that in the controls.'

Donors and Disease

Over the past decade many studies in different parts of the United States have incriminated the paid donor (and blood obtained from commercial blood banks) as the major source of infection. The most recently reported of these studies was conducted by Dr Paul Schmidt and his colleagues at the National Institutes of Health, Bethesda.

This was a controlled prospective study (unlike many previous retrospective ones) of two groups of patients 21 years and older who were undergoing cardiac surgery at the National Institutes of Health hospital. There were no significant differences between the groups with respect to age, sex, type of heart disease, type of operation and severity of preoperative symptoms. One group received 94 per cent of their blood from one or both of two commercial blood sources employing paid donors (in the Mississippi Valley area and an East Coast port city). The second group received 97 per cent of their blood from voluntary donors in the Washington area. The average number of units of blood transfused per patient was 18.5 in the commercial group and slightly more (19.6) in the voluntary group.

In the commercial group, the total hepatitis attack rate was 53 per cent; in the voluntary group, nil. This study suggests not only that there is an extremely high attack rate among cardiac surgery cases (average age 47) transfused with paid blood in the United Staes but also that an immense number of cases of infection are at present undetected. Because the number of patients involved was small (a total of 68), surveillance of the hepatitis risk is being continued and expanded on a nationwide basis. Further studies are also under way to eliminate the possibility of a geographic factor (because some of the paid blood was obtained from the Mississippi Valley area).

Nor is the problem of serum hepatitis confined to the use of whole blood. There is a serious risk in the use of whole pooled plasma and certain blood products, the production of which has been, as we saw, greatly aided by the use of plasmapheresis programmes. It has been argued, however, that, compared with the hepatitis risks involved in the use of walk-in, irregular, skid row donor types, more regular selected, longer term plasmapheresis donors have a lower carrier rate. But a great deal depends here – as it does with all donors – on two factors: the precise nature of external quality and safety controls exercised by some scientific supervisory agency (even though there are limits to effective screening) and, second, the degree of *continued* truthfulness among paid donors.

As to the controls, it has been repeatedly shown in the United States that the official public health standards designed to insure the continued safety, purity and potency of biological products are only minimal standards and in many cases are either inapplicable, inadequate or ineffective (partly because of the inherent difficulties of continually inspecting and checking all procedures at blood banks).

Under the standards set by the National Institutes of Health, an ancient physician, a nurse and a former bartender can theoretically combine their resources to form a blood bank. They can draw most of their blood from skid-row donors at the minimum fee and sell their blood to hospitals that seek the lowest bidder and are not concerned with the scientific aspects of blood banking.

Moreover, the great expansion during 1968–9 in chains of profit making hospitals (newly built hospitals as well as voluntary hospitals bought by some 33 nationwide investor owned companies) is likely to increase the risks as more blood is purchased from commercial banks. Altruistic donors can hardly be expected to give their blood to profit making hospitals.

With regard to the issues of truthfulness, again it has been repeatedly shown that paid donors – and especially poor donors badly in need of money – are, on average and compared with voluntary donors, relatives and friends, more reluctant and less likely to reveal a full medical history and to provide information about recent contacts with infectious disease, recent inoculations and about their diets, drinking and drug habits that would disqualify them as donors.

Prisoners of Commerce

The hazards involved in the commercial blood transfusion system, both to the American people and internationally, were made more explicit in 1969 by reports on the activities of Southern Food and Drug Research and its associated corporations. These corporations, operating in three states, acted as 'intermediate contractors' to some 37 major American pharmaceutical firms, a number of which have large international markets. Their main role, as commercial enterprises, was to supply plasma, hyper-immune immunoglobulin and other products and to carry out clinical trials on human beings of proposed new pharmaceutical products. The supply of hyper-immune immunoglobulin (used for therapeutic purposes in connection with mumps, whooping cough, tetanus and smallpox) involved vaccinating donors to build up the antibodies in the plasma. The technique mainly used was plasmapheresis.

With the assistance of prison physicians (some of whom were

renumerated by these corporations) extensive use was made of prisoners (who were paid for taking pills, vaccinations and supplying plasma) from 1962 to 1969. In all, these corporations are said to have conducted between 25 and 50 per cent of the initial drug tests (or first phase tests usually carried out on healthy subjects) annually undertaken in the United States.

A series of investigations and inquiries into the activities of these corporations reported:

- Potentially fatal new compounds have been tested on prisoners with little or no direct medical observation of the results.
- Prisoners failed to swallow pills, failed to report serious reactions to those they did swallow and failed to receive careful laboratory tests.
- Control records for validation purposes were totally inadequate, plasmapheresis rooms were 'sloppy', and gross contamination of the rooms containing donors' plasma was evident.
- One prisoner on plasmapheresis received back another man's red cells and was seriously damaged for life.
- Another prisoner, injected with a whooping cough vaccine, died.
- Large outbreaks of hepatitis occurred at various prisons, involving over 1,000 prisoners of whom at least six died.
- It is alleged that several agencies of the Department of Health, Education and Welfare knew for years about the activities and standards of these corporations and did not curtail or stop them.
- Many internationally known pharmaceutical firms knew of the standards of medical supervision, laboratory and quality control being exercised by these corporations. No concerted or collective action was taken to stop using these intermediaries. Some firms remained the biggest consumers of Southern Food and Drug Research and its associated corporations. Those who were still using these facilities in 1969 are reported to have defended the validity of the data provided.

This is only a brief summary of an immense amount of

documentation available in the United States. We have not included here much material raising ethical and political issues similar to those made explicit in the Nuremberg Code.

This case – or series of cases – is relevant in a number of ways to the problems raised here: the issues of donor 'truthfulness', theories of social costs in relation to blood and blood products and questions of safety, purity and potency.

In private market terms, we see that 'untruthfulness' was maximized at many points in the system, from the prisoners themselves to officials employed by the pharmaceutical firms. The social costs involved extend far beyond the areas of cost-benefit analysis conventionally studied by economists and statisticians. They embrace the prisoners and their families (many of whom were Negroes), the prison system itself, the medical profession, the pharmaceutical industry in the United States and the consumers of these products not only in the United States but in many countries of the world.

At least one conclusion can be drawn at this point. Governmental systems of licensing, inspection and quality validation appear to be helpless to control private markets in blood and blood products. Their ineffectiveness has contributed in recent years to the phenomenon in the United States of numerous legal suits based on negligence, implied warranty and various food and drug acts. What is involved, of course, is the question of whether blood transfusion is a commercial transaction or a professional service.

'Social' Versus 'Economic'

All these issues were crystallized and debated in the now famous Kansas City case of 1962. Before we pursue them it is instructive to review the causes and implications of this particular event. Briefly, the facts are these.

In 1953 a meeting of doctors, pathologists, hospital administrators and local citizens decided to form a non-profit community blood bank in Kansas City. There was a need for more blood which the local hospital blood banks were not fully supplying, and the local branch of the American Red Cross was at the time channelling the blood it collected to the Armed Forces in Korea. For the next two years there were endless disputes among the various interests involved (which need not concern us here) about power, institutional control and finance. Then, in May 1955, a commercial blood bank (calling itself the Midwest Blood Bank and Plasma Center) started operations.

The bank was owned and operated by a husband and wife team. The husband had completed grade school, had no medical training and had previously worked as a banjo teacher, second-hand car salesman and photographer. The blood bank procedures seem to have been actually directed by the wife. She called herself an RN but was not licensed as a nurse in either Kansas or Missouri and did not show any evidence of experience or training in blood banking. Originally there had been a third partner, but he had been chased out of the bank by the husband with a gun. A medical director was appointed to comply with public health regulations. He was 78, a general practitioner with no training in blood banking. The bank was inspected and licensed by the relevant federal authority, the National Institutes of Health.

Situated in a slum area, the blood bank displayed a sign reading 'Cash Paid for Blood' and drew blood from donors described as 'skid row derelicts'. It was said by one witness to have 'worms all over the floor'. In 1958 another commercial bank, the World Blood Bank, was established in Kansas City and also began operations.

From 1955 onwards pressures of various kinds were brought to bear on relatives of hospital patients, members of associations and trade unions to provide blood on a replacement basis to these commercial banks. But local hospitals refused to accept blood from these sources to discharge patients' blood fees. These and other developments seem to have forced a solution to the disputes over the control of the non-profit community blood bank, and in April 1958 it commenced operations. Subsequently, it appears from the evidence that practically all the large local hospitals entered into blood supply contracts with the Community Blood Bank and ceased operating their own banks. The Community Blood Bank thus had a virtual monopoly.

The two commercial banks then complained to the Federal Trade Commission alleging restraint of trade. In July 1962, after an investigation lasting several years, the commission issued a complaint against the Community Blood Bank and its officers, administrative director and business manager; the Kansas City

Area Hospital Association and its officers, directors and executive director; three hospitals, individually and as representatives of the forty members of the hospital association; sixteen pathologists; and two hospital administrators.

The complaint charged the respondents with having entered into an agreement or planned course of action to hamper and restrain the sale and distribution of human blood in inter-state commerce. They were charged with conspiring to boycott a commercial blood bank in the sale and distribution of blood in commerce, and that the conspiracy was to the injury of the public and unreasonably restricted and restrained inter-state commerce in violation of Section 5 of the Federal Trade Commission Act of 1952. This section of the act declares that 'uniform methods of competition in commerce, and unfair or deceptive acts or practices in commerce, are declared unlawful'. Violation of a commission 'cease and desist order', after it becomes final, subjects the violator to civil penalties up to $5,000 for each day the violation continues.

The respondents appealed. After lengthy hearings before an examiner for the commission in 1963, a further appeal and more hearings before the full Trade Commission of five members, a ruling was issued in October 1966. By a majority of three to two the commission decided that the Community Blood Bank and the hospitals, doctors and pathologists associated with it were illegally joined together in a conspiracy to restrain commerce in whole human blood.

Part of the Federal Trade Commission's case that blood was an article of commerce was based on arguments for extending the doctrine of implied warranty (fitness for use) in the financial interests of consumers – in short, to make it easier for them to sue doctors, hospitals, blood banks, laboratories and so forth. A doctor should, for example, be found guilty of negligence if he obtained human blood from a bank that failed to meet adequate standards; he 'should have known' that the hepatitis virus was present in the blood. This doctrine could be extended to all other areas of medical practice as well as to other service relationships. Non-profit hospitals would be regarded as engaged in trade or commerce for profit. Until 1964 hospitals, like churches, schools, colleges, universities, public libraries and charitable institutions not operated for profit, were exempt from the price discrimination provisions of the United States Code.

Costs of the Market System

The American Medical Association, in protesting the Federal Trade Commission ruling in the Kansas City case, warned hospitals and doctors to change their 'billing' practices and not to state the charge for blood as a separate charge. This proposal put the American Medical Association in a dilemma, however, for it struck at the basis of competition in private medical care and the association's own announced support of commercial blood banks in 1964. Other interests found themselves confronted with similar dilemmas. Pathologists and physicians working in privately owned clinical laboratories, for example, found themselves arguing against the profit motive. This was not a small group for, in 1967, 95 per cent of all clinical laboratories in the United States certified for participation in the Medicare programme were under commercial proprietary control. Most of them were approved for hematology tests. Commercial blood insurance companies, however, strongly supported the Federal Trade Commission's ruling in the interests of competition and 'sound business practices'. They were joined by sections of the pharmaceutical industry who did not wish to see commercial blood banking discouraged by 'restrictive practices'.

In January 1969 the Federal Trade Commission's ruling of 1966 in the Kansas City case was set aside by the Eighth United States Circuit Court of Appeals in Saint Louis. Up to the end of 1969 no appeal had been made to the Supreme Court.

Though this may be the end of this particular case, the fact that it happened is one illustration among many of the increasing commercialization of the blood banking system and of hospital and medical services in general. This trend must logically lead to more and more recourse to the laws and practices of the market place. There is no inconsistency in this development. If blood as a living human tissue is increasingly bought and sold as an article of commerce and profit accrues from such transactions, then it follows that the laws of commerce must, in the end, prevail. What this trend holds in store for the future of medicine in the United States as legally it is increasingly treated as a trade and as the doctrine of charitable immunity disappears into the mists of history is not a matter for this particular study. To consider all such legal ramifications would eventually lead us away from law and into the broader issues of medical ethics, the purpose of medicine and, ultimately, the value of human life.

Nevertheless, the choice of blood as an illustration and case study was no idle academic thought; it was deliberate. Short of examining humankind itself and the institution of slavery – of men and women as market commodities – blood as a living tissue may now constitute in Western societies one of the ultimate tests of where the 'social' begins and the 'economic' ends. If blood is considered in theory, in law and is treated in practice as a trading commodity, then ultimately human hearts, kidneys, eyes and other organs of the body may also come to be treated as commodities to be bought and sold in the market place.

Profitable competition for blood 'is a healthy thing', it is argued by some in the United States. It improves services, increases supplies of blood and is the answer to a 'shiftless, socialistic approach'. If competition for blood is eliminated, it is warned, it would 'be the entering wedge for the destruction of our entire anti-monopoly structure' and would threaten the interests of 'great pharmaceutical companies'.

In London, two authors, writing in a 1968 publication of the Institute of Economic Affairs, urged that payment of donors and competition for blood be introduced in Britain, where all blood is now given voluntarily, and where the incidence of tainted blood is virtually nil. Productivity would rise, the writers argue; supplies of blood would increase; 'a movement towards more efficiency in the blood market is a movement towards more efficiency in the economy as a whole'. The editor, Arthur Seldon, in a preface said that the authors 'have made an unanswerable case for a trial period in which the voluntary donor is supplemented by the fee-paid donor so that the results can be judged in practice, and not prejudged by doctrinaire obfuscation.'

In essence, these writers, American and British, are making an economic case against a monopoly of altruism in blood and other human tissues. They wish to set people free from the conscience of obligation. Although their arguments are couched in the language of price elasticity and profit maximization, they have far-reaching implications for human values and all 'social service' institutions. They legitimate, for instance, the great increase since 1967 in the number of commercial hospitals in the United States.

The moral issues that are raised extend far beyond theories of pricing and operations of the market place. Moreover, they involve the foundations of professional freedom in medical care and other service relationships with people, the concept of the hospital and the university as non-profit making institutions and the legal doctrine in the United States of charitable immunity. Charitable enterprises in that country would be subject under competitive conditions to the same laws of restraint and warranty and have the same freedoms as businessmen in the private market.

Is medical care – analyzed in its many component parts, such as blood transfusion services – a consumption good indistinguishable from other goods and services in the private economic market? What are the consequences, national and international, of treating human blood as a commercial commodity? If blood is morally sanctioned as something to be bought and sold, what ultimately is the justification for not promoting individualistic private markets in all other component areas of medical care, social work skills, the use of patients and clients for professional training and other 'social service' institutions and processes?

Where are the lines to be drawn – can indeed any lines at all be pragmatically drawn – if human blood be legitimated as a consumption good? To search for an identity and sphere of concern for social policy would thus be to search for the non-existent. All policy would become in the end economic policy, and the only values that would count are those that can be measured in terms of money and pursued in the dialectic of hedonism. To abolish the moral choice of giving to strangers could lead to an ideology to end all ideologies. This study, in one small sector of human affairs, disputes both the death of ideology and the philistine resurrection of economic man in social policy. It is thus concerned with the values we accord to people for what they give to strangers, not what they get out of society.

Note

First published in *Trans-action*, vol. 8, no. 3 (January, 1971).

CHAPTER

11

Social Policy and Economic Progress

As large scale industrialized societies get richer in material terms what is the future for social welfare? Shall we not all, or at any rate the vast majority, have incomes and assets large enough in the future to satisfy our social welfare needs in the private market without help from the state? Should not we have the right to decide our own individual resource preferences and priorities and buy from the private market our own quantities of education, medical care, housing, social security, mental health services, social work support and other services?

Such questions as these are being asked today in Britain; chiefly, I must say, by economists who are more cheerful professionals these days than they used to be when they were specialists in slump and depression, and laid claim to being the pre-eminent 'dismal scientists'. Similar questions are also being asked in Western Germany and in the United States, notably by the distinguished economist Milton Friedman[1] and his followers.

This is not, I would guess, the first time in history that the fundamental issue of the role of the state in the field of social welfare has been debated at the National Conference on Social Welfare; the conflict over individualism and collectivism developed long before the human race decided to invent the social worker. What is relatively new, and startlingly new, in the long history of man's preoccupation with poverty is the fact and the prospect of material abundance. We have only to compare the gross national products of the United States, Canada, Britain, Sweden, France, Western Germany and other industrialized countries in 1945 with the levels achieved in 1965 to realize how much richer as societies we have become in the short space of twenty years. Though there may be in the future as in the recent past periods of relative stagnation, nevertheless, on a long view our societies are steadily getting richer. Barring the utter disaster of international war, we have, therefore, to prepare ourselves and the next generation for living in very rich societies; rich in the possession of material goods and rich in leisure – or non-work time. In the next ten years, I am told, the American GNP is expected to rise to a trillion dollars.

What, then, is the future role of social policy? Is it to wither away as social welfare returns to its nineteenth-century residual function of custodial care for a small minority of the population? Are we to assume that the critical social problems of poverty, discrimination, unfreedom and violence that face our societies today will steadily disappear at the behest of economic growth and an expanding private market?

Some economic analysts in Britain noting, in recent years, the rise in national income and wealth have begun to present forcefully the case for the private market in education, medical care and social security.[2] Unlike their distinguished predecessors, they do not condemn these instruments of social policy as politically irrelevant or mistaken in the past. They are needed then as temporary *ad hoc* political mechanisms to ameliorate and reduce social conflict, to protect the rights of property, and to avoid resort to violence by the dispossessed and the deprived. This contemporary redefinition of the past role of social policy thus represents it as a form of social control; as a temporary, short term process of state intervention to buttress and legitimate industrial capitalism during its early, faltering but formative years of growth. Those, we are now told, who in the past were critical of state intervention in the guise of social policy were misguided and short-sighted. The Bourbons of today disavow the Bourbons of yesterday. The times, the concepts and the market have all changed. They have been changed by affluence, by technology and by the development of more sophisticated, anonymous and flexible mechanisms of the market to meet social needs, to enlarge the freedom of consumer choice and to provide not only more but better education, medical care, housing and social security.

In abbreviated form, these are some of the theories of private social policy now being advanced in Britain and, no doubt, by like-minded analysts in the United States. Paradoxically, at first sight, they have seized upon and welcomed the re-formulation of a 'negative income tax' (or tax allowances in reverse) extended to the poor and low wage earners. For the state to bring about in this way through the fiscal system a minimal degree of income redistribution should lead to a gradual disengagement from the direct provision of public services in kind, such as education, housing and medical care. If the poor are provided with a little more purchasing power their other needs should be treated as consumption goods to be purchased in the private market – so runs the argument.

Like other conceptions of social policy, presented in such large and all-embracing terms, this theory makes a number of assumptions about the future economic characteristics of our societies. These need to be examined; moreover, in the process of doing so, we may be helped to re-define the role of social policy in contemporary terms.

One fundamental assumption underlying this theory is that the present pattern of income and wealth differentials, which determine each individual's command over resources through time, will continue – and by implication should continue – in the future. It is accepted, of course, that absolute standards will rise for everyone; that the $3,000 family will become in x years and in real terms the $6,000 family (a doubling of purchasing power); the $100,000 family will become the $200,000 family, and so on. This assumption implies that the invisible resource allocation of the market will bring about, without the intervention of public policies, an equal proportional rise in living standards for all individuals and families. It further implies, as a social good, that the absolute differences should widen; that the gap between these two families in pre-tax incomes should double from $97,000 at present to $194,000 in the future. While this increase in inequality may, of course, be somewhat diminished by the effects of progressive taxation, there will occur, nonetheless, a sharp increase in the absolute gap unless taxation becomes far more sharply progressive in its impact than it is at present. Those who advocate this private market theory do not, however, call for a more progressive system of direct taxation. On the contrary, they argue for more tax cuts.

In short, according to this model of economic progress, within which is incorporated a declining role for social welfare, what is central is the promise of a doubling of the standard of living for everyone, including the poor. Poverty, as defined by the values and standards of 1966, will virtually disappear; meanwhile, the absolute differences in income and wealth will widen greatly. Economic models, for all their appearance of neutrality, may also be value judgment models.

A second fundamental assumption, which follows closely from the first assumption that the competitive market is and will continue to be an efficient and proportionately just allocator of resources, concerns the divergence between social costs and private costs. We know, in general, that the diseconomies and disservices involved in the production and consumption of goods do inflict damage on non-consumers and third parties – in such forms, for example, as urban blight, slum ghettos, air and river pollution, the destruction of aesthetic amenities, ill-health, industrial injuries, the invasion of privacy, and so on. Many of these damages and disservices to the 'quality of life', which may also involve harm to the values of honesty, self-development, creativity and respect for civil rights, represent non-economic variables which no statistician or economist has yet been able to quantify in dollars and pounds.

Similarly, while we may recognize the significance to human beings of the disutilities and disservices of technological and scientific changes, nevertheless, we still cannot adequately measure their effects. The social as well as the economic damages wrought by these changes are often borne by those who do not immediately benefit, and they may create new needs for more than one generation. Some of the more obvious and striking examples in this area of generational social cost benefit analysis are: the effects of automation on employment, on the obsolescence of acquired skills and on family stability; the impact of new scientific discoveries like thalidomide in generating a lifetime of personal dependency; the social, psychological and economic effects on those rejected as well as those accepted of rising standards of admission to educational systems, vocational and professional training, employment, promotion, occupational welfare, fringe benefits, middle-class housing areas, and even job corps programmes. Have we really any conception of the psychological effects on people of a continual process of social rejection and exclusion? Yet economic growth tends continuously to build ever higher these gateways to life and freedom of choice, and to widen the area over which credentialism rules;[3] the crowd outside finds it harder and harder to clamber over, squeeze through, or look over the top.

In all these sectors relating to the divergence between social costs and private costs created partly by the disutilities of progress there is in continual motion an extensive and complex system of redistribution in life chances and command over resources. It is largely an uncompensated area; almost wholly uncompensated by the competitive market and only to a limited extent by law and social policy through the agency of public assistance and other social security instruments, re-training and work programmes, public education, housing and social welfare programmes. The reasons for the lack of compensation for damages and disservices are many and various; they lie in our inability to identify the victims, to name and hold responsible the causal agents, and to measure in material terms the social costs of change and economic progress. Other and related reasons have to be sought in the realm of values; in the deeply held belief, for instance, that men who are poor and sick deserve to be poor and sick, and that those who are excluded from society merit exclusion. They are the social pathologies of other people's progress.

These two assumptions about the future concerning income and wealth differentials and social costs and private costs are, I suggest, implicit in the model of economic progress I have instanced – a model we might call the 'optimistic automated model'. It is a model which tends to create the impression that economic growth is a problem in economics alone. We thereby find ourselves, as Gross has remarked, saddled with a new form of Gresham's Law: monetary information – or dollar number magic – of *lesser* significance tends to displace other information which may be of *greater* significance.[4]

Three central questions can now, I think, be formulated. First, will economic growth in a competitive market situation result in fair shares for all in proportionate terms with social policy performing a role in the economy similar to the one it plays now? In other words, is there in the dynamics of growth in our societies a 'natural', evolutionary, inherent tendency toward equality of distribution? As we become richer do we become more equal?

Secondly, is this tendency (supposing, for the moment, that it exists) toward fair shares for all in the product of future growth strong enough to allow a run-down in the proportionate role of social policy as a redistributive agent? In other words, will a doubling of the real income of the poor as well as the rich in x years (if it should take place) make possible a progressive decline in the role of social welfare — quite apart from the issue as to whether such a decline is or is not desirable?

Now I come to my third question, the most difficult of all to project into space. What can we say about the future consequences and costs of economic growth and of scientific, technological and social change? How will these consequences and costs of change be distributed and borne, and to what extent will they (or indeed can they) be compensated for in a profit maximizing market? Can the market, for example, as an economic system resolve the problems of ethnic integration and accommodation? This is an important question now for Britain as well as for the United States.

What is indisputable is that in the last two decades the rate of change in highly industrialized societies has been rapid and pervasive, probably more rapid than in any similar period of time this century. There is, in general, no evidence that this rate of change is slowing down. It may even be expanding rapidly as more sophisticated techniques of production, distribution and supply are mastered and applied, and as medical science breaks new ground in the potential prevention of death and the prolongation of life. The addition of only five years to the existing biological life span for men as well as women, the poor as well as the rich, could present our societies with a set of immensely challenging problems.

With all that we now know, and recalling the enormous growth in scientific and technological research investment by Western society since the 1940s, it is reasonable to suppose that social and economic changes are likely to be as rapid — and probably more so — in the future as they have been in the recent past. Indeed, much of this research effort has not yet been generally applied in practice. Many years elapse before the full impact of research and innovation is experienced by the generality of individuals and families. It has also to be remembered, as Wilbert Moore has observed, that as the range of material technology and social strategies expands the net effects are additive or cumulative, despite the relatively rapid obsolescence of some procedures.[5]

This particular question concerning change is important for two reasons. First, the social costs of change rarely enter into the calculations and models of economists. They measure what they can more easily count. As yet, we cannot quantify in material terms social misery and ill-health, the effects of unemployment, slum life and Negro removal, the denial of education and civil rights, and the cumulative side effects from generation to generation of allowing cynicism and apathy to foster and grow. These are some of the costs which appear inescapably to accompany social and technical change. They are not embodied in any index of 'real' income per capita. We have, therefore, to remind ourselves continuously about their reality, partly because we happen to be living in a scientific age which tends to associate the measurable with the significant; to dismiss as intangible that which eludes measurement; and to reach conclusions on the basis of only those things which lend themselves to measurement.[6] Mathematical casework is not yet, I am glad to say, on the horizon.

Secondly, the facts of change are important because we need to ask questions about how these social costs – part of the *raison d'être* of social policy – are distributed, and may be distributed in the future, among the population by age, sex, family structure, ethnic group, income, and so forth. Is technological unemployment widely distributed or is it highly concentrated among certain groups? Who are the victims of depressed areas? Who bears the social costs of urban renewal or of 'grey area' life? The answers to these and similar questions are crucial for social policy, but, as yet, social scientists have been slow to develop techniques of analysis and indicators of positive and negative social growth. Different conclusions will be reached and different solutions required if the effects of change are widely experienced by rich and poor alike or if they are highly concentrated in certain social groups and areas.

At the heart of these speculations about the future distribution of social costs and the future of social policy lies the problem of stigma or 'spoiled identity', to use Goffman's phrase;[7] of felt and experienced discrimination and disapproval on grounds of moral behaviour, ethnic group, class, age, measured intelligence, mental fitness, or other criteria of selection–rejection. I believe that S. M. Miller was profoundly right when he wrote: 'The need in our society is for differentiation without stigma.'[8] There is, I think, no escaping the conclusion that if we are effectively to reach the poor we must differentiate and discriminate. We have to do so if we wish to channel proportionately more economic and social resources to aid the poor and the handicapped, and to compensate them as best we can for bearing part of the social costs of other people's progress.

The problem, then, is not whether to differentiate in access, treatment, giving and outcome but *how* to differentiate. What factors are or are not relevant? How in some respects can we treat equals unequally and in other respects unequals equally? We cannot now disengage ourselves from the challenge of distributing social rights without stigma; too many unfulfilled expectations have been created, and we can no longer fall back on the rationale that our economies are too poor to avoid hurting people.

This is, moreover, an issue which may well determine the future health of the professions – social work, medicine, education, nursing, public administration, and many others. They are, in many respects, the decision-makers of differentiation, the arbiters of welfare. To disengage themselves from the poor, as some social workers and physicians have tended to do in recent years,[9] is no answer for society. It could only mean, if such a trend continued, an ultimate decline in the ethical component in professional service.

But this is a controversial matter which cannot be pursued here. We must return to consider the questions and assumptions implicit in various economic models, an example of which is 'the optimistic automated model' I referred to earlier.

How valid are the assumptions, implicit and explicit, in such models? What evidence is there from the recent history of highly industrialized countries to confirm or refute these assumptions? Such questions can now be properly asked; for similar, though perhaps less sophisticated, models of economic progress played a powerful role in the shaping of policies fifteen to twenty years ago in both the United States and Britain.

I propose briefly to re-examine them; for the history of successful and unsuccessful essays in 'prediction' in the past may help us to construct more viable models for the future. At the very least, we may learn something from our failures that will help us to understand the nature of our societies and the process of change.

Around 1950 a number of propositions concerning economic growth and the role of social policy gained wide acceptance in Britain. It was said that:

(1) Inequalities in the distribution of income and wealth were diminishing at a substantial rate.

(2) Poverty would soon be virtually abolished (apart from a residual minority of incorrigibles and incompetents) under the impact of economic growth, full employment, and the redistributive effects of the social services (more vaguely described as the 'Welfare State').

(3) Educational outcomes (or achievements) as well as opportunities were rapidly widening for all classes and income groups in the population.

(4) Within a decade or so the housing problem would be largely solved, the slums abolished, and the objective of a 'decent home for every family' achieved.

(5) As a consequence of these changes, and with the added effects of a free National Health Service ('socialized medicine'), income and social class differences in mortality and morbidity would soon dissolve.

It would be wrong to describe these as scientific predictions. They were not; but they did enter into the attempts of economists and policy-makers to estimate the future of the economy, and they are representative of a large body of genuine opinion at that time. Underlying them was the assumption of a declining role for social policy in the foreseeable future.

Similar opinions were current in the United States at about the same time, though less emphasis than in Britain was given to the issue of social stratification in education and other spheres since it was believed that the United States was a more mobile, egalitarian society. The first chairman of the Council of Economic Advisers under the Eisenhower Administration reflected these opinions about the efficiency of economic growth as a just allocator of resources when he said in 1951 (before his appointment to the

Council): 'The transformation in the distribution of our national income ... may already be counted as one of the great social revolutions in history.'[10]

Economic growth spelled progress – an evolutionary and inevitable American faith that social growth would accompany economic growth. Automatically, therefore, poverty would gracefully succumb to the diffusion of abundance. All this heralded, as Daniel Bell wrote ten years later, the end of 'ideological conflict'.[11]

Since the end of the 1940s our societies have indeed prospered. Economic growth has occurred on a scale and at a rate which few experts were prepared to suggest as targets fifteen years ago. What, then, has gone wrong?

Let us suppose, for one brief moment, that we are all back at the census year 1951, looking younger, just as intelligent, but wearing clothes which would now seem a little odd. Let us further suppose that we are convinced by our economists and policy-makers that the United States and Britain would be much wealthier societies in material terms within fifteen years. How many of us would then have dared to suggest that in 1966 one American child in four would be regarded as living in poverty and three elderly persons in ten would also be living in poverty;[12] that American society would be moving toward a more unequal distribution of income and wealth;[13] that many gray areas would have become ghettos;[14] that a nationwide civil rights challenge of explosive magnitude would have to be faced – a challenge for freedom, for the right to work, for a decent home, for medical care, and against stigma;[15] that, as a nation, the United States would be seriously short of physicians, scientists, teachers, social workers, nurses, welfare aides, and professional workers in almost all categories of personal service; and that it would be importing physicians, nurses, scientists, engineers, and other categories of human capital from many less affluent nations of the world?

In Britain, in 1951, there were few who would have thought that in the years ahead the proportion of children and old people considered to be living in poverty would increase;[16] that incomes would become more unequal;[17] that the distribution of personal wealth would be found to be more highly concentrated in the top 5 per cent of the population (and much more highly concentrated than in the United States);[18] that there would be no narrowing of differentials between working-class and middle-class children in the higher sectors of the educational system;[19] that the immigration of about 750,000 'coloured' people from the Commonwealth (or less than 2 per cent of the population) would result in illiberal policies and discrimination;[20] and that, like the United States, Britain would also be facing serious shortages of physicians, nurses, teachers, social workers, town planners, and many other categories of professional workers.

These trends have occurred in both our countries in a period of not only unprecedented economic advances but of progressive developments in certain sectors of social policy: significantly, in education and social security in the United States; significantly, in medical care, employment and national (public) assistance in Britain. Had social policies been less influential during these years; had there been less intervention by government (as some social analysts had advocated in the early 1950s) then, I believe, the trend toward inequality would have been more marked.

These are some of the lessons of history. They could, of course, be more fully described and documented; for there has been, particularly in the United States, a veritable explosion in recent years of research, demonstrations, projects, reports, and books on poverty and social deprivation. The poor are showing a remarkable tolerance about their re-emergence on the national stage as subjects for investigation, inquiry and doctoral theses.

One thing I am sure we are doing by all these searchings into poverty is to raise expectations – expectations of freedom from want, stigma, ignorance and social exclusion. If we are not to fail our fellow citizens again we might do worse than ponder on some of these 'lessons of the last fifteen years of welfare'. Perhaps I might make a start by offering a few generalizations about our past errors of omission and commission.

In the climate of political and social thought around the early 1950s there was a tendency to underestimate the significance for the future of social policy of a number of major forces and trends.

(1) We underestimated the extent and rate of obsolescence of much of our social capital (houses, schools, hospitals, universities, welfare offices, public buildings, and so forth).

(2) We underestimated the rate and effects of change, scientific, technological and economic, and thus we ignored or greatly minimized the impact of social costs on the

poor, the unskilled and the underprivileged.

(3) We underestimated the effects on people of stigma, discrimination, and the denial of civil rights (see, for example, Hughes's critique of sociology for failing to foresee the coming of the civil rights movement in the United States).[21]

(4) We underestimated the cumulative forces and effects of selection through the educational system, the labour market and the housing market; in other words, we failed to conceptualize the process of cumulative causation in these areas of deprivation.

(5) We underestimated the extent of poverty and oversimplified its definition and causal origins.

But while we seriously underestimated the importance of some factors we greatly exaggerated the likely effect of others:

(1) We overestimated the potentialities of economic growth by itself alone to solve the problems of poverty, economic, educational and social.

(2) We exaggerated the trend toward equality during the Second World War in respect to income, employment and other factors – as we persistently have done for the last half century – and optimistically projected short term trends into the future.

(3) We exaggerated the effects of welfare programmes on incentives to work and moral values in general, and helped to create what we feared by nourishing systems of 'policing' and 'punishment'.

(4) We overestimated the capacity of professional organizations, particularly in medicine and social work, to expand recruitment and training to meet present and future demands.

(5) We overestimated the potentialities of the poor, without help, to understand and manipulate an increasingly complex *ad hoc* society, and we failed to understand the indignities of expecting the poor to identify themselves as poor people and to declare, in effect, 'I am an unequal person'.

(6) We greatly exaggerated the capacity of the competitive private market to resolve social problems and to meet needs

on the principle of differentiation without stigma.

(7) Lastly, and perhaps most significant of all, we have sought too diligently to find the causes of poverty among the poor and not in ourselves. Poverty, we seem to have been saying, has its origins *either* in social pathology and a lack of self-determination *or* in agency delinquency and a failure in co-ordination *or* in the shortage of social workers and psychiatrists. Now, in the poverty programme, the United States appears to be discovering a new set of causal explanations – the lack of political power amongst the poor themselves. 'The fault, dear Brutus, is not in our stars, but in ourselves, that we are underlings.'

The historical study of the concept of social policy has, I believe, something to offer us. If there is any validity in these generalizations they suggest that our frame of reference in the past has been too narrow. Thought, research and action have been focused too heavily on the poor; poverty engineering has thus been abstracted from society. Social policy has been seen as an *ad hoc* appendage to economic growth, the provision of benefits, not the formulation of rights.

If we are in the future to include the poor in our societies we shall have to widen our frames of reference. We shall need to shift the emphasis from poverty to inequality, from *ad hoc* programmes to integrated social rights, from economic growth to social growth.

And what, in the end, do I mean by 'social growth'? When our societies are spending proportionately more on the educationally deprived than on the educationally normal; when the re-housing of the poor is proceeding at a greater rate than the re-housing of the middle classes; when proportionately more medical care is being devoted to the needs of the long term chronically sick than to those of the average sick; when more social workers are moving into public programmes than into private child guidance clinics; when there are smaller differentials in incomes and assets between rich and poor, coloured and pink families.

These are a few among many of the quantifiable indicators of social growth that we could take pride in, the new status symbols of an 'affluent society'.

Notes

Lecture delivered at the American National Conference on Social Welfare in Chicago, USA, in May 1966, and published in *The Social Welfare Forum* (official proceedings) (New York: Columbia University Press, 1966).

1 Friedman, M., *Capitalism and Freedom* (Chicago: University of Chicago Press, 1962).

2 See, for example, Lees, D. S., 'Health through choice', in R. Harris, *Freedom or Free-for-all?*, Hobart Papers, vol. 3 (London: The Institute of Economic Affairs, 1965), and West, E. G., *Education and the State* (London: The Institute of Economic Affairs, 1965).

3 For example, at present in the United States between 150,000,000 and 250,000,000 copies of several thousand different standardized ability tests – IQ, aptitude and achievement – are administered annually by schools, colleges, government agencies, business firms and the military services. See Goslin, D. A., *The Search for Ability* (New York: Russell Sage Foundation, 1965) p. 13.

4 Gross, B. M., 'The social state of the union', *Trans-Action*, vol. 3, no. 1, (1965), p. 15.

5 Moore, W. E., *Social Change* (Englewood Cliffs, NJ: Prentice-Hall, 1963), p. 2.

6 This is true even though many of the things which are measured and included in national accounts and tax reports contain a great amount of statistical error and guesswork. See 1966 reports on tax assessments in California, *The Economist*, 5 March 1966, p. 901; Morgenstern, O., *On the Accuracy of Economic Observation* (Princeton University Press, 1963), and Titmuss, R. M., *Income Distribution and Social Change* (London: Allen & Unwin, 1962).

7 Goffman, E., *Stigma: Notes on the Management of Spoiled Identity* (Englewood Cliffs, NJ: Prentice-Hall, 1963).

8 Miller, S. M., 'The search for an educational revolution', in C. W. Hunnicut (ed.), *Urban Education and Cultural Deprivation* (Syracuse, NY: Syracuse University Press, 1965).

9 See, for example, Cloward, R. A., 'Social problems, social definitions and social opportunities', National Council on Crime and Delinquency (New York, 1963), mimeographed; Titmuss, R. M., 'The ethics and economics of medical care', *Medical Care*, vol. 1, no. 1 (1963), pp. 16–22.

10 Quoted in Miller, H. T., 'Is the income gap closed? "No" ', New York *Times Magazine*, 11 November 1962, p. 50.

11 Bell, D., *The End of Ideology: on the Exhaustion of Political Ideas in the Fifties* (New York: Collier Books, 1961).

12 Orshansky, M., 'Children of the poor', *Social Security Bulletin*, vol. 26, no. 7 (1963), pp. 3–13; Orshansky, 'Counting the poor: another look at the poverty profile', *ibid.*, vol. 28, no. 1 (1965), pp. 1–29; Orshansky, 'Who's who among the poor: a demographic view of poverty', *ibid.*, vol. 28, no. 7 (1965), pp. 13–32.

13 Brady, D. S., *Age and the Income Distribution*, Research Report no. 8, Social

Security Administration, US Department of Health, Education and Welfare, 1965. For other evidence on recent trends see Miller, S. M., and Rein, Martin, 'Poverty, inequality and policy' in H. S. Becker (ed.), *Social Problems* (New York: John Wiley, 1967).

14 See Hunter, D. R., *The Slums: Challenge and Response* (New York: Free Press of Glencoe, 1964); Gans, H., *The Urban Villagers* (New York: Free Press of Glencoe, 1962); Taeuber, K. E., 'Residential segregation', *Scientific American*, 213 (1965), p. 12, and Taeuber, K. E., and Taeuber, Alma F., *Negroes in Cities: Residential Segregation and Neighborhood Change* (Chicago: Aldine, 1965).

15 Office of Policy Planning and Research, US Department of Labor, *The Negro Family: the Case for National Action* (Washington, DC, 1965).

16 Abel-Smith, B., and Townsend, P., *The Poor and the Poorest* (London: Bell and Sons, 1965).

17 *Ibid.*; Nicholson, J. L., *Redistribution of income in the United Kingdom* (London: Bowes and Bowes, 1965), and Titmuss, R. M., *Income Distribution and Social Change* (London: Allen & Unwin, 1962).

18 Revell, J. R. S., 'Changes in the social distribution of property in Britain during the twentieth century', in Proceedings of the Third International Economic History Conference, 1965.

19 Moser, C. A., *Inequalities in Educational Opportunities* (London: London School of Economics, 1965).

20 White Paper, *Immigration from the Commonwealth* (London: HMSO, Cmnd 2739, 1965).

21 Hughes, E. C., 'Race relations and the sociological imagination', *American Sociological Review*, 28, (1963), 879–90.

— 12 —

The Role of Redistribution in Social Policy

In the literature of the West, concepts and models of social policy are as diverse as contemporary concepts of poverty. Historically, the two have indeed had much in common. They certainly share diversity. There are today those at one end of the political spectrum who see social policy as a transitory minimum activity of minimum government for a minimum number of poor people; as a form of social control for minority groups in a 'natural' society; as a way of resolving the conflict between the religious ethic of compassion and undiluted individualism. In this view social policy is not good business. Statistical estimates of the national income per capita look healthier if the infant mortality rate rises. At the other end of the political spectrum there are writers like Macbeath who has comprehensively stated that 'Social policies are concerned with the right ordering of the network of relationships between men and women who live together in societies, or with the principles which should govern the activities of individuals and groups so far as they affect the lives and interests of other people.'[1]

Somewhere between these extreme visionary notions lives a conventional, textbook definition of social policy.[2] The social services or social welfare, the labels we have for long attached to describe certain areas of public intervention such as income maintenance and public health, are seen as the main ingredients of social policy. They are obvious, direct and measurable acts of government, undertaken for a variety of political reasons, to provide for a range of needs, material and social, and predominantly dependent needs, which the market does not or cannot satisfy for certain designated sections of the population. Typically, these direct services are functionally organized in separate and specialized ministries, departments or divisions of government, central and local. They are seen as the 'social policy departments'. What they do is thought to be explicitly redistributive; they politically interfere with the pattern of claims set by the market. They assign claims from one set of people who are said to produce or earn the national product to another set of people who may merit compassion and charity but not economic rewards for productive service. In short, they are seen as uncovenanted benefits for the poorer sections of the community. And because these separate functional units of social service are accountable to the public their activities are, in large measure, quantifiable. We can thus measure the size of the presumed burden (as it is conventionally called) on the economy.

This, I propose to argue, is a very limited and inadequate model of the working of social policy in the second half of the twentieth century. In its distance from the realities of today it is about as helpful (or unhelpful) as some recent models of economic man maximizing his acquisitive drives. Later, I attempt to support and illustrate this statement by examining some of the lessons of experience of nearly twenty years of so-called 'welfare statism' in Britain. First, however, I want briefly to consider one or two of the factors which have contributed to this limited concept of social policy – particularly in relation to its role as a redistributive agent.

Perhaps the most important causative factor in Britain has to do with the heritage of the poor law (or public assistance). Less than sixty years ago social policy was, in the eyes of the middle and upper classes, poor law policy. This model of 'welfare use' was part of a political philosophy which saw society as an adjunct of the market.[3] As Karl Polanyi puts it, 'instead of economy being embedded in social relations, social relations are embedded in the economic system'.[4] The essential, though financially reluctant, role of the poor law was to support industrialism and the attempt in the nineteenth century to support a completely competitive, self-regulating market economy founded on the motive of individual gain. It thus had to create a great many rules of expected behaviour; about work and non-work, property, savings, family relationships, cohabitation, men in the house, and so forth.[5] Poverty, as Disraeli once said, was declared a crime by industrialism. Laws about poverty became associated with laws about crime.

This system, which legally survived in Britain until 1948, inevitably involved personal discrimination. The stigmata of the poor law test, moral judgments by people about other people and their behaviour, were a condition of redistribution. The requirements of poor law and public assistance administration were, we can now see, remarkably attuned to the characteristics of bureaucracy drawn by Weber and others.[6] It was theoretically a neat and orderly world of eligible and ineligible citizens; of approved and disapproved patterns of dependency; of those who could manage change and those who could not. From its operation for over a century Britain inherited in 1948 a whole set of administrative attitudes, values and rites; essentially middle class in structure; and moralistic in application. The new social service bottles of 1948 had poured into them much of the old wine of discrimination and prejudice. It has taken nearly two decades of sustained programmes of new recruitment, training and re-training and intraining, and the appointment of social workers to the public services, to eradicate part of this legacy of administrative behaviour.[7]

The history of the poor law and public assistance is thus still important to an understanding of social policy concepts today. If one disregards the social costs of industrialism, of allowing a large part of the disservices of technological progress to lie where they fall, then the system (of public assistance) was clearly redistributive. It directly benefited the explicit poor. Those in the greatest need did receive some benefit. But with the limited instruments of policy and administrative techniques to hand in the past, the system could only function by operating punitive tests of discrimination; by strengthening conceptions of approved and disapproved dependencies; and by a damaging assault on the recipients of welfare in terms of their sense of self-respect and self-determination. Within the established pattern of commonly held values, the system could only be redistributive by being discriminatory and socially divisive.

All this is now well documented in the archives of social inquiry and is somewhat ancient history. Equally well known is the story of society's response to the challenge of poverty during the past thirty years or so: the discovery that this system of public aid was administratively grossly inefficient; the discovery that it could not by its very nature absorb the new dimensions of social and psychological knowledge and that, therefore, it could not function effectively both as a redistributive agent and as an agent to prevent social breakdown; and the discovery that the system was fundamentally inconsistent with the need to grant to all citizens, irrespective of race, religion or colour, full and equal social rights.[8]

Gradually in Britain, as we tried to learn these lessons, we began to discard the use of discriminatory and overtly redistributive services for second class citizens. The social services on minimum standards for all citizens crept apologetically into existence. In common with other countries we invented contributory national insurance or social security and provided benefits as of right. The actuary was called in to replace the functions of the public assistance relieving officer. Free secondary education for all children, irrespective of the means of their parents, was enacted in 1944 as part of a comprehensive educational system. Public housing authorities were called upon in 1945 to build houses for people and not just for working-class people. A limited and second class health insurance scheme for working men was transformed, in 1948, into a comprehensive and free-on-demand health service for the whole population.[9]

All these and many other changes in the direct and publicly accountable instruments of social policy led to the notion that, in the year 1948, the 'Welfare State' had been established in Britain. While there was general political consensus on this matter there was, on the other hand, much confusion and debate about cause and effect.[10] There were many, for instance, who thought that these policy changes were brought about for deliberately redistributive reasons and that the effects would be significantly egalitarian. This, perhaps, was understandable. Direct welfare in the past had in fact been redistributive (considered apart from the effects of the fiscal system). Therefore it was natural to assume that more welfare in the future would mean more redistribution in favour of the poor. There were others however (among whom I count myself) who believed that the fundamental and dominating historical processes which led to these major changes in social policy were connected with the demand for one society; for non-discriminatory services for all without distinction of class, income or race; for services and relations which would deepen and enlarge self-respect; for services which would manifestly encourage social integration. From some perspectives these major changes in policy could be regarded as ideological pleas to the middle- and upper-income classes to share in the benefits (as well as the costs) of public welfare.

Built into the public model of social policy in Britain since 1948 there are two major roles or objectives: the redistributive objective and the non-discriminatory objective. To move towards the latter it was believed that a prerequisite was the legal enactment of universal (or comprehensive) systems of national insurance, education, medical care, housing and other direct services.

What have we learnt in the past fifteen years about the actual functioning of these services? What has universalism in social welfare achieved? Clearly, I cannot give you a full account of all aspects of this development during a period when, for thirteen of these years, the government in power was not, in the early stages at least, entirely committed to the concept of the 'Welfare State'. I shall therefore concentrate my conclusions, brief and inadequate though they are, on the theme of redistribution.

Up to this point I have dealt only with what I sometimes call the 'iceberg phenomena of social welfare'. That is, the direct public provision of services in kind (e.g. education and medical care) and the direct payment of benefits in cash (e.g. retirement pensions and family allowances).

I now turn to consider two other major categories of social policy which have been developing and extending their roles in Britain and other countries over much the same period of time as the category we call 'the social services'. Elsewhere, I have described the former as 'fiscal welfare' and 'occupational welfare'.[11] These are the indirect or submerged parts of the 'iceberg of social policy'. In both categories a remarkable expansion has taken place in Britain during the past twenty years.

All three categories of social policy have a great deal in common in terms of redistribution. They are all concerned with changing the individual and family pattern of current and future claims on resources set by the market, set by the possession of accumulated past rights, and set by the allocations made by government to provide for national defence and other non-market sectors. Social welfare changes the patterns of claims by, for instance, directly providing in kind education or mental hospital care either free or at less than the market cost. Fiscal welfare changes the pattern of claims by taking less in tax (and thus increasing net disposable income) when a taxpayer's child is born, when its education is prolonged, when men have ex-wives to maintain, when taxpayers reach a specified age, and so on. An individual's pattern of claims on resources is today greatly varied through fiscal welfare policy by his or her change in circumstances, family responsibilities and opportunities available (and taken) for prolonged education, home ownership and so on. In Britain, the United States and other countries the tax system has recently been regarded as an alternative in certain areas to the social security system; as a policy instrument to be used to provide higher incomes for the aged, for large families, for the blind and other handicapped groups, and for meeting part of the costs of education which today may last for up to twenty years or more.[12]

Occupational welfare, provided by virtue of employment status, achievement and record, may take the form of social security provisions in cash or in kind. Such provisions are legally approved by government and, as in the case of fiscal welfare, they may be seen as alternatives to extensions in social welfare. Their costs falls in large measure on the whole population. It is thus, like social welfare and fiscal welfare, a major redistributive mechanism.

In Britain, occupational welfare may include: pensions for employees; survivors' benefits; child allowances; death benefits; health and welfare services; severance pay and compensation for loss of office (analogous these days to compensation for loss of property rights); personal expenses for travel, entertainment and dress; meal vouchers; cars and season tickets; residential accommodation; holiday expenses; children's school fees at private schools; sickness benefits; medical expenses; education and training grants and benefits ranging from 'obvious forms of realizable goods to the most intangible forms of amenity'[13] expressed in a form that is neither money nor convertible into money.

A substantial part of these occupational welfare benefits can be interpreted – again like fiscal welfare – as social policy recognition of dependencies; the long dependencies of old age, childhood and widowhood, and such short term dependencies as sickness and the loss of job rights.

The populations to which these three categories of welfare relate differ, but a substantial section of people may be eligible for benefits in respect of all three. In Britain, most of the social welfare services (except national assistance and university education) are universalist and citizen based; they are open to all without a test of means. Thus, access to them does not depend upon achieved or inherited status. Fiscal welfare relates to a smaller population; only to those who pay direct taxes and not those who pay property taxes and social security contributions. Occupational welfare relates to the employed population and, at present, predominantly favours white-collar and middle-class occupations. Benefits are thus related to achievement.

All three categories of welfare are, as we have seen, redistributive; they change the pattern of claims on current and future resources. They function redistributively as separate, self-contained systems and they do so also in relation to the whole economy. Here is one example. Many private pension schemes, which include manual and non-manual workers, tend to redistribute claims on resources from lower paid to higher paid employees. This happens because the lower paid workers change jobs more frequently; in doing so they do not have credited to them the full amount of pension contributions or premiums. It is estimated in Britain that the cost of full preservation of pension rights for all employees in the private sector (an objective in the present government's proposals for the reform of social security) could add 15 to 25 per cent to the actuarial costs of private schemes.[14] Moreover, as at present organized, the cost to the Treasury (the whole community) of private pension schemes substantially exceeds the Treasury contribution to social security pensions for the whole population. The pensions of the rich are more heavily subsidized by the community than the pensions of the poor.[15]

This in part happens because occupational welfare and fiscal welfare benefits are fundamentally based on the principles of achievement, status and need. If there is need, then the higher the income the higher is the welfare benefit. By contrast, social welfare benefits generally take account only of needs – the need for medical care, for education and so on irrespective of income or status.

213

I have now described in very general terms three categories of social policy redistribution – with particular reference to their operation in Britain. At present, they are publicly viewed as virtually distinct systems. What goes on within and as a result of one system is ignored by the others. They are appraised, criticized or applauded as abstracted, independent entities. Historically, they have developed different concepts of poverty or subsistence; different criteria for determining approved dependencies; different standards of moral values in determining eligibility for welfare. Some examples will illustrate this point.

The social policy definition of subsistence as developed in the fiscal system for determining exemption from taxation, income needs in old age, and so on, differs markedly from the definition used in public assistance.[16] In some areas of policy the fiscal definition of poverty is employed – as, for instance, in determining grants to university students.[17] In other and similar areas of policy the public assistance definition is employed – as, for instance, in determining aid for poor parents of 16-year-old children at school.[18] It is odd, when you come to think about it, that dependency at age 16 is assessed at a lower standard of assistance than dependency at 18 or even 23 (in the case of medical students and graduates).

We have in fact two standards of poverty for determining aid from the community; both highly subjective and unscientific; both employed to assist dependent states; a working-class standard and a middle-class standard. The former has been investigated, studied, measured and argued about for long by sociologists, social workers and economists, and made the subject of many books and doctoral theses. By contrast, the latter has been virtually ignored.

One further example of double standards operating in different categories of welfare may be selected from a large field – this one to illustrate the role of moral values in social policy.

In the category of social welfare, cash aid, from public funds for unsupported mothers and their children may be stopped if it is believed that cohabitation is taking place. This is an event – or a relationship – that can rarely be legally proved. It is hardly a scientific fact. We have in Britain a cohabitation regulation;[19] you have a man in the house regulation.[20] They amount to the same thing; they cannot be spelt out in precise operational terms. Their

214

application in practice depends in large measure, therefore, on hearsay and moral judgment.

The same problem of to give or not to give aid arises in the category of fiscal welfare. As an example I quote from a memorandum by Lord Justice Hodson to a Royal Commission on Marriage and Divorce: 'A super-tax payer may, and quite frequently nowadays does, have a number of wives living at the same time since after divorce his ex-wives are not treated as one with him for tax purposes he can manage quite nicely since he is permitted' (a social policy decision) 'to deduct all his wives' maintenance allowances from his gross income for tax purposes leaving his net income comparatively slightly affected.'[21]

In both instances redistribution takes place; the community renders aid in these situations of need and dependency. But while the decision to help the public assistance mother may involve judgments about moral behaviour, in the case of the taxpayer the decision is automatic and impersonal. The logic of the double standard is not apparent. If one is socially acceptable and approved behaviour then why not the other?

Now I must begin to draw these reflections together. What have been the lessons of experience in Britain about the actual functioning of these three categories of welfare during the past fifteen years? Obviously, I cannot give you more than a fragment of an answer, and even this involves over-simplifying to a dangerous degree. To analyse and measure the redistributive effects of this process of the social division of welfare would be an immensely complex task – even if the essential statistical data were available which, in many areas, they are not. All I can offer are a few generalized conclusions.

The major positive achievement which has resulted from the creation of direct, universalist social services in kind has been the erosion of formal discriminatory barriers. One publicly approved standard of service, irrespective of income, class or race, replaced the double standard which invariably meant second class services for second class citizens. This has been most clearly seen in the National Health Service. Despite strict controls over expenditure on the Service by Conservative governments for many years it has maintained the principle of equality of access by all citizens to all branches of medical care. Viewed solely in terms of the welfare objective of non-discriminatory, non-judgmental service this is the signal achievement of the National Health Service. In part this is due to the fact that the middle classes, invited to enter the Service in 1948, did so and have since largely stayed with the Service. They have not contracted out of socialized medical care as they have done in other fields like secondary education and retirement pensions. Their continuing participation, and their more articulate demands for improvements, have been an important factor in a general rise in standards of service – particularly in hospital care.[22]

But, as some students of social policy in Britain and the United States are beginning to learn, equality of access is not the same thing as equality of outcome. We have to ask statistical and sociological questions about the utilization of the high cost quality sectors of social welfare and the low cost sectors of social welfare. We have to ask similar questions about the ways in which professional people (doctors, teachers, social workers and many others) discharge their roles in diagnosing need and in selecting or rejecting patients, clients and students for this or that service. In the modern world, the professions are increasingly becoming the arbiters of our welfare fate; they are the key-holders to equality of outcome; they help to determine the pattern of redistribution in social policy.

These generalizations apply particularly when services in kind are organized on a universalist, free-on-demand basis. When this is so we substitute, in effect, the professional decision-maker for the crude decisions of the economic market place. And we also make much more explicit – an important gain in itself – the fact that the poor have great difficulties in manipulating the wider society, in managing change, in choosing between alternatives, in finding their way around a complex world of welfare.

We have learnt from fifteen years' experience of the Health Service that the higher income groups know how to make better use of the Service; they tend to receive more specialist attention; occupy more of the beds in better equipped and staffed hospitals; receive more elective surgery; have better maternity care, and are more likely to get psychiatric help and psychotherapy than low income groups – particularly the unskilled.[23]

These are all factors which are essential to an understanding of the redistributive role played by one of the major direct welfare services in kind. They are not arguments against a comprehensive

216

free-on-demand service. But they do serve to underline one conclusion. Universalism in social welfare, though a needed prerequisite towards reducing and removing formal barriers of social and economic discrimination, does not by itself solve the problem of how to reach the more-difficult-to-reach with better medical care, especially preventive medical care.

Much the same kind of general conclusion can be drawn from Britain's experience in the field of education. Despite reforms and expansion during the past fifteen years it is a fact that the proportion of male undergraduates who are the sons of manual workers is today about 1 per cent lower than it was between 1928 and 1947. Although we have doubled the number of university students the proportion coming from working-class homes has remained fairly constant at just over a quarter.[24]

The major beneficiaries of the high cost sectors of the educational system in the 'Welfare State' have been the higher income groups. They have been helped to so benefit by the continued existence of a prosperous private sector in secondary education (partly subsidized by the state in a variety of ways including tax deductibles), and by developments since 1948 in provisions for child dependency in the category of fiscal welfare.[25] Take, for example, the case of two fathers each with two children, one earning $60,000 a year, the other $1,500 a year. In combining the effect of direct social welfare expenditures for children and indirect fiscal welfare expenditures for children the result is that the rich father now gets thirteen times more from the state than the poor father in recognition of the dependent needs of childhood.

Housing is another field of social policy which merits analysis from the point of view of redistribution. Here we have to take account of the complex interlocking effects of local rate payments, public housing subsidies, interest rates, tax deductibles for mortgage interest and other factors. When we have done so we find that the subsidy paid by the state to many middle-class families buying their own homes is greater than that received by poor tenants of public housing (local government) schemes.[26]

These are no more than illustrations of the need to study the redistributive effects of social policy in a wider frame of reference. Hitherto, our techniques of social diagnosis and our conceptual frameworks have been too narrow. We have compartmentalized social welfare as we have compartmentalized the poor. The analytic model of social policy that has been fashioned on only the phenomena that are clearly visible, direct and immediately measurable is an inadequate one. It fails to tell us about the realities of redistribution which are being generated by the processes of technological and social change and by the combined effects of social welfare, fiscal welfare and occupational welfare.

How far and to what extent should redistribution take place through welfare channels on the principle of achieved status, inherited status or need? This is the kind of question which, fundamentally, is being asked in Britain today. And it is being directed, in particular, at two major areas of social policy – social security and housing. Both these instruments of change and redistribution have been neglected for a decade or more. We have gone in search of new gods or no gods at all. It is time we returned to consider their roles afresh and with new vision. Perhaps we might then entitle our journey 'Ways of extending the Welfare State to the poor'.

Notes

Lecture delivered to the staff of the Social Security Administration Department of Health, Education and Welfare, Washington, USA, in December 1964, and published in Social Security Bulletin, Washington, June 1965.

1 Macbeath, A., *Can Social Policies be Rationally Tested?* (London: Oxford University Press, 1957).
2 For some discussion on the problems of definition see Wilensky, H. L., and Lebeaux, C. N., *Industrial Society and Social Welfare* (New York: Russell Sage Foundation, 1958); *Social Welfare Statistics of the Northern Countries* Report no. 9 (Stockholm: 1964); Myrdal, G., *Beyond the Welfare State* (Yale University Press, 1960), and Titmuss, R. M., *Essays on the 'Welfare State'* (London: Allen & Unwin, 1958).
3 See, for example, Dicey, A. V., *Law and Opinion in England during the Nineteenth Century* (London, 1905).
4 Polanyi, K., *Origins of our Time* (London: Beacon Paperbacks, no. 45, 1945), p. 63.
5 *Reports of the Royal Commission on the Poor Laws* (London: HMSO, 1909).
6 Gerth, H. H., and Mills, C. W., *From Max Weber: Essays in Sociology* (New York: Oxford University Press, 1946).
7 See, for example, *Annual Reports of the National Assistance Board, 1950–63* (London: HMSO) and *Seventh and Eighth Reports on the Work of the Children's Department*, Home Office (London: HMSO, 1955 and 1961).

8   Illustrated in the recommendations of the Beveridge Report, *Social Insurance and Allied Services*, Cmd 6404 (London: HMSO, 1942).

9   Hall, M. P., *The Social Services of Modern England* (London: Routledge, 1952).

10   Titmuss, R. M., *Income Distribution and Social Change*, ch. 9 (London: Allen & Unwin, 1962).

11   Titmuss, R. M., *Essays on the 'Welfare State'*, (2nd ed., London: Allen & Unwin, 1963).

12   *Reports of the Royal Commission on the Taxation of Profits and Income*, 1952–5 (London: HMSO, 1955).

13   *Final Report of the Royal Commission on Taxation*, Cmd 9474 (London: HMSO, 1955), p. 68. See also Rubner, A., *Fringe Benefits*, (London: Putnam, 1962).

14   See references in Titmuss, R. M., *Income Distribution and Social Change*, ch. 7, and *British Tax Review*, January–February 1964.

15   Titmuss, R. M., *The Irresponsible Society*, Fabian Tract 323 (London, 1959), chapter 3 in this volume.

16   *Reports of the Royal Commission on the Taxation of Profits and Income*, 1952–5 (London: HMSO, 1955).

17   Ministry of Education, *Grants to Students*, Cmd 1051 (London: HMSO, 1960).

18   *Report of the Working Party on Educational Maintenance Allowances* (London: HMSO, 1957).

19   National Insurance Act, 1946, section 17 (2), and *Digest of Commissioner's Decisions* (London: HMSO, 1946–64).

20   See *Report of the Public Welfare Crisis Committee*, Metropolitan Washington Chapter of the National Association of Social Workers (Washington, 1963).

21   Hodson, J., *Royal Commission on Marriage and Divorce*, MDP/1952/337 (London: HMSO, 1952).

22   Lindsey, A., *Socialized Medicine in England and Wales* (University of North Carolina Press, 1962).

23   Titmuss, R. M., *Essays on the 'Welfare State'*, App. on the National Health Service (2nd ed., London: Allen & Unwin, 1963).

24   *Robbins Report on Higher Education*, App. 2, volumes A and B (London: HMSO, 1964).

25   *The Economist*, 26 October 1963.

26   Nevitt, D., *Essays on Housing*, Occasional Papers on Social Administration, no. 9 (London: Codicote Press, 1964).

— 13 —

Equity, Adequacy and Innovation in Social Security

I

One purpose of this paper, in attempting to demonstrate some of the dilemmas of equity, is to criticize the notion that there could be some kind of final solution to the problems of social security and income maintenance in modern industrialized societies. This notion has been advanced or implied, for example, by some who advocate negative income tax or guaranteed annual income proposals. I begin, therefore with a quotation from Isaiah Berlin's *Four Essays on Liberty*[1] which expresses in a few eloquent words the dangers of such a belief:

> One belief, more than any other, is responsible for the slaughter of individuals on the altars of the great historical ideals – justice or progress or the happiness of future generations, or the sacred mission or emancipation of a nation or race or class, or even liberty itself, which demands the sacrifice of individuals for the freedom of society. This is the belief that somewhere, in the past or in the future, in divine revelation or in the mind of an individual thinker, in the pronouncements of history or science, or in the simple heart of an uncorrupted good man, there is a final solution. This ancient faith rests on the conviction that all the positive values in which men have believed must, in the end, be compatible, and perhaps even entail one another.

Not all good things are compatible, still less all the ideals of mankind, in the realm of social security as in other areas of human life. This conclusion will, I hope, emerge in more specific forms later in this paper.

It does not follow, however, that we cannot learn from each other, across national frontiers, in terms of social security ideas and strategies of innovation. That is to say, ideas and concepts about policy alternatives, principles, goals, the structure of benefits and contributions, the measurement and evaluation of needs, and so forth which may be applicable – as ideas – in another country and adaptable, in practice, to harmonize with the particular cultural and political characteristics of that country. Just as the European philosophers of the Enlightenment in the eighteenth and nineteenth centuries learnt conceptually from each other so I believe that social security 'experts' can similarly learn from each other.

The main purpose of this paper is thus to provide some illustrations of common cross-national income maintenance problems for the analysis of which we may benefit by exchanging social security ideas. The fundamental purpose of social security research and the ideas that may flow from research is not to tell other people how to do things differently but, much more modestly, to offer policy-makers a wider range of culturally adaptable possibilities and to help them to make better informed choices.

First, however, a word about definitions and language. What impresses (and sometimes depresses) me are not just the difficulties of language communication *per se* but the particular difficulties presented by the subtleties of national social security vocabularies. In English we use concepts and words such as 'poverty', 'inequality', 'inadequacy', 'subsistence', 'minimum living standards', 'low income groups', 'pauperism', and so on. They cannot be translated precisely into another language and into a different social security vocabulary. The English word 'poverty' does not, for example, seem to mean the same thing as the French 'pauvreté' or the German 'Armut'. Moreover, translation is more hazardous when we recognize that these are all relative concepts – relative in time, place, and in individual thought; when we also recognize that 'poverty', 'inadequacy' or 'insufficiency', cannot be measured solely in terms of cash resources though we find it hard to define 'non-material poverty'; and that no absolute or fixed standards of 'adequate' social security is possible – or indeed desirable.

I state these obvious facts simply as a reminder that I am conscious of the cultural diversities of international social security; diversities in goals, systems, structures and organizations which I for one respect and value.

For the purposes of this paper, the definition of the term social security covers (1) cash benefits provided without a means or needs test and (2) cash allowances provided after such a test (variously described as public assistance, national assistance, supplementary benefits and allowances[2], social aid or welfare payments).

II

It has been argued by some authorities that actuarial practice and private insurance is primarily based on principles which assure the greatest practicable degree of equity between the various classes insured whereas social security (or social insurance) is primarily governed by society's need for income protection against one or more of a number of recognized social hazards – such as old age, sickness, disability, unemployment, widowhood and so forth. While in theory the proposition concerning equity may be valid in private insurance there are substantial doubts whether it rules in actual practice.[3] However that may be, I propose to argue in this paper that considerations of equity are becoming increasingly important in all modern social security systems at the same time as considerations of adequacy of benefit also become, in the public mind, more important. People want not only higher benefits, but they are also expecting more equitable treatment for individuals, groups, classes and categories.

Equity I define as 'fairness'; that people (and classes of people) in like circumstances of need and fulfilling like conditions of eligibility should be treated alike in social security systems and in other spheres of social and economic life. It is seen as a principle – or social law – of justice. As standards of living, standards of education and standards of public information rise, people become more aware of inequities, anomalies and 'unfairness', more aware, in fact, of differential treatment and thus they come to inquire if the basis of such treatment is fair. More individual and group comparisons are made about rewards and benefits; one explanation no doubt for the phenomenon of increasing industrial disputes over pay differentials and the growth of 'welfare rights' movements in a number of countries. The increasing stress on equity by groups in like income circumstances may also be a contributory factor in pressures for earnings-related schemes of benefits geared to lifetime earnings, and for systems of inflation proof pensions. At the same time, there are other critics of 'unfairness' who see earnings-related pensions as perpetuating inequity in the wages system, while others regard higher contributions by the higher paid as inequitable because they are (or are thought to be) redistributive.

In addition, however, to these general movements of opinion there are other significant forces at work in our societies which are presenting new (or greatly enlarged) problems of equity for systems of income maintenance and the 'build-up' and inheritance of social security rights to maintenance. These 'rights', it should be noted, are today coming to constitute new forms of property rights which, once acquired, cannot be repudiated or cancelled under social security law.

Some of the more significant forces at work arise from changes of a social and demographic nature; others are resulting as a consequence of changes in the labour market, occupational status, industrial and territorial mobility. In varying degrees, they are already under way and seem likely to develop further in all modern, industrialized societies. Social security programmes cannot be immune from these forces of change. They affect, in terms of equity, not only the central policy issues of the levels of cash benefits and allowances – of current interpretations of what is 'adequacy' – but, in a myriad of ways, the whole complex pattern of eligibility, entitlement and qualification conditions which make up the body of social law governing social security systems. Before enlarging on these effects, however, we must first provide some illustrations of social change.

One significant trend is in the direction of equal status between the sexes in industrial economies. We see this expressed in demands for equal pay and equal rights for women: for better career prospects, training and re-training provisions for women; for more and wider opportunities of employment, part time and whole time, for mothers, after childbearing and child-rearing, and in demands for women to be insured and protected against industrial and social risks in the same way as men. Some countries today, it has been said, seem to be pursuing the conception of a society where most or all of the social roles of men and women will be completely interchangeable.[4]

Allied to these changes and expectations of equity is the trend, affecting both sexes in the labour market, towards more job-changing and more occupational and territorial mobility at all ages. At the same time, and as a consequence of technological and economic factors of change, there is more emphasis on re-training and on less rigidity in the labour market and in trade union rules, resulting in more changing of occupational careers, and more people being trained and re-trained. Some of these trends are leading to more frequent and more widespread periods of 'resting between work engagements' due to enforced or voluntary unemployment, job-changing, and training and re-training. They all raise questions of equity for social security systems and particularly the problem of ensuring that people do not lose pension rights through changing their jobs and for other reasons.

Simultaneously, and complicating the issues of social security 'rights' raised by greater fluidities in the world of work, we have to take account of the trends towards earlier marriage and childbearing, more illegitimate births and more adoptions, more marriage breakdowns, more legally dissolved marriages and more re-marriages and, with longer expectations of life among women, longer periods of divorced status and of widowhood. Some of these trends are leading to more demands for wives, husbands, ex-wives and ex-husbands, and those dependent on them, to have their incomes maintained on criteria of equity as 'social security rights' – a matter which is further discussed later.

These represent some broad illustrations of the trend towards a more 'open' society offering more freedoms and more choices in work and in marital relationships, affecting different countries to a greater or lesser degree; they all pose problems of equity for social security programmes.

Both the rate at which social and economic changes take place in a society (with the new expectations of equity which accompany them) and the structural character of such changes affect not only issues of equity but also questions of adequacy. Concepts of what is 'adequate' social security provision are today increasingly entangled with considerations of equity. To define equity in social security by saying that people (and classes of people) in like circumstances of need should be treated alike leads, therefore, to further questions. These are broadly of two types. One is concerned with the definition of the equity reference group or class. The other relates to time and the generation-cohort group.

As regards the first type, consider, for example, the problem of income maintenance for disabled people of working ages. What is the reference group in terms of both equity and adequacy? Is it the income and occupational group to which the disabled person previously belonged? Or the disabled group to which he may now be said to belong? [5] How is 'disability' to be assessed? What loss of working or earning capacity should give title to a pension and should a pension be payable for partial disability? Should housewives whose activities are confined to the home be included? How relevant are changes since disablement in the earnings average of the disabled person's former income group and changes in average industrial earnings and minimum wage levels? Should account be taken in the specification of equity of the cause of the disability and who was responsible (e.g. industrial accidents, non-industrial diseases and sickness, war injuries, road accidents, etc.)? Or should all disabled people be treated alike in terms of need regardless of the cause and nature of their disability and/or regardless of the current average incomes of those not disabled?

These basic issues of equity are further complicated when we take into account (as social security programmes need to) what people may get outside the programme, e.g. from common law awards, private accident insurance, special risks cover for certain industries as in mining, for example, and other forms of what are called in Britain 'alternative remedies'. The search for equity and the definition of the equity reference group becomes more difficult as more 'alternative remedies' to social security become available.

Questions of equity and adequacy of the second type are raised when these disabled groups reach 'normal' retirement ages. Is the reference group now to be the whole pensionable group? Or are those disabled before (say) age 65 to continue to be treated differently from the non-disabled retired or those disabled or sick after age 65? And in earnings-related social security schemes what account, if any, should be taken of the loss of expectations of earnings by the disabled for part of their working life for the calculation of post-age-65 benefits? What 'credit' formula (credits for involuntarily being out of the labour market) should be adopted as equitable in the absence of earnings-related contributions in the calculation of pension benefits for the individuals concerned?

All these inter-related issues of equity and adequacy are even more difficult to unravel in the case of widows and divorced wives of (again, for example) disabled men. In the past in Britain and other countries, these women have been treated differently under social security programmes according to the cause of their late husband's or ex-husband's disability and, to some extent, his contribution record. Increasingly, however, public opinion (and equal rights for women opinion) are seeing these historical considerations as irrelevant and are, in effect, demanding that equity and adequacy should be re-defined in terms of other reference groups and other reference points in time. There are, for example, demands in Britain for these women (with dependent children) to be treated alike by social security regardless of whether they are divorced, whether they have been deserted by their husbands or are widowed, and regardless of any causative factors. These demands are advanced on grounds of equity and also because when comparisons are made between these groups or classes some benefits are said to be 'inadequate' in relation to the levels of other benefits. For example, provision for deserted wives aged, say, over 50 with three dependent children is said to be inadequate if widows of the same age also with three dependent children are more favourably treated.

These are just a few random illustrations of a host of problems of equity and adequacy in social security programmes which are generated by social and economic changes and accompanying changes in public expectations.

III

At a detailed policy level, they affect a whole range of benefit entitlement, eligibility and contingent conditions in both non-means-tested and means-tested income maintenance programmes. Non-means-tested programmes (variously described as social insurance or social security under which benefits are related to contributions and/or other entitlement conditions but which exclude evidence about income for entitlement purposes) are popularly thought of in many countries as 'benefits as of right'. In part, this is because they relate to popularly accepted 'insurable contingencies' which can be administered by social security agencies. The risk of widowhood is an insurable contingency; the risk of being an unmarried mother is not.

'Benefits as of right' are, however, only acquired if the applicant satisfies — and often continues to satisfy — the administrative agency that he or she can meet a considerable number of entitlement conditions. These can include use or production of evidence concerning age, marital status and duration of marriage, family status (wives, husbands, children and other dependants), occupational or work status, residence, contribution or insured status, earnings record, medical certification, availability for work, retirement, causal conditions (e.g. in injury disability), and many other entitlement or eligibility conditions. Only in this restricted sense can benefits under such programmes be said to be 'as of right'. Moreover, parts of such programmes often include laws or regulations relating to the earnings and resources of applicants and beneficiaries and that of their wives, husbands, ex-wives, children and other 'dependants'. In short, the distinction between 'rights' schemes and means-tested schemes is not always as clear cut as is sometimes suggested.

We also have to recognize that in recent years in a number of countries there has been a growth of income-conditioned entitlement tests within 'as of right' programmes. They have been applied to defined groups of people in presumed like income circumstances. They take different forms. In some cases they represent, as in the supplementary pensions or the 'social action' of the French scheme, an extension, on a selective basis, of the 'as of right' benefits which the social insurance system provides. In others they reflect a decision to curb the application of part of the insurance programme. In Britain, for example, the government is considering applying certain pension (or deferred wages) tests to occupational pensioners aged 58–65 who, after early retirement, apply for unemployment insurance benefits and social security contribution credit benefits until they reach the social insurance retirement age of 65.[6] An example of another kind of development, but outside the social insurance scheme proper, is the scheme of supplementary pensions in Switzerland, a federal scheme, separate from social assistance, which, after the application of an income test, brings pensions to a given level.

Certain of these innovations, as, for example, Swiss supplementary pensions, illustrate attempts to find a middle way between insurance benefits as of right and conventional forms of means-tested social assistance. At the same time in other countries there are changes under way to merge or integrate under a single administrative agency non-means-tested and means-tested cash benefit programmes. To cite Britain again, for example, the public assistance programme (now called Supplementary Benefits and Allowances) has been administratively merged, nationally, regionally and locally, with the contributory insurance programme.[7] It is, moreover, something more than an 'administrative merger'. The relevant act laid down that 'every person in Great Britain of or over the age of 16 whose resources are insufficient to meet his requirements shall be entitled', subject to various conditions, to benefit or allowances as of right.[8] The concept of 'rights to maintenance' is now being further incorporated into what was at one time a wholly discretionary system (the poor law and public assistance).[9] This same trend towards social aid being provided as a right can also be observed where administrative responsibility remains separate; to give one example: in the Federal Republic of Germany the Act of 1962 reforming public assistance ensures, in the great majority of cases, a right to the appropriate kind of assistance.[10]

One important consequence of these trends is that policymakers and administrators are now confronted with new issues of equity and adequacy, particularly at the micro level of entitlement and eligibility conditions. What one part of the system ('social insurance') does or does not do in relation to issues of equity, adequacy and entitlement affects the other part of the system of cash benefits ('social assistance'). Social insurance (or security) 'as of right' can no longer be considered in a vacuum. Many of the expectations and demands for 'rights' and the inheritance of 'rights' as well as for the re-definition of equity and adequacy to which we referred earlier are simultaneously affecting both parts of the system. Many countries, for example, are faced with an acute dilemma of providing adequate pensions, to an increasing number of old people, in a form acceptable to them. In Britain another major preoccupation in social policy is the poverty of large families, even when the father is in full time work.[11]

Another area of concern, in a number of countries, is the situation of 'fatherless families'. In the USA, for instance, over a third of families with a woman head are below the poverty line.[12] There is increasing recognition of the inequitable position of these fatherless families and demands for more adequate provision for them through social security and family allowance programmes (unmarried mothers, deserted and divorced wives and widows). There are some encouraging signs that social policies are being devised and tax systems shaped to meet more realistically their particular needs. Sweden's tax system, for example, recognizes the special position of the one-parent family. Finland, to take another example, is experimenting with a scheme for paying a wage to mothers who elect to stay at home to look after their young children instead of going out to work, a scheme which is of particular help to mothers unsupported by a husband. In Hungary, after a period of twenty weeks maternity benefit at 100 per cent of earnings, mothers can be given unpaid leave and get a cash benefit until the child reaches the age of 3.

IV

Many of these expectations and demands, brought about by economic and social changes in society, are raising for both parts of the system, separately and in combination, fundamental questions of incentives and disincentives to work and to maintain the bonds of marriage and family responsibilities. Should non-working men (unemployed and sick), with or without working wives, be placed in a better income position than men who do work, with working or non-working wives? Should single (or deserted) men or women living together with children in the home be better off than married couples with the same number of children? To what extent can social security systems resolve such conflicting questions of equity and adequacy in these situations – which are often situations of poverty, hardship and low wages – when they have a duty to support the moral values that society places on work, marriage and the family?

In social security legislation in many countries (including

Britain) it is laid down under entitlement rules for various benefits that (a) a person shall not be entitled to benefit for any period during which he is engaged in remunerative full time work and (b) that a man (woman) shall be liable to maintain his wife (her husband) and children under a specific age.

It follows logically, therefore, that all parts of social security systems in attempting to meet these new and enlarged expectations and demands from poverty groups for more equitable treatment and more adequate provision have to avoid building in disincentives to full time work and disincentives to the stability of marriage and family responsibilities.

Yet such systems cannot ignore the widespread evidence of poverty and hardship caused by large families, inadequate family allowances, low wages, high rents, illegitimacy, desertion, divorce, migration, accidents, and chronic disability or handicap among both women and men. Nor can they ignore the growth in demand for equity, adequacy and rights to income maintenance which are, in some respects, the consequence of the trend towards a more 'open' society offering more freedoms in work, career opportunities and marital relationships for both sexes.

V

How these conflicts in principles and objectives are analysed and resolved in the continuing development of social security systems will depend not only on major policy decisions but on what changes are made at the detailed level of entitlement, eligibility and contingent conditions and rules. It is, I believe, at this level, as well as at the level of policy concerning adequacy, that real advances can be made towards the reduction and prevention of poverty among some of the more deprived groups in our societies.

Efforts have been made in a substantial number of countries in recent years to analyse the problems briefly set out in this paper, and to develop new instruments of policy and administration specifically designed to combat these forms of poverty and unmet needs arising, in part, from changes in society and its newer expectations of equity and adequacy. As social security provisions in all countries become more complex we have to recognize that these instruments of innovation are often small scale in scope and embedded in detailed regulations, entitlement rules and administrative codes of practice.

It is in such areas, I believe, that we can learn from each other by exchanging information, by pooling ideas, and by research studies framed to assess, compare and evaluate new social security developments in various countries.

Notes

First published in *International Social Security Review*, vol. 23, no. 2 (ISSA, 1970). I wish gratefully to acknowledge the assistance I had in the preparation of this paper from Mrs Christine Cockburn, Research Consultant to the ISSA Secretariat.

1 Berlin, I., *Four Essays on Liberty* (London: Oxford University Press, 1969), p. 167.

2 In Great Britain, supplementary benefits and allowances replaced, in 1966, the former National Assistance payments.

3 See 'Models of redistribution in social security and private insurance' (ch. 15 in Titmuss, R. M., *Commitment to Welfare* (London, 1976).

4 See, for example, Dahlström, E. (ed.), *The Changing Roles of Men and Women* (London, 1967).

5 The difficulties presented by these reference groups are illustrated in Britain in a report discussing the problems of applying the wage stop to disabled men on assistance (see *Administration of the Wage Stop*, Report by the Supplementary Benefits Commission to the Minister of Social Security London: HMSO, 1967, para. 34).

6 Report of the National Insurance Advisory Committee, *Question of the Conditions for Unemployment Benefit and Contribution Credits for Occupational Pensioners*, Cmnd 3545 (London: HMSO, Feb. 1968).

7 See *Annual Reports of the Ministry for Social Security* for 1967 and 1968 (London: HMSO).

8 Ministry of Social Security Act 1966, ch. 20 (London: HMSO, 1966).

9 The trend towards limiting the element of discretion in assistance payments has been in progress for many years – particularly since 1948 (see *Reports of the National Assistance Board*).

10 Übersicht über die Soziale Sicherung in Deutschland, 1967. *Sozialhilfe*, pp. 168–79.

11 Ministry of Social Security, *Circumstance of Families* (London: HMSO, 1967).

12 Orshansky, M., *Counting the Poor: before and after Federal Income-Support Programs* (Dec. 1967).

CHAPTER

14

Welfare 'Rights', Law and Discretion

The administrative merging in Britain in 1966 of the non-means-tested and the means-tested income maintenance programmes has made more explicit some of the fundamental issues of precedence or innovation, precision or flexibility, rule or discretion, equity or adequacy in regard to social security. They were all there and in conflict before the Social Security Act of 1966, which established the Supplementary Benefits Commission and placed it inside the Department of Social Security. Administrative discretionary powers and responsibilities for adjudicating on a comprehensive scale were, for example, built into the national insurance, industrial injuries and war pensions 'as of right' contingent schemes, just as they were in the work of the National Assistance Board. The consequences of integration have made these issues more apparent. The social policy choices that continually have to be made in income maintenance programmes between these conflicting and often overlapping principles are now clearer. The act of integration brought more choices to the political surface. It is the purpose of this paper to discuss the nature of some of these choices, and particularly the choice between legal rule and administrative discretion.[1] It will thus draw on American experience in the field of public assistance in considering the Supplementary Benefits Commission's attempts to follow a different route to individualized justice.

Dicey and Discretion

If all decisions involving social security justice to individuals were lined up on a scale with those governed by precise eligibility rules at the extreme left, and those involving complete individualized discretion at the extreme right, and those based on various mixtures of rules, principles, standards and discretion somewhere in the middle, where on the scale might be the most serious and the most frequent injustice?

It would be hard to find anyone today in Britain or North America who would publicly support in the whole field of income maintenance the principle of complete individualized discretion. To do so would involve the destruction of millions of acquired and inherited rights to social security contributory programmes. For many it would signal a reversion to a mass 'poor law age'. Powerful objections to individualized discretion would also come from others who we may describe as the new 'Diceyists', a movement that has emerged in recent years in unexpected and strange disguises in Britain and the United States.

Dicey, we may recall, was obsessed by fears of administrative discretion subject to control by administrative tribunals.[2] Discretionary power by government officials and administrative tribunals composed of lay people would both be subject to and tainted by political influence; more administrative discretion would mean more 'socialist ideas'; more administrative justice would sap the foundations of precedence and judicial case-law 'which has been for generations a leading feature of the English constitution'. In his concern for the freedom of the individual citizen, Dicey was basically opposed to the growth of public government. Less government spelt more individual freedom, dignity and self-determination. Less precedence based on case-law implied more social policy innovation and more benefits for the 'undeserving'. Less 'judicial impartiality' meant more citizen (non-legal) participation in decision-making processes.[3] In sum, he was echoing William Pitt, 'Where law ends tyranny begins'.

Modern 'Diceyism' is now to be found, on the political right, in the philosophy expounded by Professor Friedman of Chicago and many other economists, sociologists and politicians in the United States and Britain who advocate negative income taxation and

Speenhamland wage supplementation systems as the answer to the problem of 'minority poverty', and as a means of radically reducing the role of government in the direct provision of social services.

The extraordinary popularity in recent years of negative (or reverse) income taxation and other presumptive mechanical means of distributing some income to poor people is in part accounted for by a growing distrust of the exercise of administrative power in governmental systems of income maintenance, and in part as an ideological movement to transform policies into rules. Such proposals, while being advanced in the cause of less government intervention in the lives of upper- and middle-income groups, will also mean, it is argued, less bureaucratic control over the lives of poor people. More freedom for the poor, still needed by society as price stabilizers, will follow automatically from giving more freedom to the rich.

These mechanical means of distributing some income to 'poverty groups' are also seen by critics of public social services as one way of reducing lay participation in dispute and complaint procedures. The 'amateurish, inquisitorial and moralizing' participation of ordinary citizens in the work of thousands of administrative tribunals in Britain would be abolished. In so far as disputes arose in negative income taxation and similar schemes they would be handled by the courts and by lawyers.

To account fully for the widespread popularity of such schemes since the 'rediscovery of poverty' in the late 1950s would involve a lengthy digression. One further important reason should, however, be mentioned. For many supporters their appeal lies in the belief that they would concentrate income redistribution on 'those whose needs are greatest'. And they would do so with a minimum of government; a minimum of discretionary power exercised by officials, and a minimum of participation by lay people and 'social controllers' (such as social workers).

President Nixon's Family Assistance Plan (1970 version) embodies and expresses these values and beliefs.[4] It attempts to create a differential between the working rate (low wages) and the welfare rate (public assistance). Its 'new social wonder drug' is the work incentive.[5] Thus, its core proposal is wage supplementation for the 'working poor' – a new version of Speenhamland. It is aimed to apply – and the words used are similar to those in the

Act of 1795 – 'to labourers in the lower paid employments, and only to them'.[6]

In proposing to supplement the wages of the 'working poor' with dependent children it will thus discriminate against those on welfare who cannot work or who cannot get full time work who will be taxed at a higher rate on any part time earnings.

Critics of the plan have also argued that it will operate as an incentive to family break-up (the earnings of wives will be counted in 'family income'); that by contrast with universal programmes, e.g. family allowances, it will act as a divisive 'dependency-creating programme'; that it will confuse and frustrate an already heavily means-tested population; and that the recoupment of FAP payments from a deserting husband's eventual social security pension will increase the number of 'disappearing men' in North America. Lastly, and to quote Professor Burns,

> Programmes that deal only with 'the poor' run the danger, not only of being poor programmes, but also of polarising society into two groups, the poor and non-poor, the one receiving benefits and the other footing the bill. There is growing evidence of a rising resentment on the part of those just above the poverty line that everything is being done for the poor while they are neglected. A programme that perpetuates this polarisation is inefficient.[7]

It could also bring about a sharper polarization in American society between black and white because a large proportion of the 'working poor' are black people.

Some of these criticisms may also be applicable, with appropriate qualifications for differences in scale, content and objectives, to the British government's Family Income Supplements plan and associated means-testing programme.

However that may be, what is relevant to the themes of this paper is the assumption in the Nixon plan that it will reduce the area of administrative discretion. In terms of eligibility, assessment and administration it looks simpler when contrasted with the complexities of American public assistance. Hence its popularity on the political left as well as on the political right. It is seen as an impersonal plan with precise eligibility rules. The interfering, moralizing, judgmental caseworker (portrayed by many supporters of the 'Welfare Rights' movement) will have no place in its administration. Instead of the home visit and personal contact with a caseworker there will be substituted the postal application, the computer and the postal payment. The new Diceyists of welfare reform on the left and the 'economic man' Diceyists on the right both acclaim the plan on this score though they may differ on the value of the cash benefits to be provided, the scope of the plan itself and the labour control mechanisms involved.

Law and Opinion

It is a paradoxical alliance. For the Chicago School to say, in effect, 'where law ends tyranny begins' is ideologically consistent. The presumed automatism of the rules of FAP and NIT will – like the rules of monetary supply reform – assist the workings of 'the market'. Organized, militant 'consumerism' and 'tax avoidance to the limit' will be encouraged as cash is substituted for services and the market for bureaucracy and government.

All this is logical enough though it begs some fundamental questions. To understand, however, the support of welfare rights reformers we need to see it as part of the more general protest and liberation movement.[8]

It is a phenomenon which has been gathering force in recent years in most countries of Western society. In Britain it is symbolized and expressed in the growth of organized groups and associations of many different kinds; poverty groups, organizations for widows, the disabled, old age pensioners, single women, liberated women, gay people, parents of handicapped children, minority religious and ethnic groups, student action groups, anti-drug addict groups, tenants' groups, squatters, neighbourhood, territorial and amenity groups, and many others. Some are claiming equal or preferential treatment in the form of cash, goods or services. Some are demanding rights of participation in what is called 'the decision-making process'. Others more explicitly are claiming representation on committees and executive bodies of institutions which influence or affect their welfare – from secondary schools to industrial organizations. New forms of democracy are breaking out all over the place, and particularly in some politically unexpected quarters. More people are demanding rights to a greater say in what happens to them. It is an international phenomenon linked, some would argue, to a 'libertarian explosion',[9] and not peculiar to Britain or to the Supplementary Benefits Commission.

This is the social and political context within which we should discuss the growth of demand for income maintenance rights, judicialized appeal systems and equality of access to material facts contained in files or office procedural books (from confidential student files to so-called 'secret' Code As). To be the keeper of secrets these days is both a mark of stigma and a definition of old age. Only youth has no secrets.

These populist movements for social rights and participation are as difficult to define in terms of ends as democracy itself. Like democracy it is easier to say what the social rights movement is against than to say what it is for. It is against power, the arbitrary non-accountable exercise of power, against imposed stigma, against charity as opposed to rights, against the use of discretion, against discrimination on grounds of age, sex, class, colour and religion, and against moral judgments being made about claimants by social workers as well as administrators.

These, it is argued, are some of the tyrannies of the so-called bureaucrat of the public welfare system. One answer, according to leaders of the movement particularly in the United States, is increasingly to call in the lawyer and base welfare decisions on a massive body of precedent and case-law. Thus, the conclusion follows, personalized discretion in giving or withholding cash grants would be abolished. Hence the attractions to some of Nixon's Family Assistance Plan.

There are a number of basic assumptions in these arguments which may be said to relate to the functions of the Supplementary Benefits Commission in Britain and to Welfare (Public Assistance) Departments in the United States. They are all founded on the theory that case-law or lawyer's law (as in some parts of national insurance) contains no element of discretion whereas administrative discretion contains no element of law. In other words, law is as different from discretion as day is to night.

Therefore it is assumed that justice will be advanced if case-law is substituted for administrative decision; if all appeal systems are judicialized and claimants are represented by lawyers; if all discretionary cash additions are abolished; if access to the courts is made available to all claimants, and if the adversary system replaces the inquisitorial lay tribunal.

Underlying these assumptions there are many others, insufficiently defined and inadequately discussed by welfare rights reformers: that lawyers are morally infallible and do not unprofessionally 'stir up strife and litigation';[10] that they are as interested – or more interested – in poor people as in rich people; that there are enough of them everywhere to replace all administrative tribunals and to handle all disputes and complaints in the health and social services fields;[11] that citizen participation in the work of tribunals should be abolished; that the law is as speedy, cheap, effective and creative as administrative tribunals and governmental rule-making procedures; that case-law when built up in the world of public assistance will be administratively manageable and intelligible to both parties on the counter late on a Friday afternoon; and that massive case-law accumulations will be as flexibly responsive to changes in the values prevailing in society as discretionary rule-making procedures by, for example, the Supplementary Benefits Commission.

We cannot examine all these assumptions here. But the belief that lawyer's law contains no element of discretion is completely false. Law and discretion are not separated by a sharp line but by overlapping zones. Exercising discretion may be a part of finding facts and applying law, and finding facts may be a part of exercising discretion. As Roscoe Pound has said: 'in no legal system, however minute and detailed its body of rules, is justice administered wholly by rule and without recourse to the will of the judge'.[12] In the history of the administration of criminal justice in England, discretion has been more important than rule. Other criticisms of the quaint belief in the mechanistic objectivity of lawyer's law and the impartiality of judges are contained in the works cited below.[13]

To these we would add one further comment. It is insufficiently recognized today that rule-making procedure is one of the greatest inventions of modern government. In this belief we are supported by a perceptive American lawyer, Professor K. C. Davis who, after surveying the American legal system, concluded: 'the creation of new law through either statutory enactment or administrative rule-making is much more desirable than creation of new law through either judicial decision or administrative adjudication.'[14]

The American Experience

All these assumptions – intimately related to the issue of welfare 'rights' – merit more discussion than they have so far received in Britain. Meanwhile, we can ask: What evidence is there on which to test these assumptions? Do public assistance claimants as a whole – and not just one lone claimant – benefit in terms of the claims they make when systems are judicialized? Are the rights of poor people 'grossly restricted' if they are not represented by lawyers?[15] Does the 'anarchy created' by the absence of case-law in the work of the Supplementary Benefits Commission penalize claimants?'[16] Should the assistance system be judicialized on the American pattern following the precedent of the Industrial Relations Bill based, as it is, on American legal experience?[17] Does court action represent a better or more effective 'quality control' over administrative behaviour than rule-making procedures operated by administrative systems?

While we can – and, indeed, should – discuss more fully these questions and assumptions, hard evidence and unassailable facts are not easy to come by. While there is a vast literature on case-law and endless volumes of digests of decisions in the field of national insurance, there are few thorough studies of administrative rule-making and the exercise of discretion. The Franks Committee *Report on Administrative Tribunals* in 1957, for instance, and the Lord Chancellor's Advisory Committee, which considered and rejected in 1968 the possibility of extending the legal aid scheme to cover the cost of legal representation before Supplementary Benefit Appeal Tribunals, these were not founded on any searching statistical studies. This is not to say they were wrong; it is merely to point out that the conclusions of these committees were largely matters of opinion.

In the absence of any studies in depth in Britain we summarize here the findings of some American research in the public assistance field. It is moreover appropriate to do so, first, because of the widespread view that this country should adopt the American case-law approach which would encourage claimants 'to extort the last penny from the system',[18] and, secondly, because the welfare 'rights' movement originated in the States and was indirectly supported by the Federal Government's Office of

Economic Opportunity (the War on Poverty programme). The director of that Office, Mr Sargant Shriver, said in 1965 at the annual convention of the American Bar Association:

> There is a growing awareness across the country that the poor have, in fact, been deprived of their rights . . . With this awareness, there is a new appreciation of the contributions the law and lawyers can make to get poor people out of poverty.[19]

One of the more searching studies of 'welfare rights' undertaken in the States was carried out in California by Professor Scott Briar.[20] He investigated 1,088 fair hearing (welfare appeal) cases for 1965–6. All the case files were read, analysed, coded and compared statistically for relationships among them. He also observed hearings and interviewed welfare officials (variously described as caseworkers or social workers).

The legal criteria for the hearing process appear in the Federal Public Assistance statutes, the Californian statutes in the Welfare Code, and the policy interpretations and rules to be found in the Federal Handbook of Public Assistance Administration. The requirements of the hearing process include provisions for an informal demand for a hearing, notice of the right to a hearing, and specified time limits. Recipients have the right to examine evidence, to call witnesses and to employ lawyers or be represented by lawyers. There is also a provision for the publication of decisions in the form of an indexed digest. Hearings may further be reviewed by the courts. Testimony offered by clients may be criminally prejudicial.

Professor Briar remarks, in his report, on the 'incredibly complex series of statutes, rules, regulations and guidelines under which public assistance is administered'. Another student of this system, Mr Michael Evans, an ex-public welfare worker, has said: 'The volumes of case reports are fast exceeding any law library's capacity to house them.'[21]

Some of Professor Briar's findings can be summarized thus:

(1) Two-thirds of the appeal cases involved clients who would have lost public assistance altogether had they not appealed.

> These claimants, who feel they have nothing to lose, do not perceive the hearing process as a 'right'. Most are afraid to appeal if they are getting any money or services through public

assistance. They prefer to live with an inequity rather than challenge a system they consider a 'charity'.

One reason why appeals are not made is that in the American system the claimant generally has to deal with the same caseworker who has the duty of providing or determining access to social services as well as cash – a relationship reminiscent of the role of the old poor law relieving officer in Britain. Clients in the States have to 'live' with their caseworkers after a hearing.

(2) Clients who were represented at hearings did better than clients who were not. Lawyers were not markedly more successful than lay representatives.

(3) The Californian digest of all decisions (required by law) was (a) incomplete, (b) had no page numbers and (c) was not indexed. Thus, it was only helpful to those who had the time, energy and money to undertake a case-by-case search through tens of thousands of cases.[22]

(4) A large proportion of clients did not know that the police and representatives of other prosecuting agencies were present at the public hearings.

(5) As the hearings became more 'legal' (i.e. as the presence of lawyers at the hearings increased) the content became more esoteric and mystical to claimants. A similar finding has been reported by Professor Nonet in an American case study of workmen's compensation. The aims of health and rehabilitation programmes were increasingly frustrated by case-law, legal mystification and a litigious courthouse atmosphere.[23]

Professor Briar concluded:

Designed to insure against bureaucratic intransigence and programmed to encourage dignity and self-help to assistance recipients, the system instead serves frequently to reinforce the claimant's weaknesses. Confusion reigns and the client stands helpless while his complaint is processed through a system whose adversary nature is frequently invisible.

To improve the system, the lawyer had little to contribute.

In a series of studies in Wisconsin, Professor Handler and his colleagues at the Institute for Research on Poverty have demonstrated the extent to which the public assistance system in the United States is fundamentally an adversary system.[24] The essence of an adversary system is challenge. Those clothed with discretionary authority must be continually challenged – and challenged with legal hostility. Hence it is logical that the fair hearing process is set within the administrative context and is presumed to operate as a 'quality control' over administrative behaviour.[25] In Britain, by contrast, the appeal tribunals are not considered part of the administration. The Franks Committee Report said (para. 130):

> . . . we cannot accept the view that tribunals are part and parcel of the ordinary machinery of administration. We consider that they are properly to be thought of as independent organs of adjudication.

Professor Handler also found that in a system designed to create challenge the percentage of appeals heard to recipients was only 1.1 per cent (average 1959–65). This, the author said, was 'disappointingly low'.

In Wisconsin, lawyers appeared in about 12 per cent of appeal hearings. They seem to have had no effect on the success rate which was approximately the same as for those not represented. Professor Handler has clearly become sceptical of lawyers. In pointing out that there is little direct American evidence on the total and long term effects (the harm-cost equation) on relationships (and on society) of legalized hostility in the welfare system he does, however, cite evidence from studies of the administration of juvenile justice. The introduction of lawyers in juvenile justice is viewed, he says, as a hostile act (as it is in the commercial world) and

> there is evidence now that lawyers function poorly in the administration of juvenile justice. As public defenders for juveniles, they deal with cases routinely and perfunctorily, they plead the 'bad' cases to bargain the 'good ones', and they are cynical and jaded towards their clients.[26]

The Pathology of Legalism

At this point we venture on a broad generalization. The adversary public assistance system seems to produce (at one extreme) a small proportion of hostile, near desperate appellants and (at the other extreme) a very high proportion of clients characterized by Briar,

Handler and others as 'submissive', 'inert' and 'coerced', who themselves believe (in about half the cases studied on 'attitudes to welfare') that many recipients 'cheat' the welfare departments.

In this belief they were, it has been reported, simply reflecting society's attitude towards welfare recipients.[27] The stigma of receiving 'unearned benefits' – a stigma which American society apparently needs – has led to what Nonet has termed 'moral captivity' – an acceptance and incorporation by recipients of the terms and consequences of society's definition of a recipient as a person occupying a degraded role.[28] Hence, some welfare rights organizations encourage recipients to lie and 'cheat' the system: for example, by starting small fires in order to claim for fire-damaged goods.

Attitudes, behaviour and relationships which take these forms are the product of many economic, cultural and institutional factors. Certain primary ones may, however, be singled out. First, public assistance in the United States is almost entirely discretionary and it is still possible to deny eligibility on grounds of 'non-co-operation'. Secondly, in the spirit of less eligibility the great majority of welfare payments are significantly below 'official' poverty levels. Thirdly, the widespread assumption that claimants need 'rehabilitation' – hence the association of social work with money payments. Fourthly, the dominance of the work ethic as the 'final solution' involving arbitrary tests of 'work-worthiness' for women as well as men (as, for example, in Nixon's Family Assistance Plan which shifts the exercise of such discretionary power from welfare departments to labour departments so as to 'strengthen the will to work'). Fifthly, the extent to which the administration of assistance is rooted in adversariness and a pathology of 'legalism'.

By 'legalism' we mean an insistence on legal rules based on precedent and responsive only very slowly to rapidly changing human needs and circumstances. The increasing application of legalism to the public assistance system combined with rising demands for 'welfare rights' has led, all over the United States, to a massive fragmentation of entitlement. Itemized legal entitlements, in the assessment of needs and resources, now embrace hundreds of visible articles and objects – practically everything that bedrooms, living rooms, kitchens and lavatories may contain; most normal articles of clothing, day, night, summer and winter, for individuals of both sexes, all ages and nearly all shapes and sizes. For example: in New York City in 1968 (with one million people on public assistance) a man had a 'right' to possess one pair of winter trousers at $7.50 (regular sizes); the household had a right to possess in the kitchen one can-opener at 35 cents and, in the lavatory, one toilet tissue holder at 75 cents '*but only if your landlord does not have to give you one*'. And so on and on through hundreds of itemized entitlements from scrub brushes to panties.[29]

Similarly and logically, the welfare department has legal rights. It has a right to compel clients to sell things they do not need; it has a right to take over houses (owner occupied) and to sell the houses on the market, if clients are on assistance for more than one year. 'Legalism' (to quote Nonet) 'tends to weaken the authority of the law in the eyes of those whose needs and aspirations are frustrated; legal institutions come to seem ineffective and arbitrary, and tend to lose their claim to reasoned obedience.'[30] The consequences for the American public assistance system have been far-reaching: more concealed discretionary power not less (for example, in the assessment of itemized needs); more frustration, bewilderment and apathy among claimants as fair hearings become more esoteric; more inequitable treatment with the growth of itemized entitlements; more administrative inefficiencies and fewer 'quality controls'; and more hostility and fear on both sides of the counter not less.

Precision Versus Flexibility

Against this background of American experience we may now consider the Supplementary Benefits Scheme in Britain and set down some general principles relevant to the Commission's attempts since 1966 to find a balance between precision and flexibility, rule and discretion, in following an alternative route to individualized justice. In what follows I express my own views as a member of the Commission.

(1) *People should be helped to know their rights.* It must be common ground, and accepted as a fundamental principle, that everyone as citizens should know their rights. As Professor Raphael has stressed, social rights are essentially rights of access

and recipience; not rights of action.[31] It must follow that the Commission can never afford to relax its efforts to make people aware of their rights to claim and their rights to appeal. In four years, the Commission has made substantial progress in this direction, developing new leaflets and booklets and, in particular, producing the *Supplementary Benefits Handbook* – a comprehensive guide to the scheme and to the ways in which the Commission's discretion is exercised. At the outset the *Handbook* was seen to be important because helping people to know their rights is a responsibility not merely for the central department concerned but for society as a whole, and particularly for those organizations, agencies and groups who are involved in a variety of ways in meeting needs for services in kind or in cash or pressing for needs to be met – social and welfare workers, doctors, teachers, citizens advice bureaux and so forth.

(2) *The need to reduce or eliminate unnecessary discretionary power:* (a) *The need for some discretion.* The Ministry of Social Security Act lays down a minimum standard in financial terms, with discretion given to the Commission to vary these where circumstances warrant it and a right of appeal if the claimant is dissatisfied with the Commission's decision. This has the advantage of flexibility and of preserving the dignity of the individual recipient of supplementary benefit by allowing him some choice in how his income is expended. Of course it can be criticized as giving too much power to officials in the exercise of discretion and of leaving the claimant in the dark as to his precise entitlement, but both of these disadvantages can be countered through the appeals system and by action under the previous head. A definition of entitlement in precise material and itemized terms would deprive the recipient of choice, and by prohibiting flexibility would mean that whatever the level of provision it would become maximum which no official *or* tribunal could exceed. A legalized itemized prescription of minimum entitlement would become a rigid ceiling against which cases crying out by any human standards for extra help – demanding individualized justice – would press in vain. Nor would such a system eliminate arbitrary decisions – 'Your dustbin does not need renewing and your toothbrush is not worn out yet.'

In fact – and what is insufficiently recognized – the scheme does provide fully legalized basic rights, but it also provides for additional grants which allow flexible responses to human needs and to an immense variety of complex individual circumstances.

Just where the line should be drawn between legalized basic rights and discretionary additions is a problem which a fully legalized system based on case-law and precedent cannot even begin to consider. It is, however, a constant challenge to any system like the Supplementary Benefits Scheme which continues to recognize the need for individualized justice.

(3) *The need to reduce or eliminate unnecessary discretionary power*: (b) *The proper scope of discretion as the indispensable tool for the individualization of justice.* As Professor Davis has warned in another context: 'Let us not over emphasise either the need for discretion or its dangers; let us emphasise both the need for discretion and its dangers.'[32] No one wants discretion unless it serves a positive purpose, for two important reasons. First, it is an expensive way of administration; the Commission would prefer to spend money on basic entitlements rather than on administrative overheads. Secondly, more discretion means more resources by way of public education, information, advice and appeal machinery, to provide adequate safeguards against the misuse of discretion − officials, like claimants, are people.

The central concept for progress under this head is the definition of contingencies which can be met, without discretion, either by flat-rate benefits, or benefits varying with precise conditions, such as the number of children, or a fixed relationship with previous earnings, or both. The obvious example is contributory insurance programmes making provision against loss of income because of the interruption or cessation of earnings. But it is not confined to contributory schemes (both those which have contribution conditions for benefit and those which, like the Industrial Injuries Scheme, have not) but extends to non-contributory schemes like family allowances and war pensions. The latter scheme, incidentally, has the same provision by way of basic rights and discretionary additives as the Supplementary Benefits Scheme (and some of its benefits are means-tested). The balance between the two was the subject of lively controversy in the 1940s but now after thirty years' experience seems to be generally accepted as about right.

Whether a contingency can be defined in these ways is a matter for judgment on a balance of relevant considerations at any given time. Regrettably, these considerations – whether (to take one example) a benefit proposed for a particular contingency could in fact be operated in ways seen to be fair, which is closely linked with whether the contingency can be defined to this end – have received far more intensive study by government departments and their related advisory bodies (the National Insurance Advisory Committee, the Industrial Injuries Advisory Council and the Central Advisory Committee on War Pensions) than in academic circles. One of the advantages of discretionary powers is that, when for the time being it is considered impracticable to define the contingency for a non-discretionary benefit, experience can be gained in the relevant field upon which an operational definition may be formulated. An example of this process was the experience of administering discretionary additions to national assistance; this made it possible for a policy decision to be taken to introduce the long term addition as a basic benefit in the Supplementary Benefits Scheme.

(4) *The need to develop sounder and more sensitive quality controls in the administrative process*. The development of techniques of quality control is essential under any scheme containing elements of discretion. These include supervision of subordinates by superiors, the intervention of checks by one officer of another, audit and inspection controls, random sample checking, administrative surveys, the analysis of statistical data, research and so forth. The Commission has expanded the development of these techniques in a variety of ways, including utilization studies, statistical assessments of performance and the setting up of a Policy Inspectorate reporting directly to it, and is particularly anxious to respond positively to any constructive criticism of performance from outside organizations and individuals. It is sometimes assumed – particularly in the United States – that a fully judicialized system ensures better quality control but, given the desire to operate as efficiently and humanely as possible, there are at least two important and highly relevant considerations which point the other way.

First, an official who just has to apply a rigid code of case-law is not in a position of really having to justify his decision – particularly on appeal. If challenged he has in effect simply to say he did his best to apply the code; the matter is then for disputation by lawyers. But an official exercising discretion can never forget he may have to make a reasoned case for his decision to a superior and before a tribunal which has the same discretionary power as he had. Accountability to others is linked to accountability to one's own ideal of a civil servant; this, as Sir William Armstrong has said, can be a greater check than many technical checks and balances.[33]

Secondly, the aim of achieving a better quality of work in assessment is basically a matter of the quantum of resources which can be directed to the end product of adequate numbers of trained and competent staff. Given that, under either system, society will make the best allocation of resources it can against their competing demands (such as health and education services) the administrative overheads of a judicialized system will be substantially heavier. The partisan attitudes inseparable from the concept of contending parties – as distinct from the concept of a *service* – must inevitably cause heavy investment in the staff and procedures required for legalized hostility, with at least a danger that the ablest staff will be trained, and will spend their time, as advocates rather than in raising standards of local and regional office performance and in developing co-operation with those agencies responsible for services in kind.

(5) *The need for a continual process of clarification and classification in administrative rule-making.* This is vitally important when staff have to exercise discretion and need the best possible guidance. It is also an integral part of the need to inform the public of the way discretion is exercised. In a society of changing values, the substitution of clarity for vagueness is a never ending process.

It is a need which clearly does not arise in the same way in schemes based on precedent and where there is presumed to be no discretion. Such schemes, of course, require the modernization of the long itemized lists of 'rights'; the risk here, however, is that responses to changing human wants may be inordinately slow because of their legal imprisonment in precedence and the cumbrous processes of gladiatorial combat. Schemes based on a mixture of basic rights and discretionary powers can lead to more innovation and creativity in the broader context of social needs.

(6) *The need for more and better training, retraining, education and staff development programmes.* This is of crucial importance to either type of system but again the shift of resources and

priorities to cover legal processes and partisan procedures inherent in a fully judicialized system gives a decisive advantage to a mixed basic rights and discretionary system. The problem – that officials like claimants are people who reflect the limitations of their particular cultural environment – is well illustrated by Mr Michael Hill's illuminating and balanced essay 'The exercise of discretion in the National Assistance Board'.[34] It is one which the Commission have attempted to tackle in various ways, for example, by revising training programmes at all staff levels following the recommendations received from its social work consultant, Miss Olive Stevenson; by giving more prominence to the 'social services' and 'human relations' content in training programmes; and by developing integrated programmes of technical training, role-playing, behaviour and attitude assessment with the use of such aids as closed circuit television. Fundamentally, however, all the crucial issues of training and quality control are, quite simply, a matter of resources. In this area of the Commission's responsibilities as in others – as well as the personal social services – our society is failing to invest enough resources in manpower, staff development and training programmes.

(7) *The need for adequate time and adequate facilities.* The need for more and better trained manpower cannot be separated from the need to provide adequate facilities and conditions for staff in local offices. In the *Supplementary Benefits Handbook* it is written:

> [The Commission] believe that claimants have a 'right' to courtesy and understanding relations, and that Commission's staff too, have a 'right' to expect understanding from the public in the difficult tasks and pressures of work that often confront them. These are rights that cannot be laid down or ensured by law or regulation.

But they are, it must be said, extremely difficult to accord to both claimants and staff in Dickensian conditions of overcrowding, discomfort, psychological stress and overwork which, if they prevailed in the universities, would bring all (or most of) the staff and students out on the streets. While, since 1966, commendable efforts have been made to improve premises and conditions, the fact remains that there are still offices which are a disgrace in the 1970s. Administratively and financially, few objectives are as difficult to attain, without massive public support, as compensating in full for the long years of public assistance neglect. It is in essence a matter of society itself accepting – and understanding – the choices and the priorities involved.

(8) *The need to reduce the scope and coverage of means-tested supplementary benefits.* Under this last heading we return to the question of choice: the choices that continually have to be made between precedence and innovation, precision and flexibility, rule and discretion, equity and adequacy. Much of the discussion in this paper has been devoted to the issues of proportional (equitable) justice and creative (individualized) justice.

As I see it, the British income maintenance system needs both. It needs an element of flexible, individualized justice for two fundamental reasons. First, because as far as we can see ahead, and on the basis of all we know about human weaknesses and diversities a society without some element of means-testing and discretion is an unattainable ideal. It is stupid and dangerous to pretend that such an element need not exist; that all will be resolved by the automatism of negative income tax, the money market, consumerism and the lawyer. Secondly, we need this element of individualized justice in order to allow a universal rights scheme, based on principles of equity, to be as precise and inflexible as possible. These characteristics of precision, inflexibility and universality depend for their sustenance and strength on the existence of some element of flexible, individualized justice. But they do not need stigma.

The essential problem is to find the right balance. Britain has not yet done so. The situation today is one of *deteriorating unbalance*. Because, in recent years, the definition of 'subsistence' or 'poverty' has in relative terms been substantially raised, and for many other reasons besides, the Commission has attracted more and more clients, more and more duties, and more and more victims of the 'diswelfares' and moral confusions of modern society. With no immediate prospect of being relieved, it is in danger of being overwhelmed. Already it has too many claimants, too many callers, too large a case-load. For the consequence of this its staff is unjustly criticized. The more this happens the harder will it become to avoid 'the stigmatizing process' demanded – if American experience is any guide – by a materialistic market economy. I believe – because I do not wish to see poorer people stigmatized as poor people – that it is possible to develop a system of flexible, individualized justice based on considerations of dignity and self-respect. But not with millions of clients and inadequate resources in manpower. Nor will it assist to call in the lawyer – even if, by the year 2000, he was marginally interested.

Notes

This is an expanded version of a talk given at the Department of Health and Social Security Summer School, Cambridge, July 1970.

1 The distinction between 'rights' schemes and means-tested schemes is also discussed in Titmuss, R. M., 'Equity, adequacy and innovation in social security', *International Social Security Review*, vol. 23, no. 2 (1970), see ch. 13 in this volume.

2 For a recent summary of Dicey's formulation of the rule of law, see Bell, K., *Tribunals in the Social Services* (1969).

3 Dicey, A. V., *Law of the Constitution* (1885), and *Law and Opinion in England* (2nd ed., 1914). See also other references in Professor W. A. Robson's classic appraisal of Dicey's views, *Justice and Administrative Law* (1951).

4 HR 16311, the Family Assistance Act of 1970 (revised), US 91st Cong., 2nd Sess., 1970.

5 So described in an analysis by Pruger, R., 'Reciprocity and the poor', Ph.D. thesis, University of California, Berkeley, 1970.

6 Karl de Schweinitz writing on the 1795 Act in *England's Road to Social Security* (1937), p. 240, and Levi, E. G., 'Mr Nixon's Speenhamland', *Social Work* (January 1970), p. 7.

7 Burns, E. M., 'Welfare reform and income security policies', National Conference on Social Welfare paper, June 1970.

8 See, for example, Gusfield, J. R., *Protest, Reform and Revolt* (New York, 1970).

9 See, for example, Ionescu, G. (ed.), 'Anarchism today', *Government and Opposition*, vol. 5, no. 4 (LSE, 1970).

10 For a discussion of the ethics of the legal profession, see Nonet, P., *Administrative Justice* (New York, 1969).

11 The immensity of this problem in the context of a national shortage of lawyers is indicated by some statistics for tribunals under the general supervision of the Council on Tribunals. In 1969 over 150,000 cases were handled by more than 21,000 appointed members the great majority of whom were lay people' (*Annual Report for 1969–70*, London: HMSO, 1970).

12 Pound, R., *Jurisprudence* (1959), p. 355.

13 *Justice out of Reach*, a Consumer Council Study, marshals a formidable indictment of lawyers for their neglect, indifference, delays and charges in the matter of small claims by consumers. It concludes that the admission of

lawyers to a proposed small claims court should not be allowed if justice is to be obtained by consumers (London: HMSO, 1970). The harmful and undesirable effects of legal representation before administrative tribunals are discussed in Elcock, H. J., *Administrative Justice* (London: Longmans, 1969). See also *Complaints against Lawyers*, which assembles the evidence of some 4,000–5,000 complaints per year by dissatisfied consumers (A Report by *Justice*, Knight & Co., 1970); *Legal Aid as a Social Service* which criticizes lawyers for their failure to service poor people and poor areas (Cobden Trust, 1970); *Tribunals in the Social Services*, 1969, and 'Administrative tribunals since Franks', *Social and Economic Administration*, vol. 4, no. 3 (1970), by K. Bell; Abel-Smith, B., and Stevens, R. B., *In Search of Justice* (London: Allen Lane, 1968); Stevens, R. B., 'The role of a final appeal court in a democracy: the House of Lords', *Modern Law Review* (September 1965); Nonet, P., *Administrative Justice* (1969).

14 Davis, K. C., *Discretionary Justice* (Louisiana State University Press, 1969), p. 65.

15 Alleged by the Child Poverty Action Group in *Poverty*, Pamphlet One (1969), p. 3, but contradicted by *Justice out of Reach: a Case for Small Claims Courts*, A Consumer Council Study (London: HMSO, 1970).

16 Alleged by Tony Lynes in *The Fifth Social Service* (Fabian Essays, 1970). *New Society* has consistently taken the line that the 'Poor Law' will not be abolished in Britain until 'the present anarchic situation in which each appeal is considered without regard for decisions made in earlier cases' is ended (see, for example, issues of 30 April and 10 September, 1970).

17 *The Economist*, 10 October 1970.

18 Lynes, T., *The Fifth Social Justice*, p. 122.

19 *First Annual Report of the Program of the Office of Economic Opportunity to the American Bar Association* (August 1966), p. 1.

20 Briar, Scott, 'Welfare from below: recipients' views of the welfare system' in Jacobus ten Broek (ed.), *The Law of the Poor* (San Francisco: Chandler Publishing Company, 1966).

21 Evans, M., *The Courts as Social Change Agents*, National Association of Social Workers (Washington, 1969), p. 24.

22 A study in Cleveland concluded that the State Welfare Manual of case-law was incomprehensible to clients and social workers alike. 'Even experienced lawyers were puzzled.' (Stein, H. D., *The Crisis in Welfare in Cleveland*, Report of the Mayor's Commission, 1969). See also *Judicial Control of the Administrative Process*, Ditchley Paper no. 22, Ditchley Foundation (1969) especially pp. 18, 19 and 31.

23 Nonet, *Administrative Justice*, pp. 155–7.

24 See in particular, Handler, J. F., 'Justice for the welfare recipient: fair hearings in AFDO – The Wisconsin experience', *Social Service Review*, vol. 43, no. 1 (March 1969).

25 Appellate bodies consist of persons employed by welfare departments.

26 Cited from Platt, A. *et al.*, *Indiana Law Journal*, 43 (Spring 1968), p. 619.

27 Streshinsky, N. G., 'Welfare rights organizations and the Public Welfare system', Ph.D. thesis, University of California, Berkeley, 1970. This study also summarizes the results of other surveys of welfare attitudes.

28 Nonet, *Administrative Justice*, p. 91.
29 Marks. L., *Your Right to Welfare*, Citizen's Committee for Children of New York, Inc. (1968).
30 Nonet, *Administrative Justice*, p. 265.
31 Raphael, D. D. (ed.), *Political Theory and the Rights of Man* (1967).
32 Davis, *Discretionary Justice*, p. 25.
33 *Public Administration* (Summer 1970), p. 130.
34 Hill, M. J., *Public Administration*, vol. 47 (1969).

— 15 —

Developing Social Policy in Conditions of Rapid Change: the Role of Social Welfare

The first time I was honoured by being invited to address an international conference was in August 1956. That was the 8th International Conference of Social Work in Munich. Now we have doubled the number of conferences: re-styled the name of this international association – from Social Work to Social Welfare – and substantially increased the number of national delegations. To-night I am honoured again by your President, Charles Schottland, who asked me to give this opening address on a broad planetary theme; indeed, I would find it hard to imagine a broader one.

Both the change of name and the enlarged area of social concern symbolize and express something of the restless changes, social, economic and political, that have taken place in all our countries in these sixteen years since the 8th Conference was held. Social workers in many of the developed countries are less in favour today. They are no longer wholly regarded as receptacles for middle-class feelings of guilt about poor people or instruments for regulating attitudes and work behaviour. Maybe their past perception of their role (or how they wrote about it which was – and still is – often very different from what they actually do) was too limited and narrow; too client oriented in analytical terms; too preoccupied with the individual social casualties of the time. But disenchantment about social work in the West and the frustrations and lack of progress with social development in the Third World (which is also apparent today) have their dangers. Since 1956 the cost-benefit industry and the cult of management efficiency as well as the mass media denigration industry have all flourished. Material well-being for the individual, group or nation is, it is argued, quantifiable. Money as a unit of measurement permits the economist to aggregate and reduce material benefits to a common measure. Economic costs can also to some degree be fed into the model. But we cannot quantify the benefits to society of harmonious race relations; of listening and caring; of how to help people use their loneliness; of reducing corruption and nepotism among the élites of the new and old nations; of providing an irrigation project instead of a health centre in a rural area of a developing country; of crossing the boundaries (and ultimately forgetting all about boundaries) of colour, class, religion and other discriminatory barriers, national and international.

The difficulties or impossibilities of defining and measuring indicators of social growth in many areas of social policy is one among many reasons for the current disenchantments and discontents. They have resulted in two consequences which I wish to discuss later: (1) the dominance of the economic and the technocratic over the social in the approach to the problems of change and (2) trends towards the depersonalization of access to and the use of social welfare services. Both can lead to the abstraction of man from his social context; a theoretical attempt to isolate what cannot be isolated.

Your agenda for the General Meetings throughout the week should help you to avoid this abstraction though I note that you are expected to discuss – also on a global basis – housing, education, levels of living, social security, child welfare and other components of social policy. In their totality, you will be raising issues about the world's social situation: the challenge of world poverty (to use the title of Gunnar Myrdal's last book) in which he sees the equality issue as central.[1]

As background to your discussions, let me remind you of a few basic facts. During the United Nations First Development Decade, which was a period of rapid political, economic and social change and of escalating wars, violence, expenditures on arms, and catastrophe, the world's total gross national product increased by $1,100 billion.[2] Something like 80 per cent of this increase went to countries where per capita yearly incomes already average over $1,000 and where only one-quarter of the world's population resides. By contrast, only 6 per cent of the increase went to countries where per capita incomes average $200 or less but they contain 60 per cent of the world's people. While the average income in the developed countries stands today at approximately $2,400 the comparable figure for the developing countries is $180. A severe and growing maldistribution of the world's wealth and income is thus in evidence. Moreover, among many of the developing nations in which significant economic growth has occurred there is evidence that inequalities in their societies have increased; the poorest sectors of these nations may actually have grown poorer while élite groups have prospered during the First Development Decade. The price paid by the more affluent nations for, for example, coffee and sisal has dropped by more than a half in the last twenty years. This fall has had more effect on the standard of living of poor producers in Tanzania, South America and other areas than any increase in social welfare expenditures or international aid.[3]

Today, we live in a world in which children under 5 account for only 20 per cent of the population, but for more than 60 per cent of all deaths; a world in which two-thirds of the children who have escaped death will live on restricted in their growth by malnutrition – a malnutrition that stunts both bodies and minds alike; a world in which there are 100 million more adult illiterates than there were twenty years ago; a world of population explosion which adds every five days another million people to the human race; a world, in short, in which death and disease are rampant, education scarce, squalor and stagnation common, and opportunities for the realization of personal development tragically limited. Among all the limiting factors, the growth in unemployment (itself the product of many changes) is the most challenging. Whilst rates of unemployment in developed countries of around 5 to 8 per cent are deplored, the current level of unemployment (and disregarding low productivity employment and marginal producers) in developing countries has been estimated at 25 per cent or so. Moreover, a recent study of fourteen developing countries showed that unemployment is increasing at the rate of 8.5 per cent per annum.[4] These are a few facts describing the conditions of more than 95 developing countries comprising some two billion people.

Underlying the Stockholm Conference on the Human Environment in June this year a call went out for international environmental collaboration. Industrial systems in the more affluent societies do not include in the cost of what they produce such diswelfares and diseconomies of production and distribution as the spewing out of effluents into the air, the over-loading of the land with solid waste, water and food pollution, industrial and transport hazards or the lack of any charge for the eventual disposal of used-up goods. Thus, they pass on a hidden and heavy cost to the community in the destruction of amenity. This discovery of pollution, a discovery which has occurred with more remarkable rapidity in historical time among the more affluent sectors of the more affluent nations than the re-discovery of poverty, has led to a questioning of the benefits of increased economic growth and an epidemic of self-interested fear not dissimilar from the fears aroused by the spread of cholera and other infectious diseases in the nineteenth century. These fears in Britain among the higher income groups represented one of the causal factors in what was called 'The Sanitary Revolution'; a revolution that demanded more governmental intervention; fewer corrupt ministers and civil servants; more public and personal accountability, and more specific roles for social welfare — particularly in the fields of housing, education and public health.

What remains conjectural is whether this concern for the quality of the human environment at Stockholm and elsewhere is leading (or will lead to) a re-appraisal and a re-thinking of the role of social welfare in our societies. Action by government and people to mitigate and prevent environmental pollution could have far-reaching effects on public policies for housing, education, medical care, family planning and the general welfare of dependent groups in the population: children, the sick and disabled, and the elderly. It could also have in the views of many developing countries severe and deleterious effects on their economies if anti-pollution measures taken by affluent nations lead to a worsening of trade patterns, restrictions on commodities and less concern about international aid.

But less conjectural, however, for the purposes of this Conference are a number of conclusions which can usefully be drawn from the discovery of the pollution issue. In summarizing them briefly I would not wish to give the impression that I have joined the jeremiahs of science – the doom computer programmers – in predicting the extinction of the human race. I am optimistic enough to believe that man can control his environment, and that given the will – and in this case a far more determined will – the greater and more threatening problems of world poverty, unemployment and race relations can be mitigated and reduced by national and international action. There are alternatives to despair, to opting-out, and to policies of apartheid. One that is of special relevance to this Conference is the future role of social welfare.

The first conclusion I draw from the environmental debate concerns the rapidity of industrial, technological, scientific and demographic change. Equally important as established and measurable facts is that the sum of human knowledge about the consequences of change, in the form of diseconomies and diswelfares affecting the individual, the family and the group, has been greatly enlarged and deepened in recent years. We now know that the speed of change is increasing; that their effects are becoming more widespread, more subtlely non-neutral and potentially more long-run; and that increasingly more people are involved in most countries of the world. Knowledge, once gained, cannot be thrown away – that is, if we continue to believe that man can act rationally and that nation states are in some respects governable. Complexity, once understood, can only be disregarded at the risk of tyranny.

What we have also learned about increasing social costs and diswelfares – in part a corollary of increasing private affluence – is that these costs are heavily borne by poorer people; disadvantaged people, non-pink as well as pink people. Think only, for example, of urban obsolescence and decay in the West or the growth of shanty towns, the rising numbers of landless farm workers and the breakdown of kinship and cultural ties in the Third World. Read, for illustration, books like Alvin Schorr's *Slums and Social Insecurity* (1964) or Caplovitz's *The Poor Pay More* (1963) or *Development in a Divided World* (1971) edited by Dudley Seers and Leonard Joy. These and many other books about poverty and race relations which, in effect, challenge neo-classical value theory which has held that social costs are 'marginal nuisances' (they are so described in some economic textbooks) show something of the

social, economic, psychological and educational effects of exposure to the diswelfares of change. Poverty in the broadest sense is
implicated; the poverty of command over resources, whether
financial or in the form of food crops, land and cattle; the poverty
of living from day to day; the poverty of feeling; the poverty of
the senses; the poverty of language and communication; the
poverty of listening and learning; the poverty of social relations
and untouchability – all these poverties may become socially (not
genetically) inherited poverties and, according to some students of
the human condition, psychologically self-perpetuating poverties.

Those exposed to these consequences of change are at the mercy
of events (and often feel that they are) in a world of rising
expectations; the expectations of economic growth (which in the
1960s was promising – or so it was thought by many people –
that poverty would graciously succumb to growth in the West and
that economic growth in developing countries would automatically lead to social progress); the expectations of increasing
international aid, and the growth of expectations aroused in many
parts of the Third World by new national independence from
colonial power.

Given the knowledge we now have about the creative and
destructive consequences of many categories of change in all
economic and social systems (from China to Peru) and given that
medieval fatalism and the saintliness of poverty are far less
acceptable to man today, how and in what ways does or should
society respond?

Obviously, there are basic political, ideological and value issues
raised by this question. But here I wish to keep to my terms of
reference, Mr President, and concentrate the debate around the
past, present and future role of social welfare. In doing so I would,
however, point out that social welfare programmes and social
policies (however defined and determined) perform functionally
and operate differently (and often under quite different labels and
principles) in different types of societies and diverse cultural,
economic and value systems. Nevertheless, however their roles
may differ, the ends as well as the means of social welfare must be
discussed, for social policy is all about conflicting choices in
political goals as well as means. We may thus have to consider
in different cultural contexts concepts of justice as fairness;
the definition of goodness as rationality; the justification of

disobedience and compliance; the rule of law and toleration of the intolerant; rights based on needs or on capacity or on productivity or on deserts; duty and obligation; envy and equality; distributive justice, and other fundamental political and philosophical issues without which the discussion of social policy can deteriorate into sterility. To know one's chains or one's limitations is often the first step to freedom. But, as the grand inquisitor said in Dostoevsky's *Brothers Karamazov*, what men dreaded most was freedom of choice and to be left alone to grope their way in the dark. Social welfare and social and community work, as I understand the situation in Britain and many other countries, is based on opposing principles: that men should be helped to perceive and to make choices, and that it is one of the goals of social policy to provide alternatives to poverty and darkness.

All these issues of cultural diversity and conflicting choices make it much more difficult to generalize theoretically on an international or comparative basis about social policy than about economic policy. Social man, like the social structure of a society, is much more complex in many respects than economic man (if, indeed, it is permissible to make such a distinction). Moreover, as Professor Pusic has pointed out, basically different cultural and functional societies co-exist (or adjoin each other) within a nation state and he instanced, as one example, black 'ghettos' and university residential quarters adjoining each other in the United States.[5]

He provided this example in an article which argued that in order to understand what welfare is we must come to a better understanding of the nature of social development, and that in doing so it would help us to develop theoretical models in analysing the field of social welfare. One of the difficulties that confronts us, however, is the problem of how we distinguish between social welfare, occupational welfare and fiscal welfare,[6] and the further problem of the concept of welfare as betterment or as compensation for the diswelfares of change and the external effects of economic growth in different types of society.

In the past, two of the criticisms that can be levelled against students and writers in the field of social welfare and social policy are, first, that they have tended to ignore the role played by fiscal welfare in taxation systems (for example, in providing housing subsidies or benefits for home ownership, children's allowances, the costs of medical care and other welfare sectors). Simultaneously, they have also neglected to study the role played by occupational welfare in meeting a variety of needs in cash or in kind through the mechanisms of occupational status and length of service in private and public employments (for example, the provision of pensions, survivors' benefits, medical care, subsidized housing and so forth).

These writers have failed to recognize that the increasing division and specialization of labour (one significant factor in the processes of industrial and technological change) has been generally accompanied by an increasing division of welfare – much of it subsidized or paid for in the ultimate analysis by the public at large. Both fiscal and occupational welfare can thus have major redistributive effects in terms of command over resources through time by certain groups in the population. These effects may be quantitatively as significant – or even more so – in developing countries as in developed countries. They can also lead, in such countries, as public and private employees benefit from occupational and fiscal welfare, to furthering the neglect of social policy for the mass of the population.

One of the consequences of analytically leaving out of account these categories of welfare is to constrict and limit the role of social welfare or social policy. The role thus becomes a marginal one; social welfare is wholly or mainly for poor people and certain dependent groups. They therefore come to be seen as 'problems' for society; 'problems' to be solved or neglected or categorized as social pathology. One effect of isolating or selectively conceptualizing poor people as 'problems' is to generate the social processes of stigmatization; we create what we fear or we create for others what we want to create or need to create to support self-esteem and differential status systems.

Another effect of these limited and narrow approaches to social welfare is to ignore the consequences of change. An impression is thus sustained that poor people are a distinctively separate and permanent sector of the population – a class or a race or a caste apart. From these impressions or images or conceptualized 'problems' it thus seems to follow in some logical sequence that the role of social welfare is to provide benefits or betterment for poor people or only for poor people in urban areas. Where the political ideology of a society is dominated by individualistic values of personal independence, personal autonomy, self-reliance and self-mobility (as it was expressed in Britain's Poor Law Act of 1834) then the general attitude to social welfare becomes (in Professor Pusic's phrase) 'a marginalist attitude'.[7] Those who then make up the marginal group may be considered 'abnormal'. From all this can flow the view that the role of social welfare is a marginal role. An analysis of the contemporary world social situation could supply examples of marginal roles for social welfare in developing as well as developed nations.

Viewed from either an historical or a contemporary angle these values may be expressed in broad and general terms as the residual welfare model of social policy. This formulation is based on the premise that there are two 'natural' (or socially given) channels through which an individual's needs are properly met; the private market and the family. Only when these break down or fail to function effectively should social welfare institutions come into play and then only temporarily. The theoretical basis of this model can be traced back to the early days of public assistance or social aid in the West, and has found support in organic–mechanical–biological constructs of society advanced by some sociologists, anthropologists, political theorists and economists, past and present. It is, in short, a static model of social policy. It excludes all the consequences, gains and losses, diswelfares and externalities of industrial, technological, economic and other factors of change. It sees no place for social components in economic policy or economic components in social policy.

Still generalizing broadly, one can present a quite different model. This, for the sake of brevity, I will describe as the industrial, achievement–performance model of social policy. This incorporates significant roles for social welfare institutions, particularly education, public health provisions and social security (or social insurance) as adjuncts of the economy. It holds that social needs should be met on the basis of merit, achieved status differentials, work performance and productivity. Consequently, in this model, considerable emphasis is given to the meeting of such needs through fiscal welfare and occupational welfare systems.

The objectives of this model are based on and derive from various economic and psychological theories concerned with work and savings incentives, capital accumulation, effort and reward, and the formation of class and group loyalties. It is, in effect, a functional interpretation of the role of social welfare and a deterministic reading of social developments in advanced and advancing countries. It is thus argued that social welfare institutions have not come about as a result of the changing ideas, values and beliefs of individuals or because of the activities and influence of group interests and pressures but because certain economic and social institutions virtually imposed on society particular courses of social welfare action. In short, this is the functional, technocratic-servant role for social welfare. Given the values underlying this model of achievement, productivity, savings and so forth, the consequences in the long run are likely to be more inequality in the distribution of resources and command over resources by different groups in the population.[8]

Now I want to present to you a third, and again highly generalized, model of social welfare. This I describe, in shorthand, as the institutional-redistributive model of social welfare. It sees social welfare as a basic integrated institution in society providing both universal and selective services outside the market on the principle of need. Universal services, available without distinction of class, colour, sex or religion, can perform functions which foster and promote attitudes and behaviour directed towards the values of social solidarity, altruism, toleration and accountability. To use other (Kenneth Boulding's) words:

> If there is one common thread that unites all aspects of social policy and distinguishes them from merely economic policy, it is the thread of what has elsewhere been called the 'integrative system'. This includes those aspects of social life that are characterised not so much by exchange in which a quid is got for a quo as by unilateral transfers that are justified by some kind of appeal to a status or legitimacy, identity, or community . . . By and large it is an objective of social policy to build the identity of a person around some community with which he is associated.[9]

Territorially then, social policy (or social welfare) in its universalist role recognizes no human boundaries or man-made laws of residence and race. The frontiers of social growth are open. As a model, it is in part based on theories about the multiplier diswelfare and disrupting effects of change, industrial, technological, social and economic, and in part on a conception of social justice which sees man not only as an individual but as a member of groups and associations.

It follows, therefore, that this model not only incorporates and embodies the effects of past and present change but envisages a variety of roles for social welfare to play as a positive and dynamic agent of change: to promote integrative values; to prevent future diswelfares; to penetrate economic policies with social welfare objectives, and in all these ways to bring about a redistribution in command over resources through time. In doing so it challenges different societies at different stages of development and within different cultural contexts to determine a particular infrastructure of universalist services within and around which to develop selective or positively discriminating services provided, as social rights, on criteria of the needs of specific disadvantaged categories, groups and territorial areas. The fundamental problem which this model sets for government is to find the 'right' balance between the integrative role of universalist services and the social equality role of selective (or priority) developments. They are inter-dependent roles, subject to continuing adaptation and change, but often in conflict because of limited resources and the values determining priorities and choices which are set by a society at different times in different circumstances.

One of the assumptions underlying this model is that social welfare is not simply an adjunct of the economy or an ameliorative system providing services for poor people. It acknowledges the fact that not all services or grants or exchanges represent 'benefits' for individuals. Some constitute compensation for the 'diswelfares' of change experienced by the individual and the community at large because we cannot identify and legally charge the causal agents of change. But while accepting a compensatory role (for example, by providing unemployment benefits as of right to those exposed to the forces of change) it also accepts a positive role through the development of social manpower policies, corrective regional and area economic policies, re-training and further education services and other instrumentalities designed to bring about an improvement in the standard and quality of life of the individuals concerned.

The institutional-redistributive model of social welfare is, I suggest, applicable to both developing as well as developed countries. Examples of the actual application of some of the principles underlying this model can indeed be found in different parts of the world. But they are not always described or thought of as 'social welfare'. For instance, the development of the 'Ujamaa villages' involving voluntary co-operative action in Tanzania have social welfare objectives which are as significant – if not more so – as economic or technical objectives.[10] They may bring about marked improvements in public health, education and housing; areas of policy and practice normally classified in Western countries under the heading of 'social welfare'. The concept of the Ujamaa village-like community organization and social service projects in the West have much in common; they shift the emphasis from individual initiative to collective action; from economic man to social man, and from notions of employment and unemployment to 'meaningful activity'.

There are, in our societies today, few satisfactions in work for millions of men and women; hard physical labour in the fields without the use of better tools than the ancestral ones or monotonous processes on the assembly lines of mass production factories. It could be one of the future roles of social welfare to develop programmes of meaningful activity and to shift more people from the ranks of the unemployed and the under-employed to manpower-intensive social service sectors; to education in the broadest sense, to welfare activities for the old, the young, the sick and disabled, to family planning, neighbourhood projects and to all those areas sometimes described as 'community care'. Social welfare would thus be more labour intensive and less influenced by management experts advocating forms and computers in place of personal contacts.

In such ways as these, social welfare can function as an enabling agent of change and social integration and not play either a residual role or passively accept the role of an acquiescent adjunct to the economy-market, non-market or mixed. In doing so the distinction between economic development and social development will become increasingly blurred. As pointed out by the United Nations, 'the separation between the social and the economic is often an artifact of academic analysis and government departmentalization'.[11]

These three models I have presented, broad as they are and with the third one blurring the distinction between what is 'social' and what is 'economic', are only very rough approximations to variants of the real world of social policy as depicted in the many national reports produced for this Conference and which I have benefited from reading.

In conclusion, I wish to make three general points. First, I am critical of those analysts of social policy who have argued that it has failed within nation states to bring about more equality in command over resources through time. Their pessimism is part of the current disenchantment with applied forms of social welfare, social work and community development. They should remember, however, that in the long history of the human race and its struggle for social justice the corrective forces of social policy are but children of the twentieth century. For how long and in what respects have we really tried to apply what we have so recently learnt about the creative and destructive tendencies of change in both developing and developed nations? To what extent and how recently have we been prepared to shift the emphasis from the acquisitive possession of material goods to moral ideals? As R. H. Tawney put it in his *Commonplace Book* (1912):

> You cannot achieve a good society *merely* by adding one to one till you reach your millions. The social problem is a problem not of *quantities*, but of *proportions*, not the *amount* of wealth, but of the *moral justice* of your social system. If we cannot look for the realization of a peaceful and contented society merely in the diffusion of material well-being, where are we to look for it? I answer 'in rules of life which are approved as just by the conscience of mankind'. That is to say, a poor society may be a very happy and contented society. A rich society may be a very unhappy and discontented society, because the springs of happiness and contentment are to be found not in the power of man to satisfy wants, but in the power of man to regard his position in society and that of his fellows with moral approval or satisfaction.[12] (italics in original)

My second general point is one which should need little emphasis. No developments in such instruments of social policy as education, public housing, medical care, social security and social services can effect marked changes in quantifiable indices of income distribution if the prevailing systems of income and wealth taxation are regressive, inefficient or ineffective. All that such instruments may have been able to accomplish in many countries during the last twenty years is to slow down the rate of growth of inequality. If people wish to see social policies more effective in situations of scarce resources then they must demand of government higher taxation, more progressive taxation and more efficient taxation.

Finally, I want to stress that the greater the speed of change in our societies, industrial, economic, technological and demographic, the more shall we be confronted with issues of choice and priorities in social policy. The possibilities then that these issues can be resolved in any final solution become even more remote. 'One belief', wrote Isaiah Berlin in his *Four Essays on Liberty*,

> more than any other, is responsible for the slaughter of individuals on the altars of the great historical ideals – justice or progress or the happiness of future generations, or the sacred mission or emancipation of a nation or race or class, or even liberty itself, which demands the sacrifice of individuals for the freedom of society. This is the belief that somewhere, in the past or in the future, in divine revelation or in the mind of an individual thinker, in the pronouncements of history or science, or in the simple heart of an uncorrupted good man, there is a final solution. This ancient faith rests on the conviction that all the positive values in which men have believed must, in the end, be compatible, and perhaps even entail one another.[13]

Not all good things are compatible, still less all the ideals of mankind, and still less in conflicting roles of social policy.

Notes

Proceedings of the XVIth International Conference on Social Welfare, The Hague, 13 August, 1972.

1 Myrdal, G., *The Challenge of World Poverty* (1970).
2 'Survey of international development', Society for International Development, vol. 9, no. 4. (April 1972).
3 *The Internationalist*, no. 6, May–June, 1972.
4 Singer, H. W., 'A new approach to the problems of the dual society in developing countries', *International Social Development Review*, no. 3, United Nations (New York, 1971), p.27.
5 Pusic, E., 'Levels of social and economic development as limits to welfare policy', *Social Service Review*, vol. 45, no. 4 (Dec. 1971).
6 For some discussion of this problem see 'The social division of welfare', in R. M. Titmuss, *Essays on the 'Welfare State'* (1959), reproduced in this volume as chapter 2.

7 Pusic, 'Levels of social and economic development', p. 408.
8 For further discussion see Goldthorpe, J. H., 'The development of social policy in England, 1800–1914', *Transactions of the Fifth World Congress of Sociology*, 1962 (Washington, International Sociological Association, 1964).
9 Boulding, K., 'The boundaries of social policy', *Social Work*, vol. 12, no. 1 (Jan. 1967), p. 3.
10 *Tanzania Ten Years after Independence*, Report by the president of TANU (Dar es Salaam, 1971).
11 *Report on the World Social Situation*, United Nations, Sales no. 61.IV.4, p. 23.
12 R. H. Tawney's *Commonplace Book*, ed. J. M. Winter and D. M. Joslin (Cambridge: Cambridge University Press, 1972), pp. 18–19.
13 Berlin, I., *Four Essays on Liberty* (London: Oxford University Press, 1969), p. 167.

CHAPTER

— 16 —

Postscript

I was sitting on a bench with five other people in the outpatient visiting space of the radiotherapy department of the Westminster Hospital in London. We were all booked in by appointment at 10 o'clock daily week after week to go into a room called the Theratron Room. I'll explain what that means later. Next to me on the bench there was a harassed middle-aged woman, married to a postman, who had two children and who lived somewhere near a ghastly part of London called Tooting Broadway. She, like the others, had been brought to the Westminster Hospital by ambulance. She was suffering from cancer of the pelvis.

We talked, as we talked every morning, amongst ourselves and about ourselves and she suddenly said to me, 'You know, the doctors say I should rest as much as I can but I really can't do so.' I said to her, 'Why not?' And she said, 'Well, you see I haven't dared tell the neighbours that I've got cancer. They think it's infectious. Anyway, it's not very respectable, is it, to have cancer?' And then she said, 'You wouldn't tell your students would you?' By then, of course, she knew me and she knew I came from a strange, peculiar place called the London School of Economics where she thought a lot of strange, peculiar students had a lovely time at the taxpayers' expense. My answer to her was, 'Of course. Of course I would tell them; why shouldn't I use six-letter words? They can use four-letter words. Don't you know cancer is not infectious. And it is respectable. Even professors get cancer.' So you see I had to keep a promise I gave her before Christmas.

For many months last year I had experienced an acute, frustrating and annoying pain in my right shoulder and my right arm. This prevented me from doing a lot of things I wanted to do.

And, incidentally, it made it difficult for me to concentrate. It began long before the examination period and you know there is one rule that I think students might think about which is that no professor or any teacher at the university who is suffering from any kind of pain (perhaps stress is a better word) should be allowed to mark examination scripts. Anyway, apart from all that, through my local National Health Service general practitioner and my local hospital I went through a series of X-rays, tests of various kinds and they all came out with the answer that my trouble was muscular skeletal – something which the doctors in their shorthand call a 'frozen shoulder'. Later I learned that there is considerable doubt about the causes or cures or reasons for 'frozen shoulders', just as there is about a condition known as 'lower back pain' among the working classes. However, with this diagnosis I was fed into the physiotherapy department of our local hospital where I did exercises. I underwent very painful treatment of various kinds and in spite of all this and doing what I was told the pain got worse and it wouldn't go away.

Eventually, and to cut a long story short, I found myself being admitted as a National Health Service patient at 3 o'clock on Saturday, the 30th of September 1972, as an inpatient at the Westminster Hospital. Admission on a Saturday afternoon seemed to me to be very odd but I did as I was told and I was informed that if I came in on a Saturday afternoon a lot of tests and X-rays could be done on me and all would be ready for the arrival of the great men – the consultants – on Monday morning. On the Sunday, the following day, I didn't have any visitors. My wife had had to put up with a lot from me for weeks and months beforehand and so I wouldn't let her come and see me on the Sunday. By about 8 o'clock on the Sunday I decided that I would like to talk to her on the telephone. By then I had learned from the nursing staff that there was such a thing as a mobile telephone which could be dragged round the ward, plugged in and then you could have a private conversation. So I got hold of the mobile telephone and tried to get through. But every time I tried I found myself on a crossed line with another man talking to somebody else on the same line. After about ten to fifteen minutes a door opened from a side room near me where I was in the ward, a side room which was used on occasion for amenity patients or private patients. The door opened and out of it came a human being

270

about three feet five inches high in the shape of a question mark. He couldn't raise his head but in a quiet voice he said to me, 'Can I help you? You're having trouble with the telephone.' So I said, 'Yes, I can't get through; I want to talk to my wife.' And he said, 'But don't you know, there are three telephones on the third floor of this ward with the same number so you are probably talking to a patient at the other end of the corridor who is probably also talking to his wife.' Well, that cleared that one up.

The man who came to help me – let's call him Bill – I got to know very well. He was aged 53. In 1939, at the age of 19, he was an apprentice engineer in Portsmouth and he was called up for the army at the outbreak of war. In 1942 Bill got married. In 1943 he and his wife had a son, their only child. In 1944 Bill was blown up in the desert by Rommel and his back was broken in about six places. Somehow or other in 1944 in a military hospital they put him together again and he eventually came under the responsibility of a war pensioners' hospital attached to the Westminster. Since the National Health Service came into operation in 1948 Bill has spent varying periods from two to four or five weeks every year at the Westminster Hospital receiving the latest micro developments for the care and rehabilitation of people like Bill. He has never worked.

Bill and I one night worked out roughly what he had cost the National Health Service since 1948. When he was due for treatment, they sent for him by ambulance from Portsmouth where he lived in a council house and they took him back. The amount was something like a quarter of a million pounds. Now Bill was a passionate gardener – that was one of his great interests in life. While I was at the Westminster a book was published by a friend of mine, Pat Hamilton [Lady Hamilton of the Disabled Living Foundation]. This book called *Gardening for the Disabled* is a great help to seriously disabled people carrying on a hobby like gardening. Within two days of the book's publication the mobile voluntarily staffed library at the Westminster, remembering Bill's interest in gardening, sent up to him the book to read. Bill in his side room was equipped with a small television set. I joined him because while I was in the Westminster the Labour Party Conference was being held in Blackpool and I attended it, at least in spirit, most of the time. It wasn't easy to concentrate. A hospital ward between the hours of about 8 o'clock in the morning and 6 o'clock in the evening is as busy with traffic as Piccadilly Circus. There is always somebody coming in to do something. There's the mobile shop that turns up twice a day; there is the mobile library that turns up once a day; there are the people who come in to take your temperature, the student nurse who brings you the menu card for the next twenty-four hours and comes to collect it after you've decided between roast beef and chicken *vol-au-vent* for supper tomorrow; the people who come in to give you clean water; there is the lady from Brixton, homesick for Trinidad, who brings in a very noisy vacuum cleaner. And when I said to her, 'Please, take it away, Bill and I are really very clean, we haven't got any dust under the bed and the Common Market debate is going on. It's the Labour Party Conference in Blackpool' she said, 'What's the Common Market anyway – never heard of it – I've got my job to do.' Eventually I persuaded her to leave us alone in peace to follow the infighting going on in Blackpool.

After the hospital had taken about eighteen pictures from various angles of my shoulder and I had gone through a lot of other tests. I was told that what was causing all the trouble was what looked like dry rot in the top of my ribs. So they had to operate. They operated and then they had to have a conference to obtain the right histological classification of cancer. Before the operation and after the operation I had a seminar (with official permission of course) with the nursing students and I had a seminar with the medical students of one of the consultants. Somehow or other it had become known in the ward that I had written a book about blood and that I came from this strange place at LSE where many of my students became social workers. Inevitably, I was asked: What do social workers actually do? What *is* a social administrator? Two days after my operation I was allowed by the medical staff, by the house officers and the registrars, by the hierarchy in general to go down to the 'Paviour's Arms' with some of the old age pensioners where they had a pint of beer at 7 o'clock in the evening and I had a whisky. And I was also allowed to go out to a little restaurant in Ebury Street for dinner with friends and members of the staff of the Social Administration Department. So you see hospitals are flexible and this is an area where the middle classes can often get the best out of the social services. I am, I suppose, middle class. I am, I suppose, articulate whereas many of the patients are not.

After my discharge as an inpatient from the Westminster Hospital it was rather a moving experience because some of the staff of the Supplementary Benefits Commission had sent me a sort of miniature Rochford rockery and, in a little ceremony in the ward, I handed over the rockery to Bill and the staff were arranging for it to go home with him to Portsmouth, and I also handed over copies of my book, *The Gift Relationship*, to the nurses' library and the medical students' library. I think one of the best compliments I was paid as an inpatient was when I was helping two of the student nurses to make my bed one morning. They knew where I came from – they thought I was an authority on matters of this kind – and they said to me, 'We've been having an argument in the hostel about the right age to get married. What do you think, Professor? When do you think young people should get married?' Well, I really had no answer – all I could say was 'Not too soon and please not too late.'

After my discharge, I and other cancer patients had to attend every day for five to six weeks for radium treatment from a Cobalt 60 theratron machine. Capital expenditure cost was about half a million pounds and there are not many of these machines in London and the South-East. I began with an exposure of eight minutes which gradually mounted to about twenty-five minutes. I can only describe this machine by saying that as you went into the theratron room you walked past a control panel which looked like what I imagine might resemble the control panel of the Concorde cockpit. After that, you lie almost naked on a machine and you are raised and lowered and this machine beams at you from various angles radium at a cost, so I am told, of about £10 per minute. I had in all about seventeen hours. In addition, while one was on the machine, the National Health Service kindly supplied piped music free of charge in order to help patients relax.

Now, as you will have gathered from what I have said, I was extraordinarily lucky. It was a marvellous ward, staffed by some very interesting people looking after an extraordinarily interesting and diverse cross-section of the British public drawn from south-east London – south-east England in fact. If all wards in all the hospitals all over the country were anywhere near the standard of this ward at the Westminster we should have very little to complain about in evaluating standards of performance of the

National Health Service. But you know, as well as I know, that not all wards are like the ward that I was in.

When I went in on that Saturday afternoon I took with me John Rawls's book, *A Theory of Justice*, which I think is one of the most important books published in the field of social philosophy for the last twenty-five years. I took that with me and I took with me an advance copy of the present government's Green Paper on Tax Credits, and I also took a bottle of whisky. Anyway, I can tell you that while I was there I didn't get very far with *A Theory of Justice*; there wasn't time; there was too much to do; there were too many people to talk to; one had to help – one liked to help – with the tea trolley at 6 o'clock in the morning, when all the mobile patients served the immobile patients, and one shuffled around not caring what one looked like and learning a great deal about other human beings and their predicaments. But I did read the Green Paper on Tax Credits and, I don't suppose it happens very often, I did write a letter to the editor of *The Times* from the Westminster Hospital – he didn't know it came from the hospital because I signed it from my home – about the Green Paper because I thought then, indeed I still think, that the proposals, rough as they are, have considerable potentialities for extending some of the benefits of the Welfare State from the middle classes downwards to the poor.

In some of the things that I have said and in some of the things that I have written in some of my books, I have talked about what I have called 'social growth'. I believe that my experience at the Westminster provides some of the unquantifiable indicators of social growth. These are indicators that cannot be measured, cannot be quantified, but relate to the texture of relationships between human beings. These indicators cannot be calculated. They are not, as my friends the economists tell me, counted in all the Blue Books and in all the publications of the Central Statistical Office. For example, nowhere will you find any explanation or any statement about the expenditures by the National Health Service on my friend Bill and all the other expenditures -- public housing, a constant attendance allowance, a daily home help and meals-on-wheels (his wife, aged 52, went blind last year), an invalid chair, special ramps, an adapted lavatory and kitchen, lowered sinks and raised garden beds (provided by the local Parks Department). He was an example, in practice, of what a compassionate society can achieve when a philosophy of social justice and public accountability is translated into a hundred and one detailed acts of imagination and tolerance.

Among all the other experiences I had, another which stands out is that of a young West Indian from Trinidad, aged 25, with cancer of the rectum. His appointment was the same as mine for radium treatment – 10 o'clock every day. Sometimes he went into the theratron room first; sometimes I did. What determined waiting was quite simply the vagaries of London traffic – not race, religion, colour or class.

Notes

From *Social Policy: an Introduction* (London: Allen & Unwin and New York: Pantheon Books, 1974).

Index